学术英语
文献阅读与综述

ACADEMIC ENGLISH
LITERATURE READING & REVIEWING

田园 张英 董焱宁
付林 李秀立 ◎编著

清华大学出版社
北京

内 容 简 介

本教材致力于提高学生的英语论文阅读能力，兼具培养学生科学的质疑精神和批判性思维能力。教材选取高质量学术论文作为阅读材料，反映世界最新的科技发展和学术前沿；阅读技巧与策略兼顾宏观与微观，全面助力学生熟练阅读英文学术论文，掌握相关领域的最新科技发展动向和学术前沿信息；练习设计遵循学用一体原则，贴近学术生活，使学生以积极探究的态度走进英语学术阅读，全面总结并客观评价所阅读的文献。全书共设十个单元，各单元又细分为三大板块：阅读技巧与策略、学术论文精读、学术论文扩展阅读。本教材另配有练习参考答案和PPT课件，读者可登录www.tsinghuaelt.com下载使用。

本教材适用于非英语专业的硕士和博士研究生、本科高年级学生及科技和人文学科的教师和学者。

版权所有，侵权必究。举报：010-62782989，beiqinquan@tup.tsinghua.edu.cn。

图书在版编目（CIP）数据

学术英语文献阅读与综述 / 田园等编著. —北京：清华大学出版社，2023.2（2025.3重印）
ISBN 978-7-302-62492-9

Ⅰ.①学… Ⅱ.①田… Ⅲ.①英语—文献—阅读教学—高等学校—教材 Ⅳ.①H319.37

中国国家版本馆 CIP 数据核字（2023）第 025274 号

责任编辑：刘　艳
封面设计：子　一
责任校对：王凤芝
责任印制：刘　菲

出版发行：清华大学出版社
网　　　址：https://www.tup.com.cn, https://www.wqxuetang.com
地　　　址：北京清华大学学研大厦A座　　邮　编：100084
社 总 机：010-83470000　　邮　购：010-62786544
投稿与读者服务：010-62776969, c-service@tup.tsinghua.edu.cn
质量反馈：010-62772015, zhiliang@tup.tsinghua.edu.cn
印 装 者：涿州市般润文化传播有限公司
经　销：全国新华书店
开　本：185mm×260mm　　印　张：14.75　　字　数：339千字
版　次：2023年3月第1版　　印　次：2025年3月第2次印刷
定　价：64.00元

产品编号：098955-01

前言

在党的二十大报告中，习近平总书记首次将"实施科教兴国战略，强化现代化建设人才支撑"作为一个单独部分论述，充分体现了教育的基础性、战略性地位和作用。习总书记强调，我们要"全面提高人才自主培养质量，着力造就拔尖创新人才，聚天下英才而用之"。处于高等教育金字塔顶端的研究生教育在"加快建设教育强国、科技强国、人才强国"过程中发挥着重要作用。

外语素质和能力，尤其是用外语获得资料、提取信息并进行科研的能力，对于研究生的培养具有不可替代的重要作用（北京市高等教育学会研究生英语教学研究分会，2020）。熟练阅读英文学术论文，掌握相关领域的最新科技发展动向和学术前沿信息，并对所阅读信息进行恰当的分析评判是研究生开展学术研究的第一步。为了帮助研究生获得这一能力，我们编写了本教材。

本教材是清华大学研究生学术英语系列教材中的第二部。教材的编写秉承"真实语料驱动""产出导向""任务驱动"和"体验式教学"等教学理念，致力于提高学生的英语论文阅读能力，兼具培养学生科学的质疑精神和批判性思维能力。

教材选取高质量的学术论文作为阅读材料，设计贴近学术生活的阅读任务，驱动学生以积极探究的态度走进英语学术阅读，并促使他们全面总结和客观评价所阅读的文献。全书共设十个单元，各单元内容又细分为三大板块：阅读技巧与策略（Reading Skills and Strategies）、学术论文精读（Intensive Reading）、学术论文扩展阅读（Further Reading）。教材特色具体如下：

1. 选材反映世界最新的科技发展和学术前沿，时效性强。本教材阅读选材涵盖了重要学科的专业知识，文理兼顾，具体包括自动驾驶、公共卫生、批判性思维、艺术教育、语言学习、环境科学、学术写作、心理学、碳经济和人工智能等领域。学术论文精读部分的选文保留了原论文的文献著录格式，使学生可以原汁原味阅读某一学科领域的论文。另外，文末提供了常用学术词汇表，选词标准参考《非英语专业学位研究生英语教学大纲》和 Academic Word List（Coxhead, 2000），助力学生积累常用学术词汇，提升阅读能力与素养。学术论文扩展阅读部分选择了相应领域的综述类文章，使学生可以通过阅读该类文章体会如何全面、系统地总结和评价相关领域的研究。因篇幅有限，精读部分文末参考文献列表和扩展阅读部分的正文，学生可以通过扫描相应的二维码获得。

2. 阅读技巧与策略兼顾宏观与微观，实用性强。 本教材系统讲解了与学术英语阅读密切相关的技巧和策略，既包括整体阅读策略，如三步阅读法、顺序阅读法、批判性阅读，又涉及如何利用文章细节阅读，如利用文章关键引导词阅读、通过转述动词判断作者态度。阅读技巧与策略部分还介绍了如何阅读常见的期刊论文文体，如研究论文、理论性论文、综述论文、回应论文。考虑到学生在阅读文献后常常需要对文献进行综述，教材的最后两个单元将阅读技巧与策略延伸到文献综述撰写层面，讲解如何总结并撰写有注解的参考文献、如何撰写研究论文的文献综述部分，从而达到以读促写的目的，为他们撰写学术论文打好基础。

3. 练习设计遵循学用一体原则，针对性强。 每单元后的练习设计具有精准性、渐进性与多样性（文秋芳，2017），既有考查文章细节的阅读理解题，又有训练和提高学生批判性思维的开放性讨论题。通过设计与本单元阅读技巧与策略相关的练习，本教材有意识地引导学生主动将相关阅读技巧与策略应用到论文阅读中，让他们学以致用；同时，循序渐进地布置与文献综述写作相关的产出任务，如转述文中的重要观点、为论文列提纲、撰写论文总结等，驱动学生以积极探究的态度进行学术英语阅读。

本教材适用于非英语专业的硕士和博士研究生、本科高年级学生及科技和人文学科的教师和学者。教材配备练习参考答案和PPT课件，方便教师和学生学习使用，下载地址为www.tsinghuaelt.com。

本教材由田园编写第5单元和第8单元；张英编写第4单元和第6单元；董焱宁编写第3单元和第7单元；付林编写第1单元和第9单元；李秀立编写第2单元和第10单元。全书的统稿工作由田园负责。

感谢清华大学研究生教育教学改革项目的支持；感谢清华大学语言教学中心的支持；感谢清华大学出版社的支持！

编者

2023年元月于清华园

Contents

Unit 1 Autonomous Driving 1

Part 1 Reading Skills and Strategies 2
  Reading a Research Paper 2

Part 2 Intensive Reading 6
  The Moral Machine Experiment 6

Part 3 Further Reading 23
  Life and Death Decisions of Autonomous Vehicles 23

Unit 2 Public Health 25

Part 1 Reading Skills and Strategies 26
  Identifying Keywords and Formulating an Outline 26

Part 2 Intensive Reading 30
  Childhood Overweight and Obesity: Is the Gap Closing the
    Wrong Way? 30

Part 3 Further Reading 45
  Tracking of Childhood Overweight into Adulthood:
    A Systematic Review of the Literature 45

Unit 3 Critical Thinking 47

Part 1 Reading Skills and Strategies 48
  Reading Critically 48

Part 2 Intensive Reading 53
  Critical Thinking: Seven Definitions in Search of a
    Concept 53

Part 3　Further Reading 77

　　How Do English-as-a-Foreign-Language (EFL) Teachers Perceive and Engage with Critical Thinking: A Systematic Review from 2010 to 2020 77

Unit 4　Arts Education 79

Part 1　Reading Skills and Strategies 80

　　Reading Empirical Articles 80

Part 2　Intensive Reading 85

　　The Use of Folk Music in Kindergartens and Family Settings 85

Part 3　Further Reading 94

　　Education and the Arts: Educating Every Child in the Spirit of Inquiry and Joy 94

Unit 5　Language Learning 97

Part 1　Reading Skills and Strategies 98

　　Reading Conceptual Articles 98

Part 2　Intensive Reading 100

　　A Conceptual Framework to Explore the English Language Learning Experiences of International Students in Malaysia 100

Part 3　Further Reading 115

　　Twenty-Five Years of Research on Oral and Written Corrective Feedback in *System* 115

Unit 6　Environment 117

Part 1　Reading Skills and Strategies 118

　　Reading Review Articles 118

Part 2　Intensive Reading 121

　　Pesticides: An Overview of the Current Health Problems of Their Use 121

Contents

   Part 3   Further Reading 136
      Review on Mould Contamination and Hygrothermal Effect in
         Indoor Environment 136

Unit 7 English for Academic Purposes 139

   Part 1   Reading Skills and Strategies 140
      Reading Response Articles 140
   Part 2   Intensive Reading 143
      Standards of English in Academic Writing: A Response to
         McKinley and Rose..144
   Part 3   Further Reading 154
      Conceptualizations of Language Errors, Standards, Norms and
         Nativeness in English for Research Publication Purposes:
         An Analysis of Journal Submission Guidelines......................154

Unit 8 Psychology 157

   Part 1   Reading Skills and Strategies 158
      Distinguishing Reporting Verbs 158
   Part 2   Intensive Reading 160
      Procrastination, Deadlines, and Performance: Self-Control by
         Precommitment 160
   Part 3   Further Reading 174
      Academic Interventions for Academic Procrastination:
         A Review of the Literature...174

Unit 9 Carbon Economy 175

   Part 1   Reading Skills and Strategies 176
      Writing an Annotated Bibliography...176
   Part 2   Intensive Reading 178
      Operationalizing the Net-Negative Carbon Economy 178
   Part 3   Further Reading 195
      The Effects of Assigning Liability for CO_2 Removal 195

Unit 10 Artificial Intelligence (AI) 197

Part 1 Reading Skills and Strategies 198

Selecting Different Types of Literature and Writing an Effective Literature Review 198

Part 2 Intensive Reading 205

Responsible Urban Innovation with Local Government Artificial Intelligence (AI): A Conceptual Framework and Research Agenda 205

Part 3 Further Reading 222

A Systematic Literature Review of AI in the Sharing Economy 222

References 225

Unit 1
Autonomous Driving

Learning Objectives

- Summarize the three passes for reading a paper;

- Explain the three Cs in the first and second pass reading;

- Compare the differences between three-pass reading and sequential reading;

- Apply effective strategies for reading a paper.

Part 1 Reading Skills and Strategies

Reading a Research Paper

1. Introduction to Three-Pass Reading Method

When you want to keep current in your research field or do a literature survey of a new topic, you have to read a lot of research papers. Learning to read a paper efficiently is a critical skill. The three-pass reading method (Keshav, 2007) is a practical and efficient approach for reading research papers. The key idea is that, instead of reading a paper from the beginning to the end, you read the paper in up to three passes. Each pass achieves specific goals and builds upon the previous pass: using the first pass to get a general idea about the paper; using the second pass to grasp the paper's main content but not its details; using the third pass to help you understand the paper in depth.

1) The first pass

In the first pass, you quickly scan through the paper to get an overview of it. For example:

✓ Read the title, authors, abstract, and keywords;

✓ Read the section and sub-section headings, but ignore everything else;

✓ Read the conclusions.

This pass should take five to ten minutes. At the end of the first pass, you should be able to answer the following three Cs:

✓ Category: What type of paper is this? A review or an original research article? An experimental, theoretical, or numerical study? A description of a new theory/method or an application of existing theories/methods?

✓ Context: What is the research problem? Why is the problem important? How is the research problem addressed? What are the findings and conclusions?

✓ Contributions: What are the paper's main contributions? Are they significant?

After doing the first pass and answering the above questions, you may decide not to read further. This could be because the paper does not interest you, or the ideas are too vague to comprehend, or its contributions are insignificant. Incidentally, when you write a paper, you can expect that most reviewers and readers will make only one pass over it. Therefore, you have to choose a good title with coherent section and sub-section headings, write concise and comprehensive abstracts, and draw proper conclusions. If a reviewer cannot understand the gist after one pass, the paper will likely be rejected; if a reader cannot understand the highlights of the paper after one pass, the paper will likely never be read again.

2) The second pass

In the second pass, read the paper with greater care to grasp the main content, but ignore details such as proofs, implementations, and complex equations. You can do the following:

✓ Read the first sentence of each paragraph;

✓ Read carefully about any part that really interests you, e.g., the introduction section;

✓ Look carefully at the figures, diagrams, and tables;

✓ Glance over the references, tick off the ones that you have already read, and mark relevant unread references for further reading (this is a good way to learn more about the background of the research).

You may spend up to an hour on the second pass. At the end of the second pass, you should be able to answer the following three Cs:

✓ Correctness: Which previous studies is this study based on? Which theoretical bases are used to analyze the problem? Do the assumptions appear to be valid? Are the conclusions well supported by the data evidence?

✓ Creativity: How creative and original are the presented ideas or implementations? Is your mind refreshed or influenced by this paper?

✓ Clarity: Is the paper well written?

You should be able to explain the main thrust of the paper with supporting evidence to someone else. Sometimes you cannot comprehend a paper even after the second pass. This may be because the topic is new to you, or some proofs or experimental techniques are unfamiliar, or the paper is poorly written with unclear ideas and numerous forward references. You can now choose to: (1) put the paper aside and hope you do not need to understand the material to be successful in your career; (2) return to the paper later, perhaps after reading background materials; or (3) persevere and go on to the third pass.

3) The third pass

To fully understand a paper requires a third pass. The key to the third pass is to virtually reimplement the paper, that is, making the same assumptions as the authors and recreating the work. By comparing this recreation with the actual paper, you can easily identify not only a paper's innovations but also its hidden assumptions and failings.

The third pass requires great attention to detail. You should:

- ✓ Read through the paper as many times as needed;
- ✓ Identify and challenge every assumption in every statement;
- ✓ Reconstruct the current research;
- ✓ Identify hidden assumptions and failings;
- ✓ Think about how you would present a particular idea;
- ✓ Add excellent research techniques or writings in the paper to your repertoire of tools and jot down ideas for future work.

The third pass may take several hours to complete. At the end of this pass, you should be able to reconstruct the entire structure of the paper from memory as well as identify its strong and weak points. In particular, you should be able to pinpoint implicit assumptions, missing citations to relevant works, and potential issues with experimental or analytical techniques.

Do a literature survey in a field that interests you to test your three-pass reading skills.

- ✓ Use an academic search engine and some well-chosen keywords to find three to five recent or highly cited papers in the area.
- ✓ Do first-pass reading on each paper to get a sense of the work and then pick two to three excellent papers for further reading.
- ✓ Read the introduction section of the selected papers to get a thumbnail summary of the recent work, and perhaps, if you are lucky, a pointer to a recent survey paper. If you can find such a survey, read the survey paper and you will get a good overview as well as the important papers of the entire field.
- ✓ Read the bibliographies of the selected papers and find shared citations and repeated author names. These are the key papers and research in that area. Download the key papers and then go to the websites of the key researchers to see what they have published recently and where they have published them. That will help you identify the current trends and top journals in that field.
- ✓ After gathering sufficient relevant papers, do three-pass reading on these papers to build up your survey. If several papers all cite a key paper that you did not find earlier, obtain and read it, iterating as necessary.

The three-pass reading method is an incremental and iterative approach of reading a paper. The method goes from a general overview to the specific details with each step taking more time and helping you obtain a deeper understanding during each iteration. It can help you quickly read recent papers, do background research, and write reviews. This disciplined approach prevents you from drowning in the details before getting a bird's-eye-view of the papers. It allows you to estimate the amount of time required to review a set of papers.

Moreover, you can adjust the depth of paper evaluation depending on your needs and how much time you have.

2. Introduction to Sequential Reading Method

Sequential reading is to read a paper from the beginning to the end. Compared with the three-pass reading method, sequential reading may not be an effective way of reading a paper, particularly when you are doing a literature survey or reading multiple papers in a short time, since it could make you lost in details and forget the big picture. However, when you have a very relevant paper to read and you want to thoroughly process the information in the paper, you can do sequential reading to understand it in depth and extract all the details. Let's see a specific example.

Find an important paper in your research field and answer the following questions after reading through it:

✓ What are the elements in this research paper?

✓ What questions does the paper address?

✓ Is the problem relevant and important?

✓ What are the main conclusions of the paper?

✓ What evidence supports those conclusions?

✓ What is the quality of the evidence?

✓ Are the conclusions important and why?

✓ What are the limitations of the work?

✓ Can you explain the research in this paper to your friends within three minutes and in your own words?

✓ What is old and what is new to you in the paper?

You can use the following reading techniques to help you:

✓ Read actively by taking notes at the margins of the paper and writing down the key points, such as restating unclear points in your own words, filling in missing details (assumptions, algebraic steps, proofs), and challenging claims or methods, etc.

✓ Use highlighters to mark important sentences in a paper and give different colors distinctive meanings, such as definitions, catchphrases, assumptions, key ideas, etc. (develop a coloring scheme of your own and stick to it).

✓ Use mind maps or flow charts to illustrate the key information in a paper (as shown in Figure 1.1).

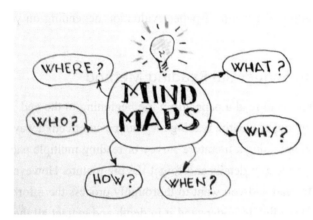

Figure 1.1　An example of the mind map for illustrating the key information in a paper

The sequential reading method can help you understand a paper in depth and obtain all the details. During reading, you can use several techniques to help you manage and organize the information. When using this method for reading a paper, you should always keep a big picture and your main questions in mind and avoid being lost in the details.

Pre-reading questions:

1. What is a moral machine?
2. What is an experiment?
3. Do you think that this title is informative for you? Why?

The Moral Machine Experiment[1]

1. Introduction

We are entering an age in which machines are tasked not only to promote well-being and minimize harm, but also to distribute the well-being they create, and the harm they

---

1　This paper is from Awad, E., Dsouza, S., Kim, R., Schulz, J., Henrich, J., Shariff, A., Bonnefon, J. & Rahwan, I. 2018. The Moral Machine experiment. *Nature, 563*(7729): 59–64.

cannot eliminate. Distribution of well-being and harm inevitably creates tradeoffs, whose resolution falls in the moral domain[1-3]. Think of an autonomous vehicle that is about to crash, and cannot find a trajectory that would save everyone. Should it swerve onto one jaywalking teenager to spare its three elderly passengers? Even in the more common instances in which harm is not inevitable, but just possible, autonomous vehicles will need to decide how to divide up the risk of harm between the different stakeholders on the road. Car manufacturers and policymakers are currently struggling with these moral dilemmas, in large part because they cannot be solved by any simple normative ethical principles such as Asimov's laws of robotics[4].

Asimov's laws were not designed to solve the problem of universal machine ethics, and they were not even designed to let machines distribute harm between humans. They were a narrative device whose goal was to generate good stories, by showcasing how challenging it is to create moral machines with a dozen lines of code. And yet, we do not have the luxury of giving up on creating moral machines[5-8]. Autonomous vehicles will cruise our roads soon, necessitating agreement on the principles that should apply when, inevitably, life-threatening dilemmas emerge. The frequency at which these dilemmas will emerge is extremely hard to estimate, just as it is extremely hard to estimate the rate at which human drivers find themselves in comparable situations. Human drivers who die in crashes cannot report whether they were faced with a dilemma; and human drivers who survive a crash may not have realized that they were in a dilemma situation. Note, though, that ethical guidelines for autonomous vehicle choices in dilemma situations do not depend on the frequency of these situations. Regardless of how rare these cases are, we need to agree beforehand how they should be solved.

The key word here is "we". As emphasized by former US president Barack Obama[9], consensus in this matter is going to be important. Decisions about the ethical principles that will guide autonomous vehicles cannot be left solely to either the engineers or the ethicists. For consumers to switch from traditional human-driven cars to autonomous vehicles, and for the wider public to accept the **proliferation** of artificial intelligence-driven vehicles on their roads, both groups will need to understand the origins of the ethical principles that are programmed into these vehicles[10]. In other words, even if ethicists were to agree on how autonomous vehicles should solve moral dilemmas, their work would be useless if citizens were to disagree with their solution, and thus opt out of the future that autonomous vehicles promise **in lieu of** the **status quo**. Any attempt to devise artificial intelligence ethics must **be** at least **cognizant of** public morality.

Accordingly, we need to gauge social expectations about how autonomous vehicles should solve moral dilemmas. This enterprise, however, is not without challenges[11]. The first challenge comes from the high dimensionality of the problem. In a typical survey, one may test whether people prefer to spare many lives rather than few[9,12,13]; or whether people prefer to spare the young rather than the elderly[14,15]; or whether people prefer to spare pedestrians who cross legally, rather than pedestrians who jaywalk; or yet some other preference, or a simple combination of two or three of these preferences. But combining a dozen such preferences leads to millions of possible **scenarios**, requiring a sample size that defies any conventional method of data collection.

The second challenge makes sample size requirements even more daunting: If we are to make progress towards universal machine ethics (or at least to identify the obstacles thereto), we need a fine-grained understanding of how different individuals and countries may differ in their ethical preferences[16,17]. As a result, data must be collected worldwide, in order to assess **demographic** and cultural moderators of ethical preferences.

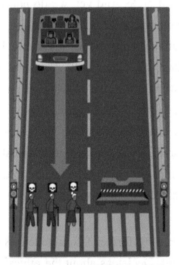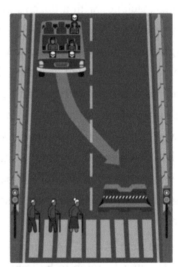

What should the self-driving car do?

Figure 1   Moral Machine interface. An autonomous vehicle experiences a sudden brake failure. Staying on course would result in the death of two elderly men and an elderly woman who are crossing on a "do not cross" signal (left). Swerving would result in the death of three passengers: an adult man, an adult woman, and a boy (right).

As a response to these challenges, we designed the Moral Machine, a multilingual online "serious game" for collecting large-scale data on how citizens would want autonomous vehicles to solve moral dilemmas in the context of unavoidable accidents. The Moral Machine attracted worldwide attention, and allowed us to collect 39.61 million decisions from 233 countries, dependencies, or territories. In the main interface of the Moral Machine, users are shown unavoidable accident scenarios with two possible outcomes, depending on whether the autonomous vehicle swerves or stays on course (Figure 1). They then click on the outcome that they find preferable. Accident scenarios are generated by the Moral Machine following an exploration strategy that focuses on nine factors: sparing humans (versus pets), staying on course (versus swerving), sparing passengers (versus pedestrians), sparing more lives (versus fewer lives), sparing men (versus women), sparing the young (versus the elderly), sparing pedestrians who cross legally (versus jaywalking), sparing the fit (versus the less fit), and sparing those with higher social status (versus lower social status). Additional characters were included in some scenarios (for example, criminals, pregnant women or doctors), who were not linked to any of these nine factors. These characters mostly served to make scenarios less repetitive for the users. After completing a 13-accident session, participants could complete a survey that collected, among other variables, demographic information such as gender, age, income, and education, as well as religious and political attitudes. Participants were **geolocated** so that their coordinates could be used in a clustering analysis that sought to identify groups of countries or territories with homogeneous vectors of moral preferences.

Here we report the findings of the Moral Machine experiment, focusing on four levels of analysis, and considering for each level of analysis how the Moral Machine results can trace our path to universal machine ethics. First, what is the relative importance of the nine preferences we explored on the platform, when data are aggregated worldwide? Second, does the intensity of each preference depend on the individual characteristics of respondents? Third, can we identify clusters of countries with homogeneous vectors of moral preferences? And fourth, do cultural and economic variations between countries predict variations in their vectors of moral preferences?

2. Methods

This study was approved by the Institute Review Board (IRB) at Massachusetts Institute of Technology (MIT). The authors complied with all relevant ethical considerations. No statistical methods were used to predetermine sample size. The experiments were randomized and the investigators were blinded to allocation during experiments and outcome assessment.

The Moral Machine website was designed to collect data on the moral acceptability of decisions made by autonomous vehicles in situations of unavoidable accidents, in which they must decide who is spared and who is sacrificed. The Moral Machine was deployed in June 2016. In October 2016, a feature was added that offered users the option to fill a survey about their demographics, political views, and religious beliefs. Between November 2016 and March 2017, the website was progressively translated into nine languages in addition to English (Arabic, Chinese, French, German, Japanese, Korean, Portuguese, Russian, and Spanish).

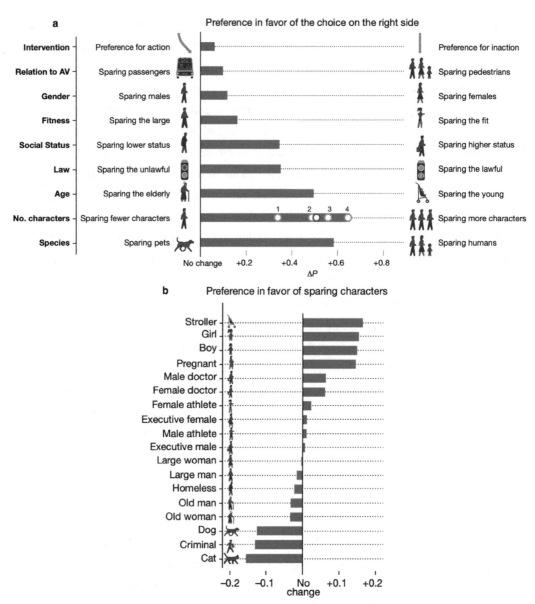

Figure 2 Global preferences. a, AMCE for each preference. In each row, ΔP is the difference between the probability of sparing characters possessing the attribute on the right, and the probability of sparing characters possessing the attribute on the left, aggregated over all other attributes. For example, for the attribute age, the probability of sparing young characters is 0.49 (s.e. = 0.0008), greater than the probability of sparing older characters. The 95% confidence intervals of the means are omitted owing to their insignificant width, given the sample size (n = 35.2 million). For the number of characters (No. characters), effect sizes are shown for each number of additional characters (1 to 4; n_1 = 1.52 million, n_2 = 1.52 million, n_3 = 1.52 million, n_4 = 1.53 million); the effect size for two additional characters overlaps with the mean effect of the attribute AV, autonomous vehicle. b, Relative

advantage or penalty for each character, compared to an adult man or woman. For each character, ΔP is the difference between the probability of sparing this character (when presented alone) and the probability of sparing one adult man or woman (n = 1 million). For example, the probability of sparing a girl is 0.15 (s.e. = 0.003), higher than the probability of sparing an adult man or woman.

While the Moral Machine offers four different modes, the focus of this article is on the central data-gathering feature of the website, called the Judge mode. In this mode, users are presented with a series of dilemmas in which the autonomous vehicle must decide between two different outcomes. In each dilemma, one outcome amounts to sparing a group of 1 to 5 characters (chosen from a sample of 20 characters, Figure 2b) and killing another group of 1 to 5 characters. The other outcome reverses the fates of the two groups. The only task of the user is to choose between the two outcomes, as a response to the question "What should the self-driving car do?" Users have the option to click on a button labelled "see description" to display a complete text description of the characters in the two groups, together with their fate in each outcome.

While users can go through as many dilemmas as they wish, dilemmas are generated in 13 sessions. Within each session, one dilemma is entirely random. The other 12 dilemmas are sampled from a space of approximately 26 million possibilities. Accordingly, it is extremely improbable for a given user to see the same dilemma twice, regardless of how many dilemmas they choose to go through, or how many times they visit the Moral Machine.

Leaving aside the one entirely random dilemma, there are two dilemmas within each session that focus on each of six dimensions of moral preferences: character gender, character age, character physical fitness, character social status, character species, and character number. Furthermore, each dilemma simultaneously randomizes three additional attributes: which group of characters will be spared if the car does nothing; whether the two groups are pedestrians, or whether one group is in the car; and whether the pedestrian characters are crossing legally or illegally. This exploration strategy is supported by a dilemma generation **algorithm**.

After completing a session of 13 dilemmas, users are presented with a summary of their decisions: which character they spared the most; which character they sacrificed the most; and the relative importance of the nine target moral dimensions in their decisions, compared to their importance to the average of all other users so far. Users have the option to share this summary with their social network. Either before or after they see this summary (randomized order), users are asked whether they want to "help us better understand their decisions". Users who click "yes" are directed to a survey of their demographic, political, and religious characteristics. They also have the option to edit the summary of their decisions, to tell us about the self-perceived importance of the nine dimensions in their decisions. These self-perceptions were not analysed in this article.

The country from which users access the website is geo-localized through the IP address of their computer or mobile device. This information is used to compute a vector of moral preferences for each country. In turn, these moral vectors are used both for cultural clustering, and for country-level correlations between moral preferences and socioeconomic indicators. The source and period of reference for each socioeconomic indicator are detailed in the Supplementary Information.

3. Results

3.1 Global Preferences

To test the relative importance of the nine preferences simultaneously explored by the Moral Machine, we used conjoint analysis to compute the average **marginal** component effect (AMCE) of each attribute (male character versus female character, passengers versus pedestrians, and so on)[18]. Figure 2a shows the unbiased estimates of nine AMCEs extracted from the Moral Machine data. In each row, the bar shows the difference between the probability of sparing characters with the attribute on the right side, and the probability of sparing the characters with the attribute on the left side, over the joint distribution of all other attributes.

As shown in Figure 2a, the strongest preferences are observed for sparing humans over animals, sparing more lives, and sparing young lives. Accordingly, these three preferences may be considered essential **building blocks** for machine ethics, or at least essential topics to be considered by policymakers. Indeed, these three preferences differ **starkly** in the level of controversy they are likely to raise among ethicists.

Consider, as a case in point, the ethical rules proposed in 2017 by the German Ethics Commission on Automated and Connected Driving[19]. This report represents the first and only attempt so far to provide official guidelines for the ethical choices of autonomous vehicles. As such, it provides an important context for interpreting our findings and their relevance to other countries that might attempt to follow the German example in the future. German Ethical Rule number 7 unambiguously states that in dilemma situations, the protection of human life should enjoy top priority over the protection of other animal life. This rule is in clear agreement with social expectations assessed through the Moral Machine. On the other hand, German Ethical Rule number 9 does not take a clear stance on whether and when autonomous vehicles should be programmed to sacrifice the few to spare the many, but leaves this possibility open: It is important, thus, to know that there would be strong public agreement with such programming, even if it is not **mandated** through regulation.

By contrast, German Ethical Rule number 9 also states that any distinction based on personal features, such as age, should be prohibited. This clearly clashes with the strong preference for sparing the young (such as children) that is assessed through the Moral Machine (see Figure 2b for a stark illustration: the four most spared characters are the baby, the little girl, the little boy, and the pregnant woman). This does not mean that policymakers should necessarily go with public opinion and allow autonomous vehicles to preferentially spare children, or, for that matter, women over men, athletes over overweight persons, or executives over homeless persons—for all of which we see weaker but clear effects. But given the strong preference for sparing children, policymakers must be aware of a dual challenge if they decide not to give a special status to children: the challenge of explaining the rationale for such a decision, and the challenge of handling the strong backlash that will inevitably occur the day an autonomous vehicle sacrifices children in a dilemma situation.

3.2 Individual Variations

We assessed individual variations by further analyzing the responses of the subgroup of Moral Machine users ($n = 492,921$) who completed the optional demographic survey on age, education, gender, income, and political and religious views, to assess whether preferences were **modulated** by these six characteristics. First, when we include all six characteristic variables in regression-based estimators of each of the nine attributes, we find that individual variations have no sizable impact on any of the nine attributes. Of these, the most notable effects are driven by gender and religiosity of respondents. For example, male respondents are 0.06% less inclined to spare females, whereas one increase in standard **deviation** of religiosity of the respondent is associated with 0.09% more **inclination** to spare humans.

More importantly, none of the six characteristics splits its subpopulations into opposing directions of effect. On the basis of a **unilateral dichotomization** of each of the six attributes, resulting in two subpopulations for each, the difference in probability (ΔP) has a positive value for all considered subpopulations. For example, both male and female respondents indicated preference for sparing females, but the latter group showed a stronger preference. In summary, the individual variations that we observe are theoretically important, but not essential information for policymakers.

3.3 Cultural Clusters

Geolocation allowed us to identify the country of residence of Moral Machine respondents, and to seek clusters of countries with homogeneous vectors of moral preferences. We selected the 130 countries, dependencies, and territories with at least 100 respondents (n range 101–448,125), standardized the nine target AMCEs of each country, and conducted a hierarchical clustering on these nine scores, using Euclidean distance and Ward's minimum variance method[20].

The first cluster (which we label the Western cluster) contains North America as well as many European countries of Protestant, Catholic, and Orthodox Christian cultural groups. The internal structure within this cluster also exhibits notable face validity, with a sub-cluster containing Scandinavian countries, and a sub-cluster containing Commonwealth countries.

The second cluster (which we call the Eastern cluster) contains many far Eastern countries such as Japan and South Korea that belong to the Confucianist cultural group, and Islamic countries such as Indonesia, Pakistan and Saudi Arabia.

The third cluster (a broadly Southern cluster) consists of the Latin American countries of Central and South America, in addition to some countries that are characterized in part by French influence (for example, **metropolitan** France, French overseas territories, and territories that were at some point under French leadership). Latin American countries are clearly separated in their own sub-cluster within the Southern cluster.

To rule out the potential effect of language, we found that the same clusters also emerged when the clustering analysis was restricted to participants who relied only on the **pictorial** representations of the dilemmas, without accessing their written descriptions.

This clustering pattern suggests that geographical and cultural **proximity** may allow groups of territories to **converge on** shared preferences for machine ethics. Between-cluster differences, though, may pose greater problems. Clusters largely differ in the weight they give to some preferences. For example, the preference to spare younger characters rather than older characters is much less pronounced for countries in the Eastern cluster, and much higher for countries in the Southern cluster. The same is true for the preference for sparing higher status characters. Similarly, countries in the Southern cluster exhibit a much weaker preference for sparing humans over pets, compared to the other two clusters. Only the (weak) preference for sparing pedestrians over passengers and the (moderate) preference for sparing the lawful over the unlawful appear to be shared to the same extent in all clusters.

Finally, we observe some striking peculiarities, such as the strong preference for sparing women and the strong preference for sparing fit characters in the Southern cluster. All the patterns of similarities and differences, though, suggest that manufacturers and policymakers should be, if not responsive, at least cognizant of moral preferences in the countries in which they design artificial intelligence systems and policies. Whereas the ethical preferences of the public should not necessarily be the primary **arbiter** of ethical policy, the people's willingness to buy autonomous vehicles and tolerate them on the roads will depend on the **palatability** of the ethical rules that are adopted.

3.4 Country-Level Predictors

Preferences revealed by the Moral Machine are highly correlated to cultural and economic variations between countries. These correlations provide support for the external validity of the platform, despite the self-selected nature of our sample. Although we do not attempt to pin down the ultimate reason or mechanism behind these correlations, we document

Unit **1** Autonomous Driving

them here as they point to possible deeper explanations of the cross-country differences and the clusters identified above.

As an illustration, consider the distance between the United States and other countries in terms of the moral preferences extracted from the Moral Machine ("MM distance"). Figure 3c shows a substantial correlation (ρ = 0.49) between this MM distance and the cultural distance from the United States based on the World Values Survey[22]. In other words, the more culturally similar a country is to the United States, the more similarly its people play the Moral Machine.

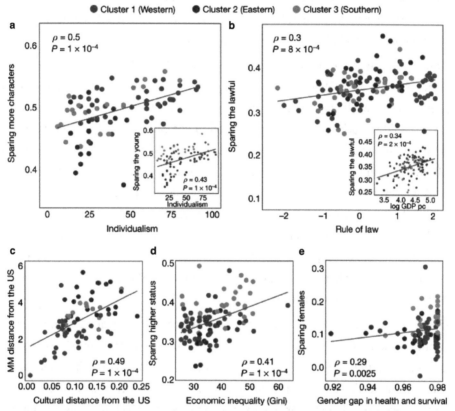

Figure 3 Association between Moral Machine preferences and other variables at the country level. Each panel shows Spearman's ρ and P value for the correlation test between the relevant pair of variables. a, Association between individualism and the preference for sparing more characters ($n = 87$), or the preference for sparing the young (inset; $n = 87$). b, Association between the preference for sparing the lawful and each of rule of law ($n = 122$) and log GDP per capita (pc) (inset; $n = 110$). c, Association between cultural distance from the United States and MM distance (distance in terms of the moral preferences extracted from the Moral Machine) from the United States ($n = 72$). d, Association between economic inequality (**Gini coefficient**) and the preference for sparing higher status ($n = 98$). e, Association between the gender gap in health and survival and the preference for sparing females ($n = 104$).

Next, we highlight four important cultural and economic predictors of Moral Machine preferences. First, we observe systematic differences between individualistic cultures and collectivistic cultures[23]. Participants from individualistic cultures, which emphasize the distinctive value of each individual[23], show a stronger preference for sparing the greater number of characters (Figure 3a). Furthermore, participants from collectivistic cultures, which emphasize the respect that is due to older members of the community[23], show a weaker preference for sparing younger characters (Figure 3a, inset). Because the preference for sparing the many and the preference for sparing the young are arguably the most important for policymakers to consider, this split between individualistic and collectivistic cultures may prove an important obstacle for universal machine ethics.

Another important (yet under-discussed) question for policymakers to consider is the importance of whether pedestrians are abiding by or violating the law. Should those who are crossing the street illegally benefit from the same protection as pedestrians who cross legally? Or should the primacy of their protection in comparison to other ethical priorities be reduced? We observe that prosperity (as indexed by GDP per capita[24]) and the quality of rules and institutions (as indexed by the Rule of Law[25]) **correlate** with a greater preference against pedestrians who cross illegally (Figure 3b). In other words, participants from countries that are poorer and suffer from weaker institutions are more tolerant of pedestrians who cross illegally, presumably because of their experience of lower rule compliance and weaker punishment of rule deviation[26]. This observation limits the generalizability of the recent German ethics guideline, for example, which state that "parties involved in the generation of mobility risks must not sacrifice non-involved parties".

Finally, our data reveal a set of preferences in which certain characters are preferred for demographic reasons. First, we observe that higher country-level economic inequality (as indexed by the country's Gini coefficient) corresponds to how unequally characters of different social status are treated. Those from countries with less economic equality between the rich and poor also treat the rich and poor less equally in the Moral Machine. This relationship may be explained by regular encounters with inequality seeping into people's moral preferences, or perhaps because broader **egalitarian** norms affect both how much inequality a country is willing to tolerate at the societal level, and how much inequality participants **endorse** in their Moral Machine judgements. Second, the differential treatment of male and female characters in the Moral Machine corresponded to the country-level gender gap in health and survival (a composite in which higher scores indicated higher ratios of female to male life expectancy and sex ratio at birth—a marker of female infanticide and anti-female sex-selective abortion). In nearly all countries, participants showed a preference for female characters; however, this preference was stronger in nations with better health and survival prospects for women. In other words, in places where there is less devaluation of women's lives in health and at birth, males are seen as more **expendable** in Moral Machine decision-making (Figure 3e). While not aiming to pin down the causes of this variation, we nevertheless provide a regression analysis which demonstrates that the results hold when controlling for several potentially confounding factors.

4. Discussion

Never in the history of humanity have we allowed a machine to autonomously decide who should live and who should die, in a **fraction** of a second, without real-time supervision. We are going to cross that bridge any time now, and it will not happen in a distant theater of military operations; it will happen in that most mundane aspect of our lives, everyday transportation. Before we allow our cars to make ethical decisions, we need to have a global conversation to express our preferences to the companies that will design moral algorithms, and to the policymakers that will regulate them.

The Moral Machine was deployed to initiate such a conversation, and millions of people weighed in from around the world. Respondents could be as **parsimonious** or thorough as they wished in the ethical framework they decided to follow. They could engage in a complicated weighting of all nine variables used in the Moral Machine, or adopt simple rules such as "let the car always go onward". Our data helped us to identify three strong preferences that can serve as building blocks for discussions of universal machine ethics, even if they are not ultimately endorsed by policymakers: the preference for sparing human lives, the preference for sparing more lives, and the preference for sparing young lives. Some preferences based on gender or social status vary considerably across countries, and appear to reflect underlying societal-level preferences for egalitarianism[27].

The Moral Machine project was atypical in many respects. It was atypical in its objectives and ambitions: no research has previously attempted to measure moral preferences using a nine-dimensional experimental design in more than 200 countries, dependencies, and territories. To achieve this unusual objective, we deployed a **viral** online platform, hoping that we would reach out to vast numbers of participants. This allowed us to collect data from millions of people over the entire world, a feat that would be nearly impossibly hard and costly to achieve through standard academic survey methods. For example, recruiting nationally representative samples of participants in hundreds of countries would already be extremely difficult, but testing a nine-factorial design in each of these samples would **verge on** impossible. Our approach allowed us to bypass these difficulties, but its downside is that our sample is self-selected, and not guaranteed to exactly match the socio-demographics of each country. The fact that the cross-societal variation we observed aligns with previously established cultural clusters, as well as the fact that macro-economic variables are predictive of Moral Machine responses, are good signals about the reliability of our data, as is our post-**stratification** analysis. But the fact that our samples are not guaranteed to be representative means that policymakers should not embrace our data as the final word on societal preferences—even if our sample is arguably close to the Internet-connected, tech-**savvy** population that is interested in driverless car technology, and more likely to participate in early adoption.

Even with a sample size as large as ours, we could not do justice to all of the complexity of autonomous vehicle dilemmas. For example, we did not introduce uncertainty about the fates of the characters, and we did not introduce any uncertainty about the classification of these characters. In our scenarios, characters were recognized as adults, children, and so on with 100% certainty, and life-and-death outcomes were predicted with 100% certainty. These assumptions are technologically unrealistic, but they were necessary to keep the project tractable. Similarly, we did not manipulate the hypothetical relationship between respondents and characters (for example, relatives or spouses). Our previous work did not find a strong effect of this variable on moral preferences[12].

Indeed, we can embrace the challenges of machine ethics as a unique opportunity to decide, as a community, what we believe to be right or wrong; and to make sure that machines, unlike humans, unerringly follow these moral preferences. We might not reach universal agreement: even the strongest preferences expressed through the Moral Machine showed substantial cultural variations, and our project builds on a long tradition of investigating cultural variations in ethical judgements[28]. But the fact that broad regions of the world displayed relative agreement suggests that our journey to consensual machine ethics is not doomed from the start. Attempts at establishing broad ethical codes for intelligent machines, such as the Asilomar AI Principles[29], often recommend that machine ethics should be aligned with human values. These codes seldom recognize, though, that humans experience inner conflict, interpersonal disagreements, and cultural dissimilarities in the moral domain[30,31,32]. We have shown that these conflicts, disagreements, and dissimilarities, while substantial, may not be fatal.

(Scan the QR code to access the list of references.)

Words and Expressions

proliferation	n.	rapid increase in the number or amount of something
in lieu of		in the place of; instead of
status quo		the existing state of affairs, especially regarding social or political issues

Unit 1 Autonomous Driving

cognizant	*adj.*	having knowledge or awareness
be cognizant of		to be aware of or have knowledge about a particular subject or issue
scenario	*n.*	a postulated sequence or development of events
demographic	*adj.*	relating to the structure of populations
geolocate	*v.*	to identify the geographical location of a person or device by means of digital information processed via the Internet
algorithm	*n.*	a process or set of rules to be followed in calculations or other problem-solving operations, especially by a computer
marginal	*adj.*	relating to or at the edge or margin
building block		a basic unit from which something is built up
starkly	*adv.*	in a way that is severe or harsh in appearance or outline
mandate	*v.*	to give (someone) authority to act in a certain way
modulate	*v.*	to exert a modifying or controlling influence on something
deviation	*n.*	the action of departing from an established course or accepted standard
inclination	*n.*	a person's natural tendency or urge to act or feel in a particular way
unilateral	*adj.*	performed by or affecting only one person, group, or country involved in a situation, without the agreement of another or the others
dichotomization	*n.*	the act of dividing into two sharply different categories
metropolitan	*adj.*	relating to or denoting a metropolis
pictorial	*adj.*	of or expressed in pictures
proximity	*n.*	nearness in space, time, or relationship
converge on		to come from different directions and meet at (a place)
arbiter	*n.*	a person who settles a dispute or has ultimate authority in a matter
palatability	*n.*	the fact or quality of being acceptable or agreeable
Gini coefficient		a statistical measure of the degree of variation represented in a set of values, used especially in analyzing income inequality
correlate	*v.*	to have a mutual relationship or connection, in which one thing affects or depends on another
egalitarian	*adj.*	believing in or based on the principle that all people are equal and deserve equal rights and opportunities

endorse	*v.*	to declare one's public approval or support of
expendable	*adj.*	of relatively little significance, and therefore able to be abandoned or destroyed
fraction	*n.*	a small or tiny part, amount, or proportion of something
parsimonious	*adj.*	very unwilling to spend money or use resources
viral	*adj.*	circulated rapidly and widely from one Internet user to another
verge on		to be very close or similar to
stratification	*n.*	the arrangement or classification of something into different groups
savvy	*adj.*	shrewd and knowledgeable; having common sense and good judgement

 Reflections and Practice

❶ Read the text and answer the following questions.

1. What are the moral dilemmas faced by car manufacturers and policymakers?
2. What are the challenges to gauge social expectations about how autonomous vehicles should solve moral dilemmas?
3. What was the Moral Machine website designed for?
4. What are the six dimensions of moral preferences examined?
5. What are the nine preferences and their relative importance explored on the Moral Machine platform?
6. What is the clash between the present study and the German Ethical Rule number 9?
7. What are the three strong preferences the authors identified as something that can serve as building blocks for discussions of universal machine ethics?
8. What are the uncertainties that the authors did not study?

❷ Discuss the following questions with your partner.

1. Should autonomous vehicles be programmed to sacrifice the few to spare the many?
2. Do you agree with the German Ethical Rule number 9, which states that any distinction based on personal features, such as age, should be prohibited?
3. How can you improve the representative level on socio-demographics of the samples collected by the Moral Machine?

4. Do you think that survey answers collected online are credible and truly represent what people think?

5. Do you want to buy a fully autonomous driving car and let the car make decisions in dangerous situations?

III Paraphrase the following sentences.

1. We are entering an age in which machines are tasked not only to promote well-being and minimize harm, but also to distribute the well-being they create, and the harm they cannot eliminate. Distribution of well-being and harm inevitably creates tradeoffs, whose resolution falls in the moral domain.

2. Autonomous vehicles will cruise our roads soon, necessitating agreement on the principles that should apply when, inevitably, life-threatening dilemmas emerge.

3. Decisions about the ethical principles that will guide autonomous vehicles cannot be left solely to either the engineers or the ethicists. For consumers to switch from traditional human-driven cars to autonomous vehicles, and for the wider public to accept the proliferation of artificial intelligence-driven vehicles on their roads, both groups will need to understand the origins of the ethical principles that are programmed into these vehicles.

4. Never in the history of humanity have we allowed a machine to autonomously decide who should live and who should die, in a fraction of a second, without real-time supervision. We are going to cross that bridge any time now, and it will not happen in a distant theater of military operations; it will happen in that most mundane aspect of our lives, everyday transportation.

5. Attempts at establishing broad ethical codes for intelligent machines, such as the Asilomar AI Principles, often recommend that machine ethics should be aligned with human values. These codes seldom recognize, though, that humans experience inner conflict, interpersonal disagreements, and cultural dissimilarities in the moral domain.

IV Do a first-pass reading of the text and answer the following questions.

1. Category: What type of paper is this? A review or an original research article? An experimental, theoretical, or numerical study?

2. Context: What is the research problem? Why is the problem important? How was the research problem addressed? What are the findings and conclusions?

3. Contributions: What are the paper's main contributions?

Ⅴ Do a second-pass reading of the text and answer the following questions.

1. Correctness: Are the assumptions of this paper valid? Are the conclusions well supported by the obtained data?
2. Creativity: Is your mind refreshed or influenced by this paper?
3. Clarity: Is the paper well written?

Ⅵ Write an outline for the text following the structure below.

1. **Research Background**
   We are entering an age in which autonomous vehicles are tasked not only to _____, but also to _____. Distribution of well-being and harm inevitably creates _____ _____.

2. **Research Question**
   How do autonomous vehicles decide to _____?

3. **Research Objective**
   To _____ about how autonomous vehicles should solve moral dilemmas and provide ethical guidelines for car manufacturers and policymakers.

4. **Methods**
   Designed the _____, a multilingual online "serious game" for collecting large-scale data on how citizens would want autonomous vehicles to solve moral dilemmas in the context of unavoidable accidents.

5. **Major Results and Findings**
   - The strongest preferences are observed for _____.
   - Some preferences based on gender or social status vary considerably across countries, and appear to reflect underlying societal-level preferences for egalitarianism.

6. **Conclusion**
   Discovered global moral preferences, individual variations in preferences, and cross-cultural ethical variation. The findings can contribute to _____ _____.

Ⅶ Write a summary for the text in 150–200 words.

Part 3　Further Reading

Life and Death Decisions of Autonomous Vehicles[1]

Abstract

How should self-driving cars make decisions when human lives hang in the balance? "The Moral Machine Experiment" (MME) suggests that people want autonomous vehicles (AVs) to treat different human lives unequally, preferentially killing some people (for example, men, the old and the poor) over others (for example, women, the young and the rich). Our results challenge this idea, revealing that this apparent preference for inequality is driven by the specific "trolley-type" paradigm used by the MME. Multiple studies with a revised paradigm reveal that people overwhelmingly want autonomous vehicles to treat different human lives equally in life and death situations, ignoring gender, age and status—a preference consistent with a general desire for equality.

Keywords: autonomous vehicle, life and death situation, decision making, moral machine, equality

 Reflections and Practice

Read the full article and answer the following questions.

1. What is the purpose of this article?
2. By what means did the authors challenge the findings reported in the MME article?
3. What is the purpose of the authors to test a forced inequality condition in their study?
4. What arguments are used to support the opinion that killing decisions made by autonomous vehicles should rely solely on structural rather than personal features?
5. What are the implications of the key findings on policy making?

1　This paper is from Bigman, Y. E. & Gray, K. 2020. Life and death decisions of autonomous vehicles. *Nature*, *579*(7797): E1–E2.

Unit 2
Public Health

Learning Objectives

- Read the keywords for the gist of a paper;

- Recognize structural indicators for predicting the information structure;

- Formulate an outline.

Part 1　Reading Skills and Strategies

Identifying Keywords and Formulating an Outline

1. Keywords in Reading

Keywords reading is a skill for improving the efficiency of reading academic papers. Keywords such as notional verbs, direction words, common structural indicators and mood qualifiers can help you quickly understand the gist of the sentences, paragraphs and entire articles.

1) Notional verbs

Notional verbs embody the main meaning of each sentence in the article. In other words, as long as the predicate verb in each sentence is understood, the main meaning of the entire article will be very clear. Let's look at the following text:

Interventions to Reduce Sedentary Behavior

This article **reports on** the proceedings as part of a joint workshop sponsored and organized by the National Heart, Lung, and Blood Institute and National Institute on Aging entitled the "Influences on Sedentary Behavior and Interventions **to Reduce** Sedentary Behavior". A panel of experts in behavioral health, physical activity (PA) interventions, and health information technology to increase activity levels convened to **discuss** the major factors that **might influence** interventions for **reducing** sedentary behaviors (SB). This workshop **was not convened to conduct** a systematic review of the literature because there are several recent publications that have done so (7, 10, 21, 31, 37). The working group **used** an overarching framework **involving** literature reviews and discussions **aimed at elucidating** the "what, how, with whom, in what context, and with what effect" of interventions for **reducing** SB. This central framework **was expanded** through bimonthly conference calls and e-mail discussions. Recommendations **evolved** from this activity were discussed and presented to an international group of SB researchers who **participated in** a 2.5-

hour webinar workshop and were **modified** according to the discussion that **ensued**. It **is important to recognize** that interventions **are substantially influenced by** the specific definitions of SB that **are being applied** and which **contribute to** elevated health risk. For example, the recommendations **put forth** below should **generally apply to** a definition of SB that **is restricted to** activities with intensities.

In the first sentence, the predicate verb "report on" reminds you that the subject information of the paper is coming, that is, "Influences on Sedentary Behavior and Interventions to Reduce Sedentary Behavior". In the sentences that follow, the non-predicate verb "reduce" recurs to focus your attention on how to make interventions to reduce sedentary behavior. Combined with the title, you can quickly grasp the purpose of this section by reading the bold letters of the verbs or verb phrases above and speed up the reading.

2) Direction words

Direction words can be considered as a kind of grammar vocabulary that helps readers to predict the focus, topic, or detailed structure, which determine your speed of reading. Let's look at the following example:

> Reports on an organization's projects may fall under **several** major functions at the same time. A report can be used to educate and gain support from key people and groups, to facilitate and inform decisionmaking about current and future projects, and to provide documentation for the organization's records.

The word "several" in the example above is an indefinite number, a direction word. When it appears in an opinion sentence or a conclusion sentence, it indicates that the noun or noun phrase will be followed: the topic or focus of the text. By recognizing it, you quickly get to know the focus of the following structure: the main function of the report which will be developed. Since you have been able to predict the center and structure of the following text, you can naturally speed up the reading.

3) Common structural indicators

Common structural indicators and sequence of process can also help predict the important detail information.

- ✓ Classification and listing indicators include: *categories, classifications, groups, pats, types, characteristics, elements, kinds, sorts, ways, classes, features, numbers, 1, 2, 3, 4, moreover, next, also, then, furthermore*, etc.
- ✓ Sequence and process indicators include: *first, second, third, after stages, now, later, before, steps, next, finally, then, the most important, furthermore, when, last*, etc.

4) Mood qualifiers

The role of mood qualifiers is to help you predict the author's tone. For example, if absolute signal words appear in an opinion sentence, it indicates that the author definitely agrees to the point of view. Thus, the following text direction will proceed towards the direction of the argument. However, if you see the possibility signal words in the opinion sentence, it indicates that the author must be skeptical of this point of view, so the following text will be in the direction of refutation or questioning. Let's look at the following example:

Does the threat of the death penalty deter people from murderous behavior more than the threat of life imprisonment? We do not yet know with anything even approaching certainty whether the death penalty does or does not deter. The question is clearly empirical, and it is **likely** that sophisticated statistical techniques will eventually permit us an answer.

Here, the word "likely", a signal word for possibility, helps you predict that the author's attitude towards precise statistical techniques is actually skeptical. Therefore, the following sentences must be a questioning or refutative one: "All statistical arguments on the death penalty are, however, excruciatingly complex and misleading."

2. Formulating an Outline

Formulating an outline of an article can also help you get the main idea of it. It is quite necessary to draw out the main points outlining the structure of the article.

1) What is an outline?

An outline is a basic writing plan which consists of a series of phrases or sentences and shows the main points that the paper will cover and the order in which these points will be mentioned.

2) The function of an outline

An outline gives you a specific guidance as to what kind of supporting details you should look for in your further research and where you can fit them into the context of your paper. The readers, on the other hand, benefit from the outline as a complete and detailed table of contents.

3) The procedure of preparing an outline

Since outlining and summarizing are two efficient ways of reading, it is necessary to formulate an outline before writing a summary of an article assigned to you by your advisor. In writing the outline, you can follow the following five procedures:

✓ Have a satisfactory thesis statement;

✓ Review all your note cards and gather related materials together under some general headings;

- ✓ Arrange these headings according to the development of your thought;
- ✓ Form a logical preliminary outline;
- ✓ Discuss your preliminary outline with your advisor.

4) A sample outline

In general, there are two types of outlines. One is called a topic outline, and the other is a complete sentence outline? The following is a sample of a topic outline.

Interventions to Reduce Sedentary Behavior

Purpose: To make people aware of the influences of sedentary behavior and to provide interventions.

Methods: Discuss interventions in the context of targeting sedentary behavior as a concept distinct from physical activity.

Recommendation 1: Focus on the assessment of the feasibility, acceptability, and effectiveness of SB interventional prognostic streams at different stages of life, with a particular concern of racial diversity.

Rationale: SB may have a significant proximal end at any age and long-term consequences for health and well-being.

Recommendation 2: Target at multiple possible levels for intervening on SB across the life course, including individual, interpersonal, organizational, environmental and policy levels.

Rationale: SB may be targeted via multiple interconnected levels of influence.

Recommendation 3: Research on how new technologies can be integrated with principles of behavioral science to reduce SB across the life course.

Rationale: Intervention studies provide some evidence in small groups of people that SB in workplaces can be effectively reduced through environmental modifications.

Recommendation 4: Make interventions by taking advantage of changes in the built and social environments including the use of social networks and the promotion of relevant public policy changes.

Rationale: Using proven behavioral strategies, incorporating messages to build awareness, and adopting new technology can provide a foundation for developing SB interventions.

Conclusions: There is a clear rationale for conducting experimentally based studies on SB interventions that are expected to lead to solutions that increase daily activity—even at a light intensity level, and the design of SB interventions should be considered as priorities.

Part 2　Intensive Reading

Childhood Overweight and Obesity: Is the Gap Closing the Wrong Way?[1]

Pre-reading questions:

✓ What is the concept of obesity? Is obesity a disease or just a person's body type?

✓ What do you think is the relationship between obesity and the social class?

✓ Are obese children more likely to become overweight adults?

✓ What diseases are obese people more likely to suffer from?

✓ What methods do you think the authors would use to investigate the relationship between obesity and social class?

Background

Obesity is considered a worldwide epidemic and a significant public health issue. Across the UK, its **incidence** and prevalence continue to rise and is estimated to cost the UK economy £3.5 billion each year (healthcare/treatment costs and sickness days off work).[1] By 2010, an estimated 12 million adults and one million children will be obese in England alone, unless lifestyle changes are made across the whole population.[2,3] Obese children and young people have an increased risk of becoming overweight/obese adults and developing adult diseases such as **cardiovascular** disease, type 2 diabetes and some cancers.[4-8] The periodic measurement of children's weight and height by school nurses and other public health professionals are a potential source of data for monitoring the development of the epidemic of childhood obesity and of evaluating the effectiveness of interventions aimed at **halting** it.

1　This paper is from Brunt, H., Lester, N., Davies, G. & Williams, R. 2008. Childhood overweight and obesity: Is the gap closing the wrong way? *Journal of Public Health, 30*(2): 145–152.

However, enquiries of English Primary Care Trusts[9] and Welsh National Health Service (NHS) Trusts and Local Health Boards[10] reveal considerable variation in the ages at which these measurements are taken, the health professionals making the measurements and the extent of population coverage. In addition, retrieving and analysing data are made overly complex by issues of data ownership, confidentiality and computer system incompatibility. Meaningful analysis is possible, but only when population coverage is high (or at least not subject to bias) and where data are available for a number of consecutive years.[11]

The body of research investigating the relationship between socioeconomic status (SES) and obesity in adults is growing. However, evidence quantifying the influence of SES on childhood overweight/obesity is fairly limited.[12–17] We know that eating habits develop early and a poor diet established in childhood and continued into adulthood can lead to later health problems.[18] We also know that economically **deprived** families often replace fresh food with cheaper processed foods.[19] Low-income households have restricted choices, especially in relation to healthier foods.[19] Healthier food items may be difficult to access and more expensive. Generally, people in more deprived households have poorer nutrient intakes than people in less deprived households and evidence suggests the gap between them has widened over the last 20 years.[19] There is also some evidence for decreased physical activity in economically disadvantaged households[20] which only **exacerbates** the problem. Perhaps for these and other reasons, there is a developing evidence base suggesting that overweight/obesity is associated with social deprivation.[12–17]

This study analyses children's height and weight data and investigates the association of family SES with overweight/obesity amongst three-year-old children in three South Wales localities, between 1995 and 2005. The selection of these localities was based on National Community Child Health Database (NCCHD) data accuracy and completeness, but also because a doubling of the prevalence of obesity in boys and girls aged five (between 1986/1987 and 2001/2002) had been reported previously.[11]

Methods

Population Measures

Height and weight data of individual (but anonymised) children were obtained from the NCCHD, a database covering children residents in Wales which receives its information from trust-based child health systems.[21] A data extract was obtained containing information which had been collected as part of the schedule of preschool health examinations by NHS trust-employed health visitors between 1995 and 2005 in the Swansea, Neath and Port Talbot areas of South Wales, UK. The final two examinations in the schedule (exams 06 and 07) are undertaken on children aged 152–160 and 182–208 weeks, respectively. Exam 06 includes a height and weight measure as standard and exam 07 includes it as an option. Data from these tests are captured by the NCCHD and mapped to the CHIRP08 examination code, enabling area comparison.

Those performing the school-entry examinations had been appropriately trained. Child height and weight measurements were taken using standardised methodology and regularly **calibrated** equipment. For both, averages of three readings were taken.

Estimates of Adiposity

Body mass index [BMI—weight (kg) divided by the square of height (m)] was used as a **surrogate** for **adiposity**, and overweight and obesity classifications were based on International Obesity Task Force (IOTF) **cut-offs**.[21] This method of assessing childhood overweight and obesity was chosen since it was used in a previous study of childhood obesity trends in the same South Wales localities.[11] BMI values were **scrutinised** to eliminate **spurious** results arising from data recording errors. As in the previous study, analysis was restricted to a BMI range of 10–27 units, regarded as biologically feasible. No **outliers** were identified.

SES Measures

Townsend material deprivation scores[22] (which comprise assessments of unemployment, overcrowding, home and car ownership) were used to determine childhood SES and was assigned according to NCCHD-recorded postcode of residence. Townsend scores, standardised to Wales, were calculated from 2001 census data at lower layer super output area (LSOA) level. LSOAs are a small area statistical geography produced by the Office for National Statistics (ONS) whose minimum and mean populations are 1,000 and 1,500, respectively. All-Wales LSOA Townsend scores were ranked and deprivation fifths (from one, least deprived, to five, most deprived) were derived.

Statistical Analysis

Data were analysed using Microsoft Access and Excel software. The NCCHD extract received for analysis contained a number of duplicates, including individuals with more than one height and weight measure. Data were "cleaned" to identify unique individuals.

Analysis of the data identified the proportion of three-year-old children who had received a CHIRP08 examination and those with a height and weight measure recorded, allowing BMI scores to be calculated. In order to minimise bias, data were analysed to show the proportion of children with a BMI score **stratified** by fifth of deprivation.

The proportion of children within the "overweight" and "obese" categories (determined by IOTF cut-offs[23]) was calculated for each deprivation fifth. This was done for the eleven-year period (1995–2005) as a whole. The proportions of overweight/obese children in the least and most deprived fifths were then calculated for each individual year to determine any time trends. This was supported by the addition of a linear regression analysis.

Results

Data Coverage

A total of 53,716 records of CHIRP08 health examinations were obtained for the period 1995–2005. Child age, as recorded on the database, ranged from 0–11 years. However, the majority of the records (92.76%) applied to three-year olds. Our analysis focuses solely on these 49,826 three-year-old children.

The CHIRP08 examination includes items other than the measurement of height and weight, e.g. vision and hearing tests. 14,266 of the 49,826 records identified were duplicate entries. This included a small number ($n = 293$) where height and weight had been measured on more than one occasion and these were excluded for the purposes of the analysis. Where there were duplicates, the most recent examination was selected.

Comparison of the number of individual children examined with office for national ONS mid-year population estimates for this age group resident in Swansea, Neath and Port Talbot (Table 1) showed that the estimated proportion of three-year-old children having a CHIRP08 exam was between 63% and 87%. Of those children who were examined, between 53% and 69% had a height and weight measurement recorded (Table 1) with a clear rise in the proportion demonstrated over the study period. This population was distributed across the deprivation fifths as shown in Table 2.

Trends in Overweight and Obesity

Amalgamating the data over the 11-year study period showed that 1,115 or 5.2% (95% CI: 4.9%–5.5%) of the 21,301 children for whom a BMI could be calculated were obese (according to the IOTF definition[23]). A further 3,202 or 15.0% (95% CI: 14.6%–15.5%) of children were overweight. The proportions of boys and girls in these categories were: overweight—boys: 14.3% (95% CI: 13.6%–14.9%) and girls: 15.8% (95% CI: 15.1%–16.5%); obese—boys: 4.9% (95% CI: 4.5%–5.3%) and girls: 5.6% (95% CI: 5.1%–6.0%). The proportion of children in the overweight and obese categories combined increased over the study period from 18.0% (95% CI: 16.1%–19.9%) in 1995 to 22.0% (95% CI: 20.2%–23.8%) in 2005. The proportion of overweight children rose from 13.9% (95% CI: 12.2%–15.6%) in 1995 to 16.8% (95% CI: 15.2%–18.5%) in 2005, whereas the proportion of obese children rose from 4.1% (95% CI:

3.1%–5.1%) in 1995 to 5.1% (95% CI: 4.2%–6.1%) in 2005.

Table 1 Three-year-old population, number and proportion of three-year-old children included on the NCCHD

Exam year	Population	Number examined (% of population)	Number of completed exams	Number with height and weight measurements taken (% of those examined)
1995	4,548	2,846 (62.6%)	3,491	1,580 (55.5%)
1996	4,425	3,840 (86.8%)	5,799	2,045 (53.3%)
1997	4,177	3,497 (83.7%)	4,946	1,955 (55.9%)
1998	3,949	3,396 (86.0%)	4,780	1,933 (56.9%)
1999	4,119	3,094 (75.1%)	4,790	1,779 (57.5%)
2000	4,140	3,339 (80.7%)	5,062	1,939 (58.1%)
2001	3,929	3,345 (85.1%)	4,900	1,952 (58.4%)
2002	3,783	2,996 (79.2%)	3,863	1,945 (64.9%)
2003	3,815	2,999 (78.6%)	3,866	2,009 (67.0%)
2004	3,884	3,097 (79.7%)	4,268	2,120 (68.5%)
2005	3,756	3,111 (82.8%)	4,061	2,044 (65.7%)
TOTAL	44,525	35,560 (79.9%)	49,826	21,301 (59.9%)

The proportion of children in the overweight and obese categories combined increased over the study period from 18.0% (95% CI: 16.1%–19.9%) in 1995 to 22.0% (95% CI: 20.2%–23.8%) in 2005. The proportion of overweight children rose from 13.9% (95% CI: 12.2%–15.6%) in 1995 to 16.8% (95% CI: 15.2%–18.5%) in 2005, whereas the proportion of obese children rose from 4.1% (95% CI: 3.1%–5.1%) in 1995 to 5.1% (95% CI: 4.2%–6.1%) in 2005. The proportion of overweight and obese girls was generally greater than for boys during the study period. Both boys and girls showed a similar rate of increase. Amongst boys, the proportion of overweight and obese individuals rose from 17.5% (95% CI: 14.9%–20.1%) in 1995 to 21.2% (95% CI: 18.7%–23.7%) in 2005 and, in girls, from 18.7% (95% CI: 15.9%–21.4%) to 22.7% (95% CI: 20.2%–25.3%). Over the 11-year period, the proportion of overweight boys increased from 14.2% (95% CI: 11.8%–16.6%) to 16.8% (95% CI: 14.5%–19.1%) and in girls from 13.6% (95% CI: 11.2%–16.1%) to 16.8% (95% CI: 11.2%–16.1%). During this time, the proportion of obese boys rose from 3.3% (95% CI: 2.1%–4.5%) to 4.4% (95% CI: 3.1%–5.7%), and girls, from 5.0% (95% CI: 3.5%–6.6%) to 5.9% (95% CI: 4.4%–7.3%).

Table 2 Distribution of study population across Townsend deprivation fifth

Townsend deprivation fifth	Height and weight recorded		
	No.	Yes	95% confidence interval %
Least deprived	2,897	4,077 (58.5%)	56.9–60.0
2	2,178	3,342 (60.5%)	58.9–62.2
3	2,545	4,000 (61.1%)	59.6–62.6
4	2,887	4,455 (60.7%)	59.2–62.1
Most deprived	3,752	5,427 (59.1%)	57.8–60.4

Table 3 Rations (compared to least deprived fifth) of the proportion of overweight and obese three-year-old boys and girls by Townsend deprivation fifth

	Townsend deprivation fifth		Proportion (n)	Ratio	95% CI
Obese	Boys	Least deprived	4.4% (92)		
		2	4.5% (78)	1.03	0.77–1.38
		3	4.8% (96)	1.08	0.82–1.43
		4	5.1% (115)	1.15	0.88–1.51
		Most deprived	5.4% (149)	1.23	0.95–1.58
	Girls	Least deprived	5.9% (118)		
		2	5.7% (92)	0.96	0.73–1.25
		3	5.3% (105)	0.89	0.69–1.15
		4	4.9% (107)	0.82	0.64–1.06
		Most deprived	6.1% (163)	1.09	0.82–1.29
Overweight	Boys	Least deprived	14.3% (298)		
		2	15.4% (264)	1.08	0.92–1.25
		3	15.2% (307)	1.06	0.92–1.23
		4	13.6% (308)	0.95	0.82–1.10
		Most deprived	13.3% (367)	0.93	0.81–1.08
	Girls	Least deprived	15.8% (315)		
		2	15.8% (256)	1.00	0.86–1.16
		3	17.0% (337)	1.07	0.93–1.24
		4	14.2% (311)	0.90	0.78–1.04
		Most deprived	16.4% (439)	1.04	0.91–1.18

Association with Socioeconomic Status

As shown in Table 3, when the data for all 11 years were amalgamated, there were no significant associations between SES and the proportions of either boys or girls considered obese or the proportions considered overweight. This was also true when overweight and obese categories were combined (not shown).

When these data were analysed by year, there was a small decrease in the proportion of children who were obese from the least deprived areas [from 5.6% (95% CI: 2.9%–8.2%) in 1995 to 4.3% (95% CI: 2.3%–6.3%) in 2005], whilst there was a more substantial increase [from 3.7% (95% CI: 1.9%–5.5%) in 1995 to 6.3% (95% CI: 4.2%–8.4%) in 2005] of the children from the most deprived areas considered obese. The proportion children resident in the least deprived fifth of areas who were overweight increased from 14.6% (95% CI: 10.5%–18.7%) in 1995 to 16.0% (95% CI: 12.4%–19.7%) in 2005, whilst for those in the most deprived fifth of areas, the increase was greater [from 12.8% (95% CI: 9.7%–16.0%) in 1995 to 18.3% (95% CI: 14.9%–21.7%) in 2005]. However, year on year variation was considerable.

Table 4 Proportion of children overweight or obese, least and most deprived fifth

Period	Least deprived (95% CI)	Most deprived (95% CI)
1995	20.2 (15.6–24.9)	16.6 (13.0–20.1)
1996	22.3 (18.0–26.7)	17.4 (14.3–20.6)
1997	18.2 (14.0–22.3)	19.3 (15.8–22.7)
1998	19.7 (15.5–23.8)	23.0 (19.3–26.6)
1999	19.8 (15.7–23.9)	21.6 (17.8–25.4)
2000	23.7 (19.2–28.2)	20.6 (17.1–24.1)
2001	21.4 (17.3–25.5)	24.2 (20.4–28.0)
2002	19.8 (15.9–23.6)	17.5 (14.1–20.9)
2003	16.9 (13.4–20.5)	23.1 (19.3–26.8)
2004	20.4 (16.6–24.1)	19.0 (15.6–22.3)
2005	20.4 (16.4–24.3)	24.6 (20.8–28.4)

For overweight and obese categories combined, once again, there was substantial annual variation throughout the study period with the most deprived fifth having the lowest proportion on five occasions and the highest on six occasions (Table 4). Analysis of the rate ratio between the most and least deprived fifths indicates that at no time during the study period was the difference in the rates statistically significant (Figure 1). The 95% confidence limits are reasonably wide due to the fairly small numbers involved.

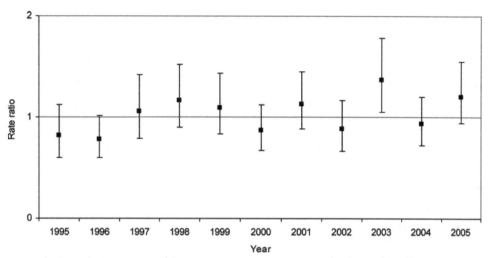

Figure 1   Rate ratio (most deprived to least deprived) of overweight and obese (combined) three-year-old children in Swansea, Neath and Port Talbot, 1995–2005.

Linear regression lines were plotted to show trends in the proportion of overweight or obese children in the most deprived and the least deprived fifths between 1995 and 2005 (Figure 2). The regression line for the least deprived fifth appears almost flat across the study period, whilst the regression line for the most deprived fifth shows some degree of a positive trend. An F test was conducted on each line to evaluate the likelihood that any observed association between time and proportion overweight and obese occurred by chance. Neither regression line produced a statistically significant result at the 5% level (Least deprived F ¼ 0.188, d.f. ¼ 9, P ¼ 0.68/Most deprived F ¼ 3.335, d.f. ¼ 9, P ¼ 0.10).

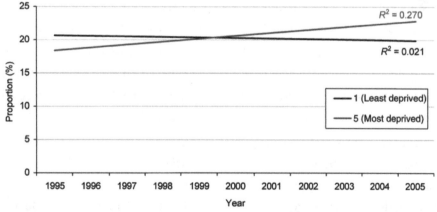

Figure 2   Proportion of overweight and obese (combined) three-year-old children in Swansea, Neath and Port Talbot from the least and most deprived areas, linear regression, 1995–2005.

These results suggest that it is not possible to reject the **null** hypothesis (that there is no relationship between time and proportions of overweight or obese children within either the most or least deprived fifths). The difference in the slopes of the two regression lines was –0.53 (95% CI: –0.22 to 0.17) and not statistically significant. In summary, the analysis suggests that the percentages overweight and obese within both the most deprived and least deprived fifths have not changed to any statistically significant degree over the study period. Furthermore, the rates of any (non-statistically significant) changes that have taken place are not statistically significantly different between the most and least deprived fifths.

Discussion

Main Findings of This Study

This study investigated the relationship between SES of three-year-old children in three Welsh localities and the prevalence of overweight and obesity in these children. When data from 1995 to 2005 were combined, there was no association. Analysis of the annual trend in overweight and obesity among children resident in the most and least deprived fifth of LSOAs showed substantial annual variation. Linear regression analysis showed that the regression line for the least deprived fifth appears almost flat across the study period, whilst the regression line for the most deprived fifth appears to show some degree of a positive trend (but not statistically significant).

What Is Already Known on This Topic

A growing body of research has investigated the relationship between SES and obesity, but with an adult focus. There is limited research specifically looking at the relationship between deprivation and obesity in children (particularly young children) over time.

One study that examined childhood overweight/obesity prevalence trends in 28,601 children (aged 5–10 years) in relation to trends in parental social class and household income, concluded that childhood obesity rates are increasing rapidly and that these increases are more **marked** amongst children from lower socioeconomic strata.[17]

Furthermore, a cross-sectional analysis of routinely collected data on Scottish preschool children suggested that obesity is associated with social deprivation.[12] The authors' reasons for this include the economics of healthier eating, the availability of, and access to, a choice of good quality healthy foods and also the likelihood that children from poorer families have reduced levels of physical activity. A similar association between deprivation and childhood obesity was found in another cross-sectional study.[13]

Another study to determine whether SES is associated with overweight and obesity in pre-pubertal children (1,420 10/11 year olds) in Italy found that the lower the cultural resources of the mother and economical resources of the family, the greater the rate of childhood weight gain.[14] A further cross-sectional study to determine if neighbourhood SES is systematically related to the prevalence of overweight children in Canada (5–17 year-olds) found that the prevalence of overweight is inversely and statistically significantly related to neighbourhood SES, observed a gradient of increasing overweight prevalence by decreasing neighbourhood SES quartiles and stated that a child's odds of being overweight increases if living in a low versus a high SES neighbourhood (OR ¼ 1.29, 95% CI ¼ 1.14–1.46).[15]

A review that examined predictors of childhood obesity found no clear relationship between SES in early life and childhood fatness.[16] However, a strong consistent relationship was observed between low SES in early life and increased fatness in adulthood. Studies investigating SES were generally large but very few considered confounding by parental fatness.

What This Study Adds

This analysis shows that the relationship, between overweight and obesity on the one hand, and social deprivation on the other, is dynamic. It showed signs of change in these South Wales localities over the study period, from one in which the prevalence of overweight and obesity appeared to be greater in the least socially deprived fifth of children to one where the prevalence of overweight and obesity appeared to be greater in the most deprived fifth. It should be noted, however, that substantial variation in overweight and obesity prevalence was observed over time and results obtained were not statistically significant.

There are important wider public health implications associated with this analysis. The fact that only 59.9% of examined children had corresponding height and weight measurements reinforces the need for improved data quality and **surveillance** of overweight and obesity amongst children. The observed trends highlight the influence socioeconomic factors may have on childhood overweight/obesity and suggest that directing lifestyle-changing messages and interventions towards those in more deprived population groups could have a greater impact on addressing this issue.

Limitations of This Study

This is an ecological analysis with all the limitations of such analyses—difficulties of dealing with confounding and identifying cause and effect relationships. There is limited coverage for height and weight measurements. We have estimated that, over the study period, around 80% of children appear on the NCCHD with at least one CHIRP08 entry. Of these, an average of 60% have a valid height and weight measurement recorded, although improvements were observed over the study period. This raises the probability of selection bias if either BMI or deprivation, or both, are associated with the probability of heights and weights being recorded, or indeed appearing on the database with a CHIRP08 exam in the first instance. The fact that there were no differences related to deprivation in the probability of data being recorded provides some assurance that, if such bias exists, it does not have a major influence over the conclusions of the study.

The problems with NCCHD coverage exemplify the need for investment in a proper surveillance system for this important public health area. As mentioned above, height and weight measurements were only recorded in around two thirds of the records on the NCCHD, despite the study focusing on three localities where coverage is believed to be better. Had national coverage been higher, this would have enabled the analysis to take place across Wales, yielding larger numbers and more statistically robust findings.

A further limitation of this study is that data coverage constraints determined that the focus of the study had to be on three-year-old children. It is likely that the effect of socioeconomic disadvantage in increasing the risk of overweight and obesity in children will **manifest** itself more strongly as they become older. In order to make comparisons with other studies, it would have been interesting to have undertaken a similar analysis looking at the relationship between overweight/obesity and deprivation in older children, but poor data coverage issues for older children prevented this.

BMI is a widely used, but increasingly questioned, **proxy** for adiposity. Other measures, particularly waist circumference and more sophisticated estimates of body fat may be more relevant in relation to the prediction of future cardiovascular morbidity. However, as a proxy measure of changes in the prevalence of overweight and obesity, BMI is a practical measure on a population basis and should be retained at least until a better and equally practical measure is available.

As with the previous study using similar data,[11] the range of acceptable BMI values was restricted to the range 10–27 kg/m^2. The upper limit of this range may well be inappropriate given current trends in childhood obesity. However, unless the accuracy and recording of measurements improve, such a restriction on the range of valid BMI values is probably required.

(Scan the QR code to access the list of references.)

 ## Words and Expressions

obesity	n.	more than average fatness
incidence	n.	the extent to which something happens or has an effect

Unit **2** Public Health

cardiovascular	*adj.*	(medical) connected with the heart and the blood vessels (= the tubes that carry blood around the body)
halt	*v.*	to stop; to make somebody or something stop
deprived	*adj.*	without enough food, education, and all the things that are necessary for people to live a happy and comfortable life
exacerbate	*v.*	to make something worse, especially a disease or problem
calibrate	*v.*	to mark units of measurement on an instrument so that it can measure something accurately
surrogate	*n.*	a person appointed to represent or act on behalf of others; a person or thing that takes the place of somebody or something else
adiposity	*n.*	having the property of containing fat
cut-off	*n.*	a point or limit when you stop something
scrutinise	*v.*	to examine carefully for accuracy with the intent of verification
spurious	*adj.*	false, although seeming to be genuine
outlier	*n.*	an extreme deviation from the mean
stratify	*v.*	to form, arrange, or deposit in layers
amalgamate	*v.*	to join or unite to form a larger organization or group, or to make separate organizations do this
null	*adj.*	having the value zero
marked	*adj.*	easy to see
surveillance	*n.*	close observation of a person or group (usually by the police)
manifest	*v.*	(formal) to show something clearly
proxy	*n.*	something that you use to represent something else that you are trying to measure or calculate

 Reflections and Practice

❶ **Read the text and answer the following questions.**

1. How could obesity be considered a worldwide epidemic and a significant public health issue?
2. On what basis did the authors claim that the incidence and prevalence of the obesity are rising?

3. Why is it significant to study obesity rates in children?
4. What do the Townsend material deprivation scores comprise of?
5. What are the limitations of this study?

II Discuss the following questions with your partner.

1. On what basis did the authors claim "obesity is considered a worldwide epidemic and a significant public health issue"? Do a lot of African people also suffer from obesity?
2. To what extent is the socioeconomic status of Chinese families related to overweight or obesity? Can children born in disadvantaged families grow up into adults without becoming obese through their own perceptions of healthy lifestyle and taking up physical exercises?
3. The article claims that, based on eleven years of statistics, the overall obesity rate of three-year-old children has little to do with the socioeconomic status of their parents (though it varies from year to year). But it is closely related to social deprivation. What is the relationship between parents' socioeconomic status and social deprivation?

III Paraphrase the following sentences.

1. The periodic measurement of children's weight and height by school nurses and other public health professionals are a potential source of data for monitoring the development of the epidemic of childhood obesity and of evaluating the effectiveness of interventions aimed at halting it.
2. Generally, people in more deprived households have poorer nutrient intakes than people in less deprived households and evidence suggests the gap between them has widened over the last 20 years. There is also some evidence for decreased physical activity in economically disadvantaged households which only exacerbates the problem.
3. Analysis of the data identified the proportion of three-year-old children who had received a CHIRP08 examination and those with a height and weight measure recorded, allowing BMI scores to be calculated. In order to minimise bias, data were analysed to show the proportion of children with a BMI score stratified by fifth of deprivation.
4. The proportion children resident in the least deprived fifth of areas who were overweight increased from 14.6% (95% CI: 10.5%–18.7%) in 1995 to 16.0% (95% CI: 12.4%–19.7%) in 2005, whilst for those in the most deprived fifth of areas, the

increase was greater [from 12.8% (95% CI: 9.7%–16.0%) in 1995 to 18.3% (95% CI: 14.9%–21.7%) in 2005].

5. One study that examined childhood overweight/obesity prevalence trends in 28,601 children (aged 5–10 years) in relation to trends in parental social class and household income, concluded that childhood obesity rates are increasing rapidly and that these increases are more marked amongst children from lower socioeconomic strata.

IV Locate at the Background section and underline the key verbs. Then fill in the blanks with the key verbs you underlined.

1. Across the UK, its incidence and prevalence continue to _____ (升高) and is estimated to _____ (花费) the UK economy £3.5 billion each year (healthcare/treatment costs and sickness days off work).

2. The periodic measurement of children's weight and height by school nurses and other public health professionals are a potential source of data for _____ (监测) the development of the epidemic of childhood obesity and of _____ (评估) the effectiveness of interventions aimed at _____ (阻止) it.

3. Generally, people in more deprived households have poorer nutrient intakes than people in less deprived households and evidence suggests the gap between them has _____ (加大) over the last 20 years.

4. There is also some evidence for decreased physical activity in economically disadvantaged households which only _____ (加重) the problem.

5. This study _____ (分析) children's height and weight data and investigates the association of family SES with overweight/obesity amongst three-year-old children in three South Wales localities, between 1995 and 2005.

V Locate at the Methods section and underline the key nouns. Fill in the blanks with the key nouns you underlined. You may fill in one, two, three or four nouns for each blank.

1. _____ (身高和体重数据) of individual (but anonymised) children were obtained from the NCCHD, a database covering children residents in Wales which receives its information from trust-based child health systems.

2. Child height and weight measurements were taken using _____ (标准方法) and regularly calibrated equipment.

3. Body mass index [BMI—weight (kg) divided by the square of height (m)] was used as a _____ (肥胖症的代表).

4. _____ (汤森德物质剥夺分数) (which comprise assessments of unemployment, overcrowding, home and car ownership) were used to determine childhood SES and was assigned according to NCCHD-recorded postcode of residence.

5. In order to minimise _____ (偏差), data were analysed to show the proportion of children with a BMI score stratified by fifth of deprivation.

Ⅵ Locate at the Discussion section and underline direction words or connectors. You may fill in one, two or three words for each blank.

1. Analysis of the annual trend in overweight and obesity among children resident in the most and least deprived fifth of LSOAs showed _____ (重大的) annual variation.

2. Linear regression analysis showed that the regression line for the least deprived fifth appears almost flat across the study period, _____ (而，同时) the regression line for the most deprived fifth appears to show some degree of a positive trend.

3. _____ (并且), a cross-sectional analysis of routinely collected data on Scottish preschool children suggested that obesity is associated with social deprivation.

4. Studies investigating SES were generally large but _____ (很少，非常少有) considered confounding by parental fatness.

5. This analysis shows that the relationship, between overweight and obesity on the one hand, and social deprivation _____ (在另一方面), is dynamic.

Ⅶ Write an outline for the text following the structure below.

1. **Background**

   Obesity, as an epidemic, costs the UK economy £3.5 billion a year, and obese children have an increased risk of cardiovascular disease, type 2 diabetes and certain cancers when they grow into adults.

2. **Methods**

   A statistical approach: Measurement of body mass index data of three-year-old children living in different areas of the Welsh and analysis of the socioeconomic status of their parents.

   Population measures: Measuring the height and weight of three-year-old children from populations living in three different Welsh neighborhoods between 1995–2005 to make a comparative analysis.

Estimates of adiposity: _____

SES measures: _____

Statistical analysis: _____

3. Results

Data coverage: _____

Trends in overweight and obesity: _____

Association with socioeconomic status: _____

4. Discussion

Main findings of this study: _____

_____

What is already known on this topic: _____

_____

What this study adds: _____

Limitations of this study: _____

_____

(VIII) Write a summary for the text in 150–200 words.

Part 3   Further Reading

Tracking of Childhood Overweight into Adulthood: A Systematic Review of the Literature[1]

Abstract

Overweight and obesity in youth are important public health concerns and are of

---

1   This paper is from Singh, A. S., Mulder, C., Twisk, J. W. van Mechelen, W. & Chinapaw, M. J. 2008. Tracking of childhood overweight into adulthood: A systematic review of the literature. *Obesity Reviews: An Official Journal of the International Association for the Study of Obesity*, 9(5): 474–488.

particular interest because of possible long-term associations with adult weight status and morbidity. The aim of this study was to systematically review the literature and update evidence concerning persistence of childhood overweight. A computerized bibliographical search—restricted to studies with a prospective or retrospective longitudinal design—was conducted. Two authors independently extracted data and assessed the methodological quality of the included studies in four dimensions: (i) study population and participation rate; (ii) study attrition; (iii) data collection, and (iv) data analysis. Conclusions were based on a rating system of three levels of evidence. A total of 25 publications were selected for inclusion in this review. According to a methodological quality assessment, 13 studies were considered to be of high quality. The majority of these high-quality studies were published after 2001, indicating that recently published data, in particular, provide us with reliable information. All included studies consistently report an increased risk of overweight and obese youth becoming overweight adults, suggesting that the likelihood of persistence of overweight into adulthood is moderate for overweight and obese youth. However, predictive values varied considerably. Limiting aspects with respect to generalizability and methodological issues are discussed.

Keywords: adulthood, childhood, overweight, systematic review, tracking

Reflections and Practice

Read the full article and answer the following questions.

1. What is the updated evidence concerning the persistence of childhood overweight?
2. How is computerized bibliographical research designed and conducted?
3. What did the authors do to ensure that the collected data provide reliable information?
4. How are the data analyzed?
5. What important findings are revealed?

Unit 3
Critical Thinking

📝 Learning Objectives

- Understand the meaning and importance of critical reading;

- Understand the strategies for reading critically;

- Compare different perceptions of critical thinking;

- Apply critical reading skills to academic and general reading activities.

Part 1 Reading Skills and Strategies

Reading Critically

1. Understanding the Meaning of Critical Reading

To understand the meaning of critical reading, it is imperative to clarify the meaning of "critical". Like how it is used in the term of "critical thinking", the word "critical" is often translated as *pipan* in Chinese, which prompts people to associate it with the meaning of "critique", "criticizing", or "criticism" (Dong, 2018). It seems that critical reading is a technique that requires readers to find something wrong with the text they are reading. In fact, however, "critical" implies the ability of reasoning. Critical reading prompts readers to make reasonable judgements about "what a text says" and "how it says what it does" (DiYanni, 2017: 4).

Critical reading is a process which involves readers' critical thinking skills to analyze and evaluate a text. It is defined as "very high-level comprehension of written material requiring interpretation and evaluation skills that enable the reader to separate important information, use inference to come to logical conclusions, distinguish between facts and opinions, and determine a writer's purpose and tone" (Pirozzi et al., 2014: 234).

As the definition implies, critical reading is a complex process which requires more than reading the text and understanding what is said. A lot of effort is expected to be put into the reading process to reason through the text. Wallace & Wray (2011: 12–13) provide a self-assessment checklist. Take a look at Table 3.1 and consider if you are doing all or any of these tasks when reading academic texts.

Table 3.1 Critical reading: A self-assessment checklist

When I read an academic text, I:	
1. try to work out what the authors are aiming to achieve	☐
2. try to work out the structure of the argument	☐
3. try to identify the main claims made	☐

	(Continued)
When I read an academic text, I:	
4. adopt a skeptical stance towards the authors' claims, checking that they are supported by appropriate evidence	☐
5. assess the backing for any generalizations made	☐
6. check how the authors define their key terms and whether they are consistent in using them	☐
7. consider what underlying values may be guiding the authors and influencing their claims	☐
8. keep an open mind, willing to be convinced	☐
9. look out for instances of irrelevant or distracting material, and for the absence of necessary material	☐
10. identify any literature sources to which the authors refer, that I may need to follow up	☐

It is fine if you have not yet been doing all these tasks when reading academic texts. Critical reading is a skill that requires learning and practice. Review the list, identify the tasks that you have not ticked, and consider how you might do so in your future reading.

2. Understanding the Importance of Critical Reading

As a postgraduate student, you are required to read academic texts all the time. However, you are not expected to accept everything you read because a text is the product of the author's decisions and is created for a purpose. It contains messages that reflect the author's attitudes, viewpoints, and conclusions based on his or her experiences, knowledge, beliefs, values, interests and positions. It applies to both general readings and academic texts. Although authors of academic texts are expected to present objective views and reliable evidence, it is possible, for example, that:

✓ The authors mean to be honest, but may have been misled by the evidence into saying something that you consider untrue;

✓ The authors mean to be logical, but may have developed a line of reasoning that contains a flaw;

✓ The authors mean to be impartial, but may have incorporated into the account some assumptions that you don't share;

✓ The authors mean to tell you something new, but may not have taken into account other information that you possess. (Wallace & Wray, 2011: 5)

The above scenarios highlight the necessity of obtaining a deep understanding of the text that is beyond its face value, which requires readers to read critically so that they can identify the authors' perspectives and stances, examine the authors' evidence and reasoning, and make connections between their ideas with those of the authors. It is not only important for your learning as a postgraduate student but also essential for your research as an emerging scholar.

3. Using Critical Synopsis Questions for Critical Reading

Critical reading requires readers to actively engage with the text they are reading. Strategies for critical reading are often closely related to the analysis and evaluation of a text. One approach to critical reading is the use of five critical synopsis questions (Wallace & Wray, 2011: 37):

- ✓ Why am I reading this?
- ✓ What are the authors trying to do in writing this?
- ✓ Is what the authors are saying relevant to what I want to find out?
- ✓ How convincing is what the authors are saying?
- ✓ In conclusion, what use can I make of this?

These questions facilitate readers to first analyze the purposes from the perspectives of both the readers and the authors, then evaluate the quality of the ideas provided by the authors, and finally identify their responses to the text. Table 3.2 presents the explanation of the five questions and some example responses.

Table 3.2 Five critical synopsis questions and example responses

Questions	Explanations	Example responses
Why am I reading this?	Identifying the purposes of why you choose to read a text is the first step toward critical reading. It allows you to make critical decisions on what to read and how to read it. Even if it is not a self-selected reading, finding a meaningful purpose for reading the given text helps you benefit from the reading as much as possible.	✓ I am reading this because it is related to the central question of my literature review: What has been done in the area of critical thinking and second language writing? ✓ I am reading this because it is a required reading task of an applied linguistics course. I am expected to figure out the what, how, and why of "critical reading".

(Continued)

Questions	Explanations	Example responses
What are the authors trying to do in writing this?	The authors' purposes of writing a text often influence what they write and how they write it. Identifying the authors' purposes helps you think beyond what is written and make meaningful connections between the authors' purposes and the information, viewpoints, and conclusions that the authors provide. Sometimes, the authors' purposes are clearly stated in the text, for example, in the abstract or introduction of a research paper. In many cases, you should go beyond the purposes that the authors have claimed based on careful consideration of who the authors are, who the target readers are, as well as where and when the text is published to examine if there are any unstated purposes.	✓ The authors are trying to report the results of a study that focused on teaching critical thinking in China. ✓ Since the paper was written in Chinese and published in a journal that targets English teachers in China, the authors are trying to convince Chinese English teachers that this approach can be used effectively in their classrooms.
Is what the authors are saying relevant to what I want to find out?	This question directs your attention to the content of the text and aims at locating the overlapping areas of the content of the text and your purposes for reading it. You are expected to focus on the most relevant information since it is unlikely that you pay attention to all the details of a text.	✓ The author used Paul & Elder's (2001) critical thinking model in her research design. Since I'm considering using this model as the theoretical framework of my study, I want to find out if the model applies to the context of my research and if the findings can support my explanation of why I use this model in my study.

(Continued)

Questions	Explanations	Example responses
How convincing is what the authors are saying?	This question invites you to evaluate the text based on critical thinking standards, such as the ones offered by Elder & Paul (2019): clarity, precision, accuracy, depth, breadth, relevance, logic, significance, and fairness. Questions related to these standards can be used as tools to help evaluate academic texts. For example: Is the supporting evidence relevant to the argument? Have the authors considered the most important problem? Do the authors need to look at the issue from another perspective?	✓ The author used both an experimental group and a control group to compare the pre-test and post-test scores, which makes the results very convincing. However, as the author only examined students' critical thinking scores without evaluating their language proficiency, it is not clear if language proficiency was an important factor that might have influenced the final results.
In conclusion, what use can I make of this?	The last question prompts you to consider your responses to the text, for example, whether you agree with the author's arguments or not. It also reminds you of your initial purposes of reading it and allows you to evaluate how the text fulfils your goals.	✓ The research findings reported in this article will be useful for supporting the argument about the connection between critical thinking and writing. ✓ It is a good example of how Paul & Elder's (2001) model can be used to design critical thinking approaches, but a few influential factors should be carefully considered if the approach is to be used in a multilingual context.

Table 3.2 provides only a few examples of how to approach these questions. It is possible that you answer them in different ways based on the features of the text you read and the purposes of your reading. Start thinking carefully about these questions when reading academic texts in your discipline and consider how you would gain a critical understanding of the texts through answering these questions.

Unit 3 Critical Thinking

Part 2 Intensive Reading

Pre-reading questions:

✓ What is the key concept of this article?
✓ What is your understanding of the key concept?
✓ What are some key questions relevant to the concept?
✓ What might be the purpose of this article?

Critical Thinking: Seven Definitions in Search of a Concept[1]

Introduction

In contemporary debates about the nature of higher education, a concept that **looms** particularly large is the idea of critical thinking. It has become, as Barnett (1997) suggests, "one of the defining concepts of the Western University" (3). The manifest importance of critical thinking is **evident** in many of the educational practices of teaching academics (Chanock 2000). For example, in many of the assignments and essays academics set for students, the basic intellectual task is often framed around the idea of being critical in some way: critically analyse X or provide a critical discussion of Y. The term is often prominent in the written feedback provided to students once a task has been completed: "This essay would have benefited from a more critical approach" or "You need to criticise, not just summarise". In the broader domain of educational policy, the idea of critical thinking has also assumed major importance in the current emphasis that is placed on the development of student's generic skills and **attributes** on academic programs (Barrie and Prosser 2004).

But, while there is broad agreement about the importance of critical thinking as an educational ideal, a view often expressed in the literature is that academics are not always so clear about what the concept means, and also not so certain about how the idea is best conveyed to students in their studies. Atkinson (1997) describes the situation thus:

---

[1] This paper is from Moore, T. 2013. Critical thinking: Seven definitions in search of a concept. *Studies in Higher Education*, *38*(4): 506–522.

Academics normally considered masters of precise definition seem almost unwilling or unable to define critical thinking. Rather they often appear to take the concept on faith, perhaps as a self-evident foundation of Western thought—such as freedom of speech. (1997, 74)

For Fox (1994), the difficulties of critical thinking arise from academics typically learning these practices themselves in an **intuitive** way, and so as a part of their professional habitus (Bourdieu 1977), the concept becomes a largely unspoken and **ineffable** one:

Because it is learned intuitively, critical thinking is easy [for academics] to recognize, like a face or a personality, but it is not so easily defined and it is not at all simple to explain. (Fox 1994, 125)

Barnett (1997) sees the problem stemming from a lack of conscious reflection by practitioners about this key notion: "Higher education," he says, "which **prides itself on** critical thought, has done no adequate thinking about critical thinking." (3) The evident importance of critical thinking in higher education, as well as the seeming pedagogical uncertainty surrounding the concept, suggests there is a need to find out more about how the idea is actually understood and used by academics in their teaching in the disciplines. The present study is motivated by this interest.

Background Literature: The Critical Thinking Movement and the Definition Question

Although there appears to be some uncertainty surrounding the concept of critical thinking, this is not to suggest that the idea has remained an unexamined one, and that it has somehow entered the educational practices of our institutions without some effort to properly **interrogate** and understand it. A group of academics have devoted themselves conscientiously to these definitional questions—the "critical thinking movement" (Davies 2006; Ennis 1992, 2001; Facione 1990; Paul 1996; van Gelder 2000). Emanating largely out of the US, these scholars, consisting mainly of educational philosophers and psychologists, have worked hard to develop "clear and distinct" understandings of the term. Their efforts have been notable for seeking to establish a single overarching definition (Norris 1992). Ennis, for example, a key member of the movement, emphasises the rational basis of critical thinking, defining it as: "reasonable, reflective thinking that is focused on deciding what to believe or do" (1987, 10). Siegel (1988), another important contributor, frames his account in similar terms, describing critical thinking as "the educational **cognate** of **rationality**", and a critical thinker, "as the individual who is appropriately moved by reasons" (25).

Other thinkers, however, have **shunned** the idea of a single unitary definition and have suggested that critical thinking, of its nature, necessarily takes in a variety of cognitive modes. Clinchy (1994), for example, sees the forms of critical thinking required in the academy falling roughly into two types: a "separated knowing" which, she says, has the qualities of "detachment" and "impersonality" and a "connected knowing" which is concerned more with an **empathic** understanding—trying to "get into the heads" of those one wishes to understand. Barnett (1997) identifies at least four modes; what he describes as critical thinking are "disciplinary competence", "practical knowledge", "political engagement" and a form of "strategic thinking". In his account, Barnett stresses the distinctiveness of these different versions of critical thinking, insisting that the concept resists reduction to any single mode: "Critical thought is not all of a piece. Of the four forms in the university" (or at least the ones that Barnett identifies) "none is reducible", he says, "to any of the others" (1997, 14).

Despite the major theoretical effort that has gone into analysing and explicating the idea of critical thinking, it is questionable whether these processes have managed ultimately to make the concept a comprehensible one in our institutions. Capossela dismissively describes the situation thus:

> It seems reasonable to suppose that a concept so frequently invoked would long ago have acquired a clear-cut definition, but in fact the opposite is true: With each new appearance, critical thinking becomes less, rather than more, clearly defined (1998, 1).

The term, as critical theorist Raymond Williams has suggested, is a "most difficult one" (1976, 74). Commenting on this apparent confusion, Norris (1992) has suggested the problem underlying the multiplicity of views and the resultant blurring of the concept is the lack of an empirical basis in the various attempts at characterizing critical thinking. Thus, there has been a tendency, Norris suggests, to treat the concept as an abstract and philosophical one, and to rely mainly on methods of introspection and intuition to develop and refine its meanings. Some critics have suggested that what is produced ultimately out of such processes are definitions of a more normative nature than ones based in any actual reality, thus casting some doubt on the validity of many of the ideas proposed (Atkinson 1997).

Such a position is very much apiece with Wittgenstein's famous critique of introspective forms of philosophical inquiry, and the "never-ending" quest in that discipline to define concepts in some abstract way. For Wittgenstein, there are no such abstract meanings. Instead, words and expressions only take on meanings, he suggests, from the way they are used "in the stream of life". As he famously declared in his *Philosophical Investigations:*

> For a large class of cases in which we employ the word "meaning" it can be defined thus: the meaning of a word is its use in the language (1958, 20, sect. 43).

Wittgenstein believed that many philosophical problems stem from looking at words in isolation, in a static way. "The confusions which occupy us", he declared, "arise when language is like an engine idling, not when it is doing work" (1958, 51, sect. 132). Indeed, this may be a way of understanding the definitional **impasse** that the critical thinking movement seems to have found itself in; that is, there has been a tendency to detach the concept from its actual uses, and then to attach to it either notions that are thought to be somehow intrinsic to it, or else notions that one desires it to have. A concept treated in this way will inevitably yield many different meanings, and lead us into what Wittgenstein called a state of "puzzlement". The way out of such confusion, according to Wittgenstein, is to engage in a form of linguistic empiricism—not to rely on what one thinks a word means, but instead to look at those situations in which it is being used. "Don't think, but look" was Wittgenstein's **blunt** instruction to his fellow philosophers.

These ideas formed the basis for the study described in this article. Instead of relying on the literature to establish the likely meanings of critical thinking as an educational goal, it was thought useful to seek out the actual understandings of the concept as held by practicing academics, and to find out how the term is used by them in their teaching activities. The approach, a deliberately **"emic"** practice-based as opposed to an **"etic"** systems-based one (Pike 1967), sought to reverse conventional research processes—not to seek to understand an idea (such as critical thinking) and then see how it is applied in educational practice, but instead to see how the idea is used as an educational practice and then to draw on these findings to form an understanding of it as a concept.

The Study

The study was conducted at an Australian university, and involved interviewing academics from a range of disciplines: philosophy, history and literary/cultural studies. This choice of disciplines was a deliberate one. The intention was to cover areas that were closely related in an educational sense; that is to say, ones that students on an undergraduate program may find themselves studying concurrently, and where any variation in conceptions of critical thinking may have a bearing on their experience of study. Seventeen academics (10 men and 7 women) took part in the study, with approximately equal numbers from each discipline. Table 1 provides details of these participants, including their disciplinary backgrounds and research interests (pseudonyms have been used in each case). All participants were tenured staff, with some occupying, or having previously occupied, senior positions in the faculty. One, for example, was a former dean; another three at the time of the study were heads of school or centre. All participants were strongly involved in teaching on undergraduate programs.

Table 1   Summary of informants (discipline, research interests)

Discipline area	Informant*	Research interests**
History	Edward (M)	European social history; Enlightenment; French Revolution
	Hannah (F)	Ptolemaic and Roman Egypt; Greek and Roman history; early Christianity
	Katherine (F)	Southeast Asian history; Vietnam War
	Nell (F)	Australian social, political and religious history; women's history
	Michael (M)	British 19th-century urban and working class history; Australian regional political history
	Nigel (M)	Australian history; American history
Philosophy	Eric (M)	Ancient Greek and Roman philosophy; metaphysics; aesthetics; moral philosophy
	Henry (M)	philosophy of language; philosophy of science; philosophy of religion, aesthetics, logic, metaphysics
	Jonathon (M)	cognitive science; metaphysics; critical thinking
	Kim (M)	bioethics; ethical theory; moral psychology
	Lauren (F)	history of women's ideas; philosophy of language; continental philosophy; Sartre and de Beauvoir
Literary/cultural studies	Bruce (M)	19th- and 20th-century novel; Dickens
	Quentin (M)	literary stylistics; translation studies; poetry and prosody; Shakespeare
	Brian (M)	literature politics, and society; cultural studies; utopia, dystopia and science fiction; Bourdieu, Jameson, Williams
	Nora (F)	modernism, postmodernism in European literature and film; realism in Russian, French and English literary canon; Dostoyevsky
	Lois (F)	romanticism; ecophilosophy; ecocriticism
	Zoe (F)	media and communication; modernity and postmodernity, the culture of the everyday

* pseudonyms used; M = Male, F = Female
** as indicated on school websites

Interviews ran from between one to two hours. The central questions asked of informants were whether they found the term "critical thinking" relevant to their practice as a teacher; and then, if this was the case, how they understood the term, especially in relation to the qualities and attributes they were seeking to encourage in their students. An interview schedule was used in the sessions, although the nature of the exchange was typically conversational and open-ended. Interviews were recorded, transcribed, and then analysed for key themes (see Jones 2007 for a similar approach).

Findings from Interviews

The first point to note from the interviews is that, without exception, all informants thought the idea of being "critical" absolutely central to their teaching, and to their academic outlook generally. Thus, for example, one of the philosophers (Jonathon) described critical thinking as "absolutely our discipline's bread and butter"; for one of the historians (Nigel), "the demonstrating of a critical approach" was the quality, more than anything else, that "distinguished the really successful students"; and for an informant from literary/cultural studies (Nora), it was teaching students to be "critics" that "we're basically on about in this discipline". But, while there was broad agreement about the need for students to be "critical" in their studies, much variation was evident in their commentaries about how the term was understood, as well as how these understandings were conveyed to students on programs. In what follows, I seek to give an account of this definitional variety. The findings have been grouped into two broad categories: (i) major themes, which were those understandings of critical thinking given some airing by most informants; and (ii) minor themes, which were understandings expressed by only some.

Critical Thinking as Judgement

Arguably the most prominent idea expressed in the interviews was to see critical thinking fundamentally as the making of judgements. This was true across the three discipline areas. Thus, for one of the historians (Nell), critical thinking always meant "judgement and the making of distinctions of some kind". A literary/cultural studies academic (Nora) also identified judgement ("the taking of a stand") as a key element to being critical in her discipline area:

> Being critical, it's about taking a stand. You have to commit as a critic.

One of the philosophers, Eric, saw the activity in similar terms—as the "**rendering** of **verdicts**" on the ideas students need to engage with. As he **pithily** put it:

> I like to say to students—would it profit you to read the entirety of Aristotle's work, and form no view whether it's bullshit or not?

In elaborating on this idea of judgement, informants also gave a sense of the types of judgements they expected students to be making. As suggested in Eric's blunt account, the most basic type of judgement is perhaps one between "good" and "bad". A number of informants discussed the judgements students are required to make in these broad terms. Henry (philosophy) talked about how in one of his subject areas, philosophy of religion, the main task for students was to engage with the "primary question of whether there are *good* arguments for or against the existence of God" (all italics in quotes indicate my emphases). Similarly, Hannah, an historian, spoke of the importance in her field of students being able to make judgements about the types of sources they might rely on in their work—to decide between "*good* historical and archaeological sources" and ones that "they should really steer well away from".

A number of other, perhaps more precise, evaluative terms were mentioned in discussion. The more prominent of these were notions of "validity" and "truthfulness". For Edward (history), the idea of validity was central in his particular account of critical thinking:

> Critical thinking would be thinking about an historical account in an evaluative sort of way and thinking particularly about the ways in which it might be *valid* or *invalid*.

In literary/cultural studies, Brian likewise spoke of the need for students to understand what a "*valid*...interpretation of a text" might entail. For the philosophers, the concept was particularly **salient**. Eric (philosophy), for example, discussed "validity" as one of a number of key evaluative concepts that students needed to learn as part of the procedures in that discipline for assessing the quality of arguments ("We explain validity as structural goodness—that is, if the premises lead to the conclusion").

"Truthfulness" was also mentioned as an evaluative criterion, though accompanied in most cases, by a degree of qualification along the way. Nigel, an historian, for example, said he sought to impress upon students the need to maintain "their capacity for judgements about what is more likely to be a *true*, or correct interpretation of an historical event", while at the same time seeing the need to **warn students off** "the idea of big T truths" in the discipline. Judgements of "truthfulness" were also discussed by the philosophers, especially in relation to the protocols typically used in the discipline to critically evaluate arguments. Thus, as Eric explained, within the traditions of analytical philosophy, "students need to assess the validity of arguments, and a part of this is to make a judgement about whether such arguments are founded on premises that are in fact *true*". A number of the philosophers however, **alluded to the difficulties** of relying too heavily on notions of truthfulness in one's judgements:

> The word that I would prefer to use with students is *acceptability*. Are the premises acceptable, which is not necessarily asking them to judge whether they are *true*. But whether in your judgement someone else who believed them or failed to

believe them would thereby show themselves to be irrational. (Henry)

Other key criteria to emerge from the interviews, and which it was thought should inform students' critical judgements, were notions of reliability, usefulness and persuasiveness.

Critical Thinking as a Skeptical and Provisional View of Knowledge

Another major theme that emerged in discussions—one very much related to the idea of judgement—was the idea of critical thinking as a skeptical thinking. Skepticism might be viewed as a particular form of judgement; that is, as a propensity to judge in a negative way, or at least to be permanently cautious about accepting the judgements and ideas of others. This version of critical thinking was discussed very much in these terms by informants:

Well. I suppose that...critical thinking is not just *accepting* what somebody tells you. (Lauren, philosophy)

In general terms, I would say critical thinking is the capacity to cut through *accepted* ideas...to recognize and examine them. (Katherine, history)

The best essays begin by *taking issue* either with the question, or with certain critics and...to argue against them and produce some kind of interesting response. (Quentin, literary/cultural studies)

The philosophers had a good deal to say on this issue—perhaps not surprisingly, seeing a skeptical outlook as fundamental to that particular discipline's spirit of inquiry. Eric, for example, chose to invoke one of philosophy's more iconic images to convey the centrality of this notion—that of Socrates famously challenging the assumptions of his hapless interlocutors.

What's Socrates' characteristic activity? It's to **buttonhole** somebody who has **pretensions** about knowing something and show that his beliefs are inconsistent. And there is I think this important emphasis in philosophy in not **acquiescing** and believing things for inadequate reasons.

A similar view was expressed from within literary/cultural studies. For Lois, a skeptical outlook was particularly called for in the type of literature she taught, because of the tendency, for students (and scholars as well) to "accept certain theories as dogma"—attributable, she thought, to the sense of "**charisma** attaching to the originators of these theories". A good example of this for Lois was Freudian theory.

I mean, for example, Freudian psychoanalysis. There is a certain amount of evidential basis for it. However, there is also a high degree of imagination and sort of creative modelling involved in Freud's theory. Yet, students, indeed not only students, will often be tempted to adopt it... as some kind of truth. And you then get this phenomenon of the theory being accepted without question.

Along with adopting a skeptical attitude towards the ideas one is presented with on a course, several informants thought it equally important for students to apply the same critical view towards their own ideas, beliefs and assumptions.

> Interviewer: So in the context of your teaching, which qualities or capacities do you most associate with critical thinking?
>
> Michael (history): Well challenging attitudes. I want to challenge students' assumptions, as much as challenge the ideas that we put to them in what they read.

Michael went on to explain the importance in the study of history of being aware of the constructed nature of many of the precepts one relies on in their understanding of historical processes. He cited here the example of the idea of the "nation state":

> I try to get students to the idea...that the nation state is not the only way of organizing and seeing the world, which is so central to our understandings of 20th-century history... Some students just can't get past the idea that things are just natural, that they're permanent and that's how things will continue.

A similar view was expressed by informants from the other disciplines. In literary/cultural studies, it was explained that students often come to the course with their own preconceptions about what "literature" is, and what kinds of literary works might be the **legitimate** objects of study in the discipline. Some of the first work set for students on the course, it was explained, was to have students interrogate their understandings of the nature of literature—what one lecturer described as their "taken-for-granteds":

> What we're really asking [students] to do is to critique their own commonsense understandings of things...such as what literature is, and we want to challenge their "taken-for-granteds". (Lois)

In philosophy, this habit of mind was described as the need to "wonder about and question" one's acquired beliefs about things:

> These students are still very young, and they have just left high school, so we say to them, "Look you know there are lots of things in life that we all acquire when we are young, all sorts of beliefs and views and so on. And you can wonder about them, and question them". And I think that is something that everybody, not just in philosophy, does around the university. (Jonathon)

Critical Thinking as a Simple Originality

While many informants were sure that a key to being critical was adopting a skeptical and questioning view of knowledge—whether the extant knowledge students bring to the academy, or that to which they are exposed once they arrive—there was an interesting **dissenting** view that emerged in the interviews, one that took issue, or indeed was "critical" of, a routinely skeptical outlook. For these informants, to be "critical" involved not only the challenging of ideas, but also an effort to actually "produce" them:

> A critical thinker has to argue on the basis of the critical thought. But it is not enough just to have critically negative thoughts. You actually have to...put them into something, to produce something. (Nigel, history)

Henry, also picking up on this theme, was bothered that his discipline, philosophy, was inclined towards an excessive negativity (the overvalued practice of "poking holes in arguments", as he described it), though he thought this a tendency across the faculty as a whole:

> Because of the nature of philosophy, it's much easier to publish a paper in which you take an argument and *poke some holes in it*. So I think we can systematically overvalue critique. But I don't think it's just...philosophers who do that, I think it's true of large parts of the faculty that we place too high a value on critique.

The alternative account was to see critical thinking more in terms of students coming to conclusions about issues, and making their own modest contributions to knowledge. This view was characterized in a variety of ways. One was to see it in terms related to the idea of "construction" or "manufacture". Henry (philosophy), for example, talked about students needing "to *make* a case", and "to take some reasonably interesting proposition or theory and *make something of it*"; Edward (history) spoke of the need for students to "*build* on their historical sources, or *organize* them in a particular way to *construct* a particular...picture of the past".

Another type of characterization was one that evoked less a sense of "the building up" of knowledge, and more a kind of "moving across", or having a lateral engagement with it. For a number of informants, this type of engagement was suggestive of some originality of thought. Michael (history), for example, spoke about a group of students he had taught that year who had impressed him by offering their own particular interpretations of a historical period: "They were quite creative", he said, for "taking things *outside* the accepted...historical interpretations". For Lois (literary/cultural studies), the type of thinking to be encouraged was one where students "headed in a different direction". In elaborating on her concerns about students being too readily **dismissive** of certain ideas—the "doing of hatchet jobs", discussed earlier—Lois thought that a genuinely "critical" approach was one where students did not see a text primarily as an object to be evaluated, but rather as something that might stimulate them to pursue a different course:

> What I've been trying to impress upon students is that to be critical you don't just go in and do a hatchet job, you have a look and see if there is...a redeeming element here that you could pick up and run with, *to head in a different direction.*

Brian, from the same discipline, saw the contribution students can make in the same lateral terms—as a "sideways" movement, involving the drawing of "connections" between different sources.

> Well, the most exciting thing is when in a sense students *move sideways*—where they make a connection between the text that you've given and something else that you haven't given at all...It's the *lateral thinking* that counts.

Critical Thinking as a Careful and Sensitive Reading of Text

A final major theme was to see critical thinking as a "careful and sensitive reading" of material. For some informants, the idea of being able to grasp the basic meaning of texts was seen as fundamental to the activity of critical thinking. This notion was particularly emphasized by the philosophers—perhaps as a consequence of the generally difficult types of reading required in that discipline. Jonathon, for example, suggested that the ability to make basic sense of texts lay at the heart of all critical practices:

> Put rather bluntly, just trying to figure out what somebody is on about is what underlies everything that we are looking at. I think the connection of critical thinking between all disciplines would be a connection of careful reading.

There was some emphasizing of this notion by informants from the other disciplines. Bruce (literary studies), for example, stressed its overwhelming importance in literary criticism:

> First of all, being critical is something that's really dependent on students having demonstrated a working understanding of the text that is being used.

Other dimensions of critical reading were also identified. One of these was the ability to read beyond a text's literal meanings and to be able to engage with its broader rhetorical purposes. For those who spoke about this aspect, it was important, they said, for students to develop a sensitivity to the circumstances in which a text might be written, and to be able to give some account of its underlying "motives", "intentions" and "agendas". This characterization of reading was especially strong among the historians, who saw such an approach to text as a crucial part of a student's training in the discipline, particularly in their engagement with primary source material. Nell, for example, spoke of the need for students to "go further into a historical document" and to have "a go at working out its intentions".

Michael also emphasized the importance of going beyond a literal understanding:

> So in being critical we want students to understand the assumptions within...these documents...why are they being produced, the agendas, that sort of thing.

This type of contextual reading was not the sole province of the historians. Lauren, for example, mentioned that, although the more conventional approach in philosophy was to lay out the content of arguments "as they appeared on the page", there were occasions when students needed to see these ideas within some broader domain.

> In the philosophical arguments that they read sometimes students are asked to fill...in the historical background...to consider what the philosopher is saying, what are their arguments, and why in the context of the time are they saying these things.

Another type of "critically interpretive" reading was one focused not so much on identifying the underlying intentions and purposes of individual authors and texts, as on understanding a text in relation to broader paradigms of writing and thinking that existed at the time of its production. Thus, Nell (history) thought that a "really critical reading" was one that showed awareness of "the kind of code that an author writes in because of the particular form that they were using...and the particular discourse they had to write in". This type of discursive approach, one that seeks to understand a text in relation to its own conventions, was elaborated on by a number of the literary/cultural studies informants:

> Another aspect of critical thinking I bring to bear is an appreciation of the historical context in which these people theorists are writing and thinking...that you can't necessarily expect people to have the same kinds of assumptions that you're making. (Lois)

For Lois, this type of reading involved an "empathic" kind of engagement with a text, and, for her, needed to be understood as critical, but at the same time as fundamentally non-judgemental:

> The point about this critical approach to reading is not to try to condemn, but rather to understand the legacy of a certain way of thinking which became predominant under a particular circumstance, and at a certain time.

The preceding themes discussed are what I have termed major themes. The remaining discussion is focused on the minor themes, which were those given coverage by a more limited number of informants.

Critical Thinking as Rationality

One of the less prominent themes was the conceiving of critical thinking as a form of rationality. As we saw in the earlier review of literature, this conception figures substantially within the critical thinking movement (Ennis 1987; Siegel 1988). In the interviews, it was the philosophers who most emphasized this dimension of critical thinking. Jonathon, for example, was sure it was this spirit of rationality that lies at the heart of all critical activities:

> There is a sense that to some extent all intellectual work is engagement with a rational project.

Eric also saw rationality as a universal method, suggesting that central to this method was a propensity to believe in things for certain explicit and specifiable reasons:

> We in philosophy think of the teaching of critical thinking as passing on certain sorts of skills which we think are more or less universal...One thing we want...students to do is develop a fondness for believing things in accordance with the best reasons.

While the philosophers gave particular weight to students having a reason-based approach to their thinking, several informants from other disciplines also touched on this notion, though discussing it in not quite the same explicit terms. Bruce (literary studies), for example, spoke of the common problem of his students arguing by assertion, without providing a "rational basis" for the assessments they made of a work of literature. For Bruce, it was this mode of thinking that needed to be particularly emphasized:

> For me that's one of the main things that I assess an essay on...whether it supports an argument not just by assertion, but by demonstration with reference to the texts that's being discussed.

Whilst informants generally agreed about the need to instill principles of reason and logic, some were uneasy about just how much these should be stressed. Nell (history), for example, felt it was necessary for students to understand not only the potential of a certain logical habit of mind, but also the limitations that such an approach could impose upon one's thinking:

> I do believe there are processes of logic that are appropriate and inappropriate. But where I have problems with logic is that it's just a tool...and it's a tool that within its own rules can actually stop you doing things, as well as allow you to do things.

Critical Thinking as the Adopting of an Ethical and Activist Stance

Those who saw an ethical and activist dimension to critical thinking were informants who emphasized the broad social mission of universities—that is, to see a university education being concerned as much with "life in the world" (as one informant described it), as with training in specific discipline areas. Thus, for these informants, the definitions of critical thinking needed to be extended beyond acts of cognition, and to incorporate some notion of critical action.

> It's important for students to confront issues in a fairly personal way and to try and figure out for themselves where they stand on these issues and to be able to defend them. (Kim, philosophy)

Some informants were specific about the nature of the "stand" they thought the term implied. For some, being "critical" meant being broadly critical of the political, social and also academic "establishment". Bruce (literary/cultural studies), for example, spoke of a commonly held view that saw "the duty of the university as in some sense being opposed to the establishment in society". Such a role he likened to a "corrupting of youth":

> We like to say to students—that's the monolith over there and the university's job [and your job] is to be in a sense subversive of it.

Nell (history) also spoke about for this form of socially engaged critique:

> There is a sense of "critical" being critical of the established order...So it's critical in the sense of having—not exactly a radical—but at least kind of a reformist kind of agenda, in other words not being satisfied with the status quo.

Other informants were more specific about the kinds of values and ideals they thought should inform this socially critical view, including such notions as "**emancipation**", "liberation", "freedom from oppression" and "a general **egalitarianism**". Brian (literary/cultural studies) mentioned how the approach he sought to develop in students was strongly rooted in the critical traditions of the Frankfurt school:

> For the Frankfurt school...knowledge is not neutral. They argue that it's often implicated in man's oppression...And the point of this kind of critique is to liberate human beings...it's the idea of emancipation, which is to do with the idea of enlightenment critique.

This "transformational" form of critique was also elaborated on by Nigel (history). Whilst less explicit about the theoretical basis for such an outlook, Nigel was sure of the need to have this activist ethic included as one of the goals of higher education. For him, the key attribute to develop in students was a sense of "critical responsibility":

> So there is a sense of being critically responsible...one of the burdens of being a capable person is the burden of feeling responsible for the state of the world.

This is not to suggest, however, that this version of critical thinking was embraced by all. One notably dissident voice was Nora's (literary/cultural studies). Far from encouraging students into some form of activist thinking, Nora was most disapproving of the tendency for students to push (and be encouraged to push) a particular moral position in their work (for example, to take a view that "all violence is bad"). At best, Nora thought such intrusions irrelevant; at worst they demonstrated for her an unthinking form of "political correctness":

> There are no value judgements in critique, as in this is a good way to be, this is a bad way to be. So, for example, if you're talking about violence you don't have a contentious judgement which proclaims "all violence is bad" because that's sort of not relevant.

In contrast to other informants, who thought the taking of an ideological stance always implicit in the idea of being critical, for Nora, the two notions were wholly "**incompatible**":

> If in one's thinking there is a kind of element of good or bad, that is not being critical, that is not critique. That is value judgement of a subjective and emotional kind, and it always reduces to ideology. You don't have ideology in critique.

Critical Thinking as Self-Reflexivity

A final notion was an understanding of critical thinking as a form of self-reflexiveness. In many of the previous themes considered so far, "critical thinking" has typically been thought of as a type of thinking that students need to direct at the knowledge (or whatever it is they are engaged with) in their studies. In this final theme, the particular type of thinking identified is not one directed at a form of knowledge as such, but rather turned back at the originator of these thoughts—the thinking self. This particular understanding of critical thinking was perhaps articulated most succinctly by Zoe (literary/cultural studies).

> When students are given material to consider, then for me critical thinking is...about not only being able to critique the material in front of you, but also to critique your own assumptions about what's in front of you...So it's a sort of self-consciousness, or self-reflexiveness.

The first of the definitional strands discussed in this article was the idea of critical thinking as the making of judgements. For those informants who discussed the idea of **reflexivity**, critical thinking needed to be understood as much as a developing "awareness" or a "self-consciousness" about how judgements are made, as the actual judgements (or "interpretations") themselves:

> What we try to assist the students in doing is to become much more self-conscious about the way that they are making sense of texts. So critical thinking in that context is very much to do with students being aware of how they have arrived at the interpretations that they're making. (Lois, literary/cultural studies)

Lois also thought of critical thinking as an irredeemably "**contingent**" activity, one in which the thinker's own subjectivity invariably plays a role. For Lois, such a view—one held in many parts of the academy, she thought—has its basis in a Kantian **epistemological** outlook, which precludes the possibility of any entirely objective knowledge (or indeed objective critique) of things:

> In the back of my mind is Kant's first critique—the critique of pure reason. That's something that I think a lot of people basically now just assume—that one can't know things in themselves, that one's knowledge is always contingent, and is always shaped by one's own perceptual and conceptual apparatus.

For Lois, part of becoming a "reflective" critical thinker was in a sense to come to terms with this indeterminacy, and to understand the contingent and variable nature of one's beliefs and judgements. Brian, from the same discipline area, also emphasized this contingent quality and thought that to have an appreciation of the "problem of knowledge"—as well as one's permanently "fraught" relationship with it—lay at the heart of a genuinely critical outlook. For Brian, it was those students whose engagement with the subject gave no indication of this type of "reflexivity" who really struggled:

> Knowledge of whatever is a much more fraught process than we might initially think...The worst writing from students is those who do not give a sense that all this is problematic.

Discussion and Implications for Teaching

The preceding discussion has outlined the ways that academics from a range of disciplinary backgrounds understand the notion of critical thinking. There are several conclusions that can be drawn from their various commentaries. The first is that far from being a largely "buried" and "ineffable" concept within university education, as is suggested in the research literature (Atkinson 1997; Fox 1994), it would appear that academics—or those in the study at least—have quite developed understandings of the notion that they are able to articulate in cogent and often very engaging ways. Evidence from the interviews also suggests that these understandings are often well conveyed to students.

Another conclusion is that the idea of critical thinking clearly **defies** reduction to some narrow, and readily identifiable cognitive mode, of the type, for example, promoted from within the critical thinking movement (Ennis 2001; Facione 1990; Ikuenobe 2001). Instead, in the interviews, we saw much variety in the way that academics understood the term, a finding more in keeping with those advocating a more multidimensional view of critical thinking (Barnett 1997; Clinchy 1994; McPeck 1992). In the interviews, this variety was evident not only in the differing accounts of various informants, but also on occasions in a variety of conceptions articulated by a single informant.

Along with seeing critical thinking as a term having multiple meanings, the interviews suggested that it is also a contested notion. This was evident in a number of quite **divergent**, even incompatible, accounts by informants—for example, in the different views expressed about whether critical thinking is at heart an "evaluative" mode, or a more "constructive" one; or whether the term necessarily entails the adopting of an ethical and activist stance towards the world; or how much being critical involves a logical and rational outlook. Although not investigated in any systematic way, there would appear to be a disciplinary basis for some of the variation observed. Thus, we saw for example, that the philosophers seemed generally to favour a more rational and evaluative approach, while in the other disciplines, the preference, on the face of it, appeared to be for looser, more interpretative forms of critique (see Jones 2009; Moore 2011a, 2011b for more detailed discussion of this point).

In presenting the study's finding, it is important to stress that there is no attempt here to establish any definitive or **exhaustive** account of the varieties of critical thinking. This is for the reason that the research was restricted to a limited range of disciplines, and indeed to the views of a limited number of representatives from each of these. One can indeed posit other possible understandings of the concept, ones that might emerge from investigation of other fields and disciplines—for example, to see critical thinking, at heart, as a form of "problem-solving", as is the tendency among some of the more applied disciplines (Boud and Felitti 1991; Hoey 1983, 2001). What we can say with certainty, though, is that the notion is a complex one, and that in this complexity there is the potential for a fair degree of confusion for students in the way they engage with the idea in their studies.

What implications then does this situation have for teaching? One can cite several. The first concerns the issue of institutional **meta-languages**, and the need for key terms like "critical" to be clarified as well as they can be to students in their studies. As a first step, it seems important for teaching academics to take on board an idea that is now well-accepted within contemporary linguistics, but not necessarily in other fields; this is that words are fundamentally "**polysemous**" in nature. As Gee (2004) explains:

> Words do not have just general dictionary-like meanings. They have different and specific meanings in different situations where they are used, and in different specialist domains that recruit them (41).

This suggests then that clarification will come not from some generic exposition of meaning, as occurs, for example, in the common practice of providing students with glossaries of key terms in university study; e.g. "discuss", "argue", etc (Davies and Devlin 2007). What is needed instead are acquisition processes that are rooted within quite specific study contexts, and which involve deliberate acts of "dialogue and interaction" (Gee 2004, 54). This might take in a range of teaching activities: helping students to identify in specific assignments how critical thinking might enter into their work; showing students textual instantiations of the thinking that is being asked of them in specific situations; allowing students the opportunity to express their queries, doubts—fears even—about the requirements of critical thinking on a course of study. It is a source of some optimism that methods such as these seemed a part of the teaching routines of many of the informants who took part in the study.

A second implication concerns the variety of critical modes identified in the study. One would not want to suggest here that what students need is to be taught, in some separate and discrete way, a whole range of different ways of being critical. In such a project, there would be the potential for additional confusions. In any teaching program aimed at clarifying the idea of critical thinking, it is important to recognize that, while the term connotes a variety of cognitive modes, we need also to assume that there exists some common thread of meaning, or what Wittgenstein (1958, 31) famously referred to as a "family resemblance" of meanings. This suggests the need for a transdisciplinary approach, where students are encouraged to reflect on the variety of educational and intellectual processes they experience in the "different specialist domains" of their studies, and to seek to recognize any coherences that might exist in these processes. Figure 1 outlines an imaginary assignment task, one which, in the way that undergraduate study is presently structured, is difficult to imagine being enacted. It is one though that seeks to capture in a practical way some of the ideas about "critical thinking" being proposed in this article.

> **An imaginary assignment task**
>
> At University X, it is claimed that students will develop, among other things, the ability to **think critically**. Think about several subjects you have completed on your course.
>
> In what ways (if at all), do you think work in these subjects has helped you to develop your abilities as a **critical thinker**? How would you describe the type of **critical thinking** you needed to develop in each case? Did this seem to be the same, or was it different in some sense? Is it somehow easier being **critical** in one subject than another?
>
> In what ways (if at all), do you think these **critical capacities** might have relevance to your life (e.g. as a student, as a worker, as a citizen etc.)?
>
> Does University X, in your judgement, make good its claim that it teaches students to be **critical**?

Figure 1　Imaginary assignment task

Conclusion

In his now famous text, *Keywords*, Williams (1976) explored the complexity of a range of keywords and concepts that for him characterize modern intellectual life—a shared, but "imperfect" vocabulary, as Williams described it, that lies at the heart of our discussions of life's "most central processes" (12). In terms rather similar to Wittgenstein, Williams suggests that any effort that seeks to simplify the meanings of difficult words (such as we have seen within the critical thinking movement) is unlikely to help resolve confusions:

> I do not share the optimism, or the theories which underlie it...which suppose that clarification of difficult words would help in the resolution of disputes conducted in their terms and which are often visibly confused by them. (20)

Instead of seeking to "purify the dialect of the tribe", an expression borrowed from Eliot, Williams suggests we need to see the "imperfections" and uncertainties of words as matters of "contemporary substance", and as "variations" to be insisted upon:

> Variations and confusions of meaning are not faults in a system, or errors of feedback, or deficiencies of education. They are in many cases, in my terms, historical and contemporary substance. Indeed they are often variations to be insisted upon, just because they embody different experiences and readings of experience, and this will continue to be true in active relationships and conflicts, over and above the clarifying exercises of scholars or committees. What can really be contributed is not resolution, but perhaps at times that extra edge of consciousness. (21)

Thus, in the act of trying to understand and appreciate these "varieties of tradition and experience", what might emerge, Williams suggests, is an "extra edge of consciousness". This evocative expression, which suggests a mainly empathic view of knowledge and of its creators and purveyors, may be as good a definition as any for the difficult term we have been considering in the preceding pages. Indeed, in trying to make sense of "critical thinking", and in working out how it might be best taught, it may be that it is above all this quality—"an extra edge of consciousness"—that we should hope to encourage in our students, and also in ourselves, and in the world generally, in spite of the many challenges that we all face.

(Scan the QR code to access the list of references.)

Words and Expressions

loom	*v.*	to appear as a large, often frightening or unclear shape or object

evident	adj.	easily seen or understood
attribute	n.	a quality or characteristic that someone or something has
intuitive	adj.	based on feelings rather than facts or proof
ineffable	adj.	causing so much emotion, especially pleasure, that it cannot be described
pride oneself on		to value a skill or good quality that one has
interrogate	v.	to ask someone a lot of questions for a long time in order to get information, sometimes using threats or violence
cognate	n.	a word that has the same origin as another word, or is related in some way to another word
rationality	n.	the quality of being based on clear thought and reason, or of making decisions based on clear thought and reason
shun	v.	to avoid something
empathic	adj.	having the ability to imagine how someone else feels
impasse	n.	a situation in which progress is impossible, especially because the people involved cannot agree
blunt	adj.	saying what you think without trying to be polite or considering other people's feelings
emic	adj.	relating to a way of studying or describing a language or culture from the point of view of the people who use the language or live in the culture
etic	adj.	relating to a way of studying or describing a language or culture from the point of view of people who do not use the language or who live outside the culture
render	v.	to cause someone or something to be in a particular state
verdict	n.	an opinion or decision made after judging the facts that are given, especially one made at the end of a trial
pithily	adv.	in a clever way that uses only a few words
salient	adj.	most noticeable or important
warn someone off		to tell someone not to do something because of danger or some other reasons
allude to someone/something		to mention someone or something without talking about him, her, or it directly

Unit 3 Critical Thinking

buttonhole	v.	to stop someone and make him or her listen to you
pretension	n.	a false or unsupportable claim
acquiesce	v.	to accept or agree to something, often unwillingly
charisma	n.	a special power that some people have naturally that makes them able to influence other people and attract their attention and admiration
legitimate	adj.	reasonable and acceptable
dissenting	adj.	showing a strongly different opinion on a particular question, especially an official suggestion or plan, a legal decision, or a popular belief
dismissive	adj.	showing that you do not think something is worth considering
emancipation	n.	the process of giving people social or political freedom and rights
egalitarianism	n.	the belief in or practicing of egalitarian principles (= the idea that all people should have the same rights and opportunities)
incompatible	adj.	not able to exist or work with another person or thing because of basic differences
reflexivity	n.	the fact of someone being able to examine his or her own feelings, reactions, and motives (= reasons for acting) and how these influence what he or she does or thinks in a situation
contingent	adj.	depending on or influenced by something else
epistemological	adj.	relating to the part of philosophy that is about the study of how we know things
defy	v.	to refuse to obey a person, decision, law, situation, etc.
divergent	adj.	different or becoming different from something else
exhaustive	adj.	complete and including everything
meta-language	n.	a language or system of symbols used to discuss another language or system
polysemous	adj.	having more than one meaning

Reflections and Practice

I Read the text and answer the following questions.

1. What is the purpose of the study?
2. What are the challenges that the author indicated regarding the definition of critical thinking?
3. Can you briefly talk about the "critical thinking movement"? For example: Where did it occur? What was the purpose? How did some of its key members define critical thinking? What was the "impasse" it faced?
4. What disciplines were involved in this study? Why were these disciplines selected?
5. What are the major and minor themes identified in the findings?
6. What are the major conclusions and teaching implications?

II Discuss the following questions with your partner.

1. What is the significance of clarifying the concept of critical thinking?
2. As the author mentioned in the article, some researchers preferred to seek a single unitary definition for critical thinking, yet others viewed it as having multiple meanings. What is your view on this, and why? Which do you think is more beneficial to critical thinking instruction in higher education?
3. The study found seven definitions of critical thinking. How do you understand these definitions? What is your response to each of them or how would you comment on these views? What are some other possible perceptions of this concept?
4. What are the perceptions and practices of critical thinking in your discipline? How are they similar to or different from the findings reported in the study?
5. How would you comment on the design of this study? How would you design the research differently if you were to fulfil the same research purpose?

III Paraphrase the following sentences.

1. The evident importance of critical thinking in higher education, as well as the seeming pedagogical uncertainty surrounding the concept, suggests there is a need to find out more about how the idea is actually understood and used by academics in their teaching in the disciplines.
2. It seems reasonable to suppose that a concept so frequently invoked would long ago have acquired a clear-cut definition, but in fact the opposite is true: With each new

appearance, critical thinking becomes less, rather than more, clearly defined.

3. Indeed, this may be a way of understanding the definitional impasse that the critical thinking movement seems to have found itself in; that is, there has been a tendency to detach the concept from its actual uses, and then to attach to it either notions that are thought to be somehow intrinsic to it, or else notions that one desires it to have.

4. This suggests the need for a transdisciplinary approach, where students are encouraged to reflect on the variety of educational and intellectual processes they experience in the "different specialist domains" of their studies, and to seek to recognize any coherences that might exist in these processes.

5. Indeed, in trying to make sense of "critical thinking", and in working out how it might be best taught, it may be that it is above all this quality—"an extra edge of consciousness"—that we should hope to encourage in our students, and also in ourselves, and in the world generally, in spite of the many challenges that we all face.

IV Read the text and form a critical synopsis of the text by answering the five questions.

Questions	Your response
1. Why am I reading this?	
2. What is the author trying to do in writing this?	
3. Is what the author is saying relevant to what I want to find out?	
4. How convincing is what the author is saying?	
5. In conclusion, what use can I make of this?	

Ⓥ Write an outline for the text following the structure below.

1. **Introduction**

   Research context: The idea of critical thinking is _____.

   Literature review: Scholars have devoted great effort to _____ by either trying to find a single unitary definition or by viewing it as having a variety of cognitive modes.

   Research niche: Although critical thinking is considered to be significant in higher education, there lacks _____
   _____.

   Research objective: The purpose of this study is to _____
   _____.

2. **Methods**

   Participants: The study involved interviewing seventeen academics _____
   _____.

   Procedure: The participants took part in _____.

   Data collection and analysis: Interviews were _____ for key themes.

3. **Findings**

   At least seven definitional strands were identified in the informants' commentaries, and have been grouped into two broad categories: _____.

   Major themes: _____;

   Minor themes: _____.

4. **Discussion/Conclusion**

   Explanations for the findings:

   - The participating academics have _____
     that are often well conveyed to their students.
   - Critical thinking is viewed as not only a term that has multiple meanings but also
     _____.

   Implications of the study:

   - The first implication concerns _____, and the need for key terms like "critical" to be clarified as well as they can be to students in their studies.

> - The second implication concerns _____.
>
> **Limitations of the study:** The research was restricted to _____
> _____.
>
> **Recommendations for future research:** One can indeed posit _____
> _____, ones that might emerge from investigation of other fields and disciplines.

Ⅵ **Write a summary for the text in 150–200 words.**

Part 3 Further Reading

How Do English-as-a-Foreign-Language (EFL) Teachers Perceive and Engage with Critical Thinking: A Systematic Review from 2010 to 2020[1]

Abstract

This article presents a critical review of 25 empirical studies on English-as-a-foreign-language (EFL) teachers' perceptions of and engagement with critical thinking (CT) in a wide range of educational contexts from 2010 to 2020. Through a systematic process of paper selection and review, three central themes were identified, namely, (1) EFL teachers' understanding of CT and CT instruction; (2) EFL teachers' CT instructional models and strategies; and (3) the impacts of EFL teachers' CT instruction on students and themselves with various influencing factors at individual, interpersonal, and environmental levels. The review sheds light on the gap between the curriculum rhetoric and classroom reality due to the lack of attention to CT in current language teacher education. It also provides a critical analysis of the research methodologies adopted in the existing literature and outlines new

---

1 This paper is from Yuan, R., Liao, W., Wang, Z. Kong, J. & Zhang, Y. 2022. How do English-as-a-foreign-language (EFL) teachers perceive and engage with critical thinking: A systematic review from 2010 to 2020. *Thinking Skills and Creativity*, *43*: 101–102.

directions for interested researchers in the fields of language teaching and teacher education.

Keywords: critical thinking, skills and dispositions, English-as-a-foreign-language (EFL) teachers, systematic review

 Reflections and Practice

Read the full article and answer the following questions.

1. What is the aim of this review article?
2. What was the review process?
3. What important findings are revealed?
4. What are the major contributions of the review article?
5. What suggestions for further research are proposed?

Unit 4
Arts Education

 Learning Objectives

- Understand the overall structure and components of empirical articles;

- Evaluate the ideas and research design in empirical articles;

- Apply the appropriate reading strategies in an empirical article.

Part 1 Reading Skills and Strategies

Reading Empirical Articles

1. Understanding the Overall Structure and Components of Empirical Articles

An empirical article usually structures around IMRAD or other variants. In the IMRAD structure, "I" means Introduction, "M" represents Method, and "RAD" refers to Results and Discussion (Swales, 1990; Hu, 2000; Pang, 2008; Lin & Evans, 2012; Cargill & O'Connor, 2013, etc.). In fact, an empirical article includes at least ten parts: Title, Author(s)' Name(s) and Affiliation, Abstract, Introduction, Literature Review, Method, Results, Discussion, Conclusion and References. All parts closely correlate in the empirical article, with their unique roles. Below is a brief introduction to the major sections, as indicated in Table 4.1.

- ✓ **Title:** Explicit and concise, the title is the gist of an empirical article.

- ✓ **Abstract:** Not beyond a prescribed word limit, an abstract summarizes the research background, research question, method, results and discussion, as well as research conclusions and recommendations.

- ✓ **Introduction**: This section introduces the research background, puts forward the research question or hypothesis, and states the research purpose and significance. In some cases, the definition of a certain concept and the overall structure of the empirical article could be identified.

- ✓ **Literature review**: It critically reviews the development of a certain subject area, indicating the research gaps to be further filled in research. In some cases, Literature Review mingles with Introduction as an indispensable part in the section of Introduction.

- ✓ **Method:** This section clarifies how the research is conducted. Usually, it exhibits the normal research methods used, such as the qualitative method, quantitative method, or mixed methods.

- ✓ **Results:** As one of the essential parts, this section usually presents data in tables, charts, histograms, line graphs, photos and others, apart from the written words. It pinpoints the important data and offers a contextual explanation of the data.

- ✓ **Discussion:** By comparing the present results with the previous literature, this part analyzes the reasons for the similarities or differences between the latter and former. It also discusses the theoretical implications and practical applications, as well as the limitations of the research. In some cases, Results integrates with Discussion as an unitary section.
- ✓ **Conclusion:** On the basis of a brief summary of the end results, this section draws conclusions for the research. This last part would direct for the future research while leaving readers a sense of completeness of the present work.

Table 4.1 Overall structure and components of empirical articles

Section	Function	Focused questions
Title	Clarifying the research thesis	✓ What is the research about?
Abstract	Summarizing the main points	✓ What is the main focus of study? ✓ What are the salient findings of the research?
Introduction	Introducing the research question	✓ What is the purpose of the study? ✓ What is the research question?
Literature review	Recalling research development	✓ How is the previous work? ✓ What are the differences between the previous work and the present study?
Method	Describing the methods used	✓ Who or what was involved in this study? ✓ When and where was the study done? ✓ What instruments were used? ✓ How was the variable controlled? ✓ How was the study conducted?
Results	Presenting results	✓ What are the research findings? ✓ In which way are the findings presented?
Discussion	Analyzing the results from different perspectives	✓ Do the results agree or disagree with the previous study? ✓ What are the implications and/or applications? ✓ What are the novelties of the research?
Conclusion	Ending the present work	✓ What are the conclusions? ✓ What are the contributions? ✓ What are the recommendations for future work?

2. Applying Different Reading Strategies in an Empirical Article

For the purpose of effective reading of an empirical article, readers may deploy different reading strategies. These strategies include target-focused reading, frame-work reading, note-taking reading, multi-time reading, etc. In different cases readers may take different approaches to the information processing.

1) Target-focused reading

This strategy is used to read the title and abstract for the overview of a research. The title reveals the gist of a research while the abstract tells the most extracted information as to the research question, method, results and conclusion.

Target-focused reading is also used for the easy and rapid access to the lead-in information in the section of Introduction and the summing-up remarks in the section of Conclusion. This reading strategy enables readers to find the research background, the questions raised or hypothesis put forward, as well as the research purpose and significance. Likewise, it helps readers find the research contribution to the relevant fields and suggestions for the future work.

Before reading through the whole article, many experienced readers are very inclined to focus on the information located in tables and figures in the section of Results. They are eager to catch the novelties or the comparative advantages of the research. Instinctively, they hope the information in the tables or figures could bring insight into their own research.

2) Frame-work reading

Feasible and effective, frame-work reading is used to recognize the outline by scanning the major headings and subheadings of an empirical article, as well as some sketchy ideas in each heading and subheading. While processing the information mostly at a surface level, this strategy contributes to the command of a global view of the article without reading the details. This could be a heuristic and pragmatic approach to information retrieval.

Below are two examples of framework of empirical articles. Sample 1 is from the field of arts education, without subheadings, and Sample 2 is from the field of biology and medicine, with subheadings.

Sample 1:

Arts and Scholastic Performance

1. Introduction

2. Methods

3. Results and Discussion

4. Conclusion

Sample 2:

> Interstitial Fluid Micro Flows Along Perivascular and Adventitial Clearances Around Neurovascular Bundles

1. Introduction

2. Materials and Methods

2.1 Experimental animals

2.2 Surgical operation

2.3 Fluorescing imaging

2.4 Histological staining

3. Results

3.1 Histological analysis of the structure of the PAC around neurovascular bundles

3.2 High-speed heart-orientated ISF micro flow along PAC (p)

3.3 Double-belt ISF flow along PAC (v) around neurovascular bundles

3.4 Waterfall-like ISF flow induced by the small branching vessel or torn fascia along PAC

4. Discussion

4.1 The PAC is the kernel structure for flood-like ISF flow

4.2 The diversity of ISF flow within PAC

4.3 The kinematic laws of ISF flow along PAC around neurovascular bundles

5. Conclusion

3) Note-taking reading

Note-taking reading is known as deep reading, which encourages readers to probe into the information at both global and regional levels. This reading strategy asks readers to note-take or mind map (see Figure 4.1) the ideas coming from both the article and the readers by following a series of questions, such as: (1) What is the research about? (2) What is the purpose of this research? (3) How does the previous research work? (4) What are the theoretical underpinnings? (5) Are the research gaps addressed? (6) What are the specific questions raised in this article? (7) How is this research conducted? (8) Are the methods used appropriate? (9) Are the methods distinctive? (10) How is the data dealt with? (11) What are the findings? (12) Is the data reliable and credible? (13) What are the conclusions? (14) Are the conclusions convincing? (15) What are the contributions of this research to the relevant fields?

(16) What are the limitations of this research? (17) What are the suggestions for the follow-up work? (18) What are the originality and novelty of this research? (19) What are the profound implications of this research? (20) What have I learned from this research? (21) Is it a research breakthrough in the relevant fields? (22) What follow-up work could I do? or (23) Can my research surpass this study?

Note-taking reading asks readers to both identify the essential information and evaluate the strengths and weaknesses of the research. It may arouse readers' appetite for further investigation. Cognitively processing the information at a deep level, it tests readers' information extraction ability, as well as the critical thinking ability, dialectical thinking ability and creative thinking ability.

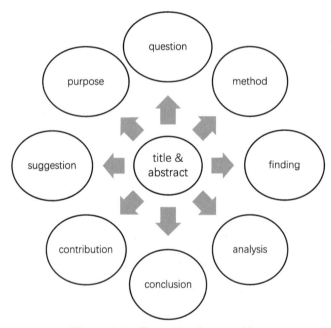

Figure 4.1   Example of note-taking

4) Multi-time reading

Some empirical articles indeed deserve multi-time reading. These articles may discover unexpected experimental phenomena, report new research methods, mark a great technology breakthrough, or represent a huge milestone in the development of the discipline. They may also enlarge researchers' views, improve their knowledge, lead them out of the blind alley, or help them blaze a new trail. Reading these articles is a great source of research inspiration. As a lighthouse, they will inspire researchers' creative thinking for further innovation. Therefore, careful reading of innovative literature is the mother of research success.

Unit 4 Arts Education

Part 2 Intensive Reading

Pre-reading questions:

✓ What is the topic/area of the research article?

✓ What might be the purpose of this article?

✓ How will the research be conducted?

The Use of Folk Music in Kindergartens and Family Settings[1]

1. Introduction

Folk music is an integral part of the culture and lifestyle of each nation. Omerzel Terlep (1984) notes that the music that we refer to as folk music is the music of broad masses in a particular time and place, who accept, change, and adapt the creations produced by individuals according to their **aesthetic** sense (p. 3). Knowing the nation's musical **treasure trove** is a key **prerequisite** for the preservation of its folk tradition. The family or parents and grandparents, being a child's first teachers, are a key factor in introducing a child to folk art during preschool. Kindergartens also play an important role in preserving folk traditions, encouraging, developing, and arousing love of folk music among preschool children by way of systematic music education. The **integration** of activities regarding folk music in kindergartens is connected with facilitation of children's individual development (Fu, 2010) and development of social competences (Zalar, 2015). It is **paramount** that children are allowed to recognize and experience musical activities (singing, playing, listening, and creating) that are connected and **intertwined** with folk themes.

According to Zmaga Kumer (2002), folk song is an integral part of Slovenian culture even today, equal in value to artificial poetry and music and at the same time independent of the two, as it **abides by** its own rules. A man's first encounter with folk song is one of the earliest experiences a human being can grasp and feel the consequences **thereof** without fully understanding them.

---

1 This paper is from Denac, O. & Žnidaršič, J. 2018. The use of folk music in kindergartens and family settings. *Creative Education, 9*: 2856–2862.

Children's folk songs should be present in children's lives on a daily basis. Furthermore, Žgavec (2004) strongly recommends that integration of folk songs is conscious and systematic on all levels of education. Since folk songs are generally short and simple in terms of their text and music, they can be sung by the youngest of children. In that regard, we must be aware about the criteria when we choose the song **repertoire**. As Borota (2010) states, one needs to consider two fundamental aspects besides the song's artistic merit, namely, their diversity and developmental appropriateness. Naturally, this also means that we choose a folk song based on its theme, form, language, or rhythmic and melodic structure. According to Kumer (1987), "The content variety of children's songs depends on the environment a child is raised in. The songs of children living in the country reflect the child's contact with nature and animals, while the creativity of urban children is inspired more by the technical sphere. Children's folk songs are frequently merely playful rhyming games or voice imitations. They are also about weather, food, adventures in the **pastures** or at home; in short, they are about anything that children experience or feel close to" (p. 169). Thus, they can be classified into songs on animals, nature and seasons, songs for playing and amusement, funny songs, counting rhymes, riddle songs, teasing songs, and lullabies.

Playing folk instruments is equally important as folk singing. Along with some of the oldest instruments, such as pan's flute, cross flute, dulcimer, cimbalom, double flute, horns, ocarina, clay pot bass, tambouritza, etc., there are many children's folk instruments and sounders made of different material or common objects, plants, or fruits, such as corn fiddle, rattles, rhythm instruments (pot lids), ratchet, wind rattles, thin paper and a comb, whistles, whit-horns, birch flute, etc. Children's instruments and sound toys in fact include anything that children can use to produce music, sounds, or rhythm; in other words, anything they can blow, **clatter**, **rattle**, rub against different surfaces, **pluck**, **strum**, or pound (Cvetko, 1991).

One of the main goals of music education in the preschool period is to arouse children's interest in singing folk songs, playing folk instruments, and listening to folk music. However, we need to be conscious of the fact that the attitude towards music education has changed significantly in recent years. Today it is no longer taken for granted that children are happy to sing, play, and create. The underlying reason for that is the plurality of **acoustic** stimuli, resulting in passive attitude of children towards musical activities. Children's playful creativity, socializing, or merrymaking is often distracted by television, radio, and computer. In order to preserve our folk tradition through our children and create a positive attitude towards cultural heritage, we need a systematic approach to the planning, **implementation**, and evaluation of music education.

2. Aims and Method of the Empirical Research

The survey, which was based on the identified problem, involved preschool teachers and parents of preschool children attending kindergarten. The objective of our study was to identify:

- ✓ the position folk music occupies in kindergartens—singing folk songs, playing children's folk instruments, listening to folk songs;
- ✓ the level of children's interest in singing folk songs, playing children's folk instruments, and listening to folk songs in kindergarten;
- ✓ the position folk music occupies at home—singing folk songs, playing children's folk instruments, and listening to folk songs by both children and their parents.

The study addressed the following research questions:

- ✓ How often do preschool teachers incorporate folk music in their education process?
- ✓ How many and which children's folk songs did children learn over a period of one year?
- ✓ Which music activities related to folk tradition preschool children are happy to take part in?
- ✓ How often do parents engage in music activities related to folk tradition with their families?
- ✓ How often do children engage in music activities related to folk tradition with their families?
- ✓ What significance is **attributed to** folk music by parents?

Our research sample included preschool teachers ($n = 240$) who teach groups of children of different ages (from 3 to 6) and the parents of the children ($n = 4,312$). Information was collected using a questionnaire for the teachers and another one for the parents. The data was then processed quantitatively and summarized by means of frequency distribution (f, f %).

3. Results

3.1 Research Results Based on the Questionnaire for the Teachers

How often do preschool teachers incorporate folk music in their education process?

Most teachers frequently **incorporate** singing folk songs in the education process, though they rarely play folk instruments or listen to folk music in class. When dealing with folk music, one needs to make sure that all musical activities are equally represented. One of the teacher's tasks is to encourage children to sing folk songs, produce music using folk instruments and sounders, construct simple folk instruments, and actively listen to folk music (Table 1).

Table 1 Frequency of incorporating folk music in the education process

Activities Answers	Singing folk songs		Playing folk instruments		Listening to folk music	
	f	f%	f	f%	f	f%
Very frequently	22	9.2	23	9.6	29	12.1
Frequently	133	55.4	85	35.4	41	17.1
Rarely	85	35.4	88	36.7	101	42.1
Never	0	0	44	18.3	69	28.7
Total	240	100	240	100	240	100

How many and which children's folk songs did children learn over a period of one year?

Table 2 clearly shows that on average, preschool children learned 1.7 songs in one year. Preschool teachers should aspire to maintain a certain balance with regard to the number of artificial and folk songs included in the learning process. In other words, they should teach children at least as many folk songs as artificial ones over the period of one year. Judging by the list of song titles, the teachers frequently chose songs that were evidently too difficult in terms of their rhythmic and melodic structure. However, they did make sure that the songs were extremely varied in terms of their content, including songs on animals, nature and seasons, and songs for playing and amusement, as well as, though to a lesser extent, teasing songs, funny songs, and **lullabies**.

Table 2 Number of folk songs learned

Children's age	3–6 years
Number of songs learned	401
Number of teachers/units	240
Average number of songs learned	1.7

Which music activities related to folk tradition preschool children are happy to take part in?

According to the teachers, most children are often and very often happy to participate in the singing of folk songs, playing folk instruments, and listening to folk music. As children are obviously fond of all music activities, the teachers should include those related to folk themes in the education process more frequently than they presently do. This means that more attention should be paid to playing folk instruments and listening to folk music (Table 3).

Table 3 Activities children are happy to take part in

Activities Answers	Singing folk songs		Playing folk instruments		Listening to folk music	
	f	f%	f	f%	f	f%
Very frequently	73	30.4	103	42.9	52	21.7
Frequently	124	51.7	98	40.8	121	50.4
Rarely	43	17.9	39	16.3	67	27.9
Never	0	0	0	0	0	0
Total	240	100	240	100	240	100

3.2 Research Results Based on the Questionnaire for the Parents

How often do parents engage in music activities related to folk tradition with their families?

Our results clearly indicate that most parents never listen to folk music, play folk instruments, or actively participate in various folk events. In addition, they rarely sing folk songs at home or attend events with folk themes. Over a half of the interviewed parents rarely acquires sheet music with folk songs. The activities which some of the interviewed parents engage in frequently include singing folk songs and purchasing songbooks with folk music or folk songs (Table 4).

Table 4 Frequency of parents engaging in music activities with their families

Activities Answers	Never		Rarely		Frequently		Total	
	f	f%	f	f%	f	f%	f	f%
Singing folk songs	234	5.4	3,089	71.6	989	22.9		
Listening to folk music	2,567	59.5	1,513	35.1	232	5.4		
Playing folk instruments	2,308	53.5	1,806	41.9	138	4.6		
Attending events where folk music is played	1,424	33	2,789	64.7	99	2.3	4,312	100
Active involvement of parents in groups producing folk music (choir, folk band, folk dance group)	4,155	96.3	112	2.6	45	1		
Purchase of CDs with folk music	1,997	46.3	1,892	43.9	423	9.8		
Purchase of sheet music with folk songs (songbooks)	1,312	30.4	2,236	51.9	764	17.7		

How often do children engage in music activities related to folk tradition with their families?

Based on our survey results we can further conclude that a majority of children never play folk instruments or listen to folk music at home. We can partly attribute that to the inactivity of the parents who do not encourage children to produce or listen to folk music by setting an example and to teachers who rarely incorporate listening to folk music and playing folk instruments in the education process. Children do tend to sing folk songs at home, as this is the one activity that both parents and teachers pay more attention to (Table 5).

Table 5 Frequency of children engaging in music activities with their families

Activities / Answers	Never f	Never f%	Rarely f	Rarely f%	Frequently f	Frequently f%	Total f	Total f%
Singing folk songs	122	2.8	2,698	62.6	1,492	34.6		
Listening to folk music	2,433	56.4	1,691	39.2	188	4.4	4,312	100
Playing folk instruments	2,750	63.8	1,517	35.2	45	1.0		

What significance is attributed to folk music by parents?

Although the results showed that more than half of the parents do not sing folk songs, play folk instruments, or listen to folk music at home, the majority of parents (91.9%) do attribute great importance to folk music. This is evident from the following answers: Folk music is a memory of the past; it is part of our lives; it is our cultural heritage which cheers us up; it is about respect for tradition; it is part of Slovenian tradition which needs to be preserved; it is the basis of our past, present, and future.

4. Conclusions

Our survey results suggest that musical activities related to folk music are not sufficiently incorporated into education process or home environment. Children should learn more folk songs in the kindergarten, and sing them more frequently. Preschool teachers should be familiar with the criteria for the selection of appropriate folk songs, **taking into consideration** the level of children's musical skills. Furthermore, they should pay more attention to listening to folk music and playing folk instruments. The world of children's musical instruments and sounders is extremely varied. A child can see a toy in nearly any object and can easily turn it into a musical instrument, which they can listen to or use to produce different sounds, thus encouraging their own creativity. When discussing folk music tradition, the teacher must aim at all musical activities being equally represented.

In the past, the family and the life within a community were two paramount factors in preserving music as cultural heritage. Nowadays, however, our lifestyles have been changing continuously while our taste in music has been increasingly influenced by the media, kindergarten, school, and cultural institutions. For this reason, the family which represents a key element in preserving folk traditions should take a more active role in transferring knowledge to younger generations. Parents should motivate children more than they do and promote their interest in and love of folk music at home through their own active engagement. Parents that are passive towards producing and listening to folk music will have a direct impact on the attitude their children will have towards such activities.

What can be done to raise the awareness of one's cultural heritage and children's interest in it?

Plevnik (2010) believes that in Slovenia, we need to raise the awareness of the role cultural education plays within the education system, improve the level of cultural **literacy**, and establish a proper connection between education and culture. We need to realize that key success factors include preschool teachers with a vision that incorporates the integration of folk music into the education process and parents who promote love of and a proper attitude towards cultural heritage in their children through their own knowledge and engagement from the child's earliest years on.

(Scan the QR code to access the list of references.)

Words and Expressions

aesthetic	*adj.*	concerned with beauty and art and the understanding of beautiful things
treasure trove		a place, book, etc. containing many useful or beautiful things
prerequisite	*n.*	something that must exist or happen before something else can happen or be done
integration	*n.*	the act or process of combining two or more things so that they work together
paramount	*adj.*	more important than anything else
intertwine	*v.*	to become mutually involved
abide by		to accept and act according to a law, an agreement, etc.
thereof	*adv.*	of the thing mentioned
repertoire	*n.*	all the plays, songs, pieces of music, etc. that a performer knows and can perform
pasture	*n.*	land covered with grass that is suitable for feeding animals on
clatter	*v.*	to make a rattling sound

rattle	v.	to make a series of short loud sounds when hitting against something hard
pluck	v.	to play a musical instrument by pulling the strings with fingers
strum	v.	to play a guitar or similar instrument by moving your fingers up and down across the strings
acoustic	adj.	related to sound or to the sense of hearing
implementation	n.	the act of accomplishing some aim or executing some order
attribute to		to say or believe that something is the result of a particular thing
incorporate	v.	to include something so that it forms a part of something
lullaby	n.	a soft gentle song sung to make a child go to sleep
take into consideration		to take account of something
literacy	n.	the ability to read and write

Reflections and Practice

I Read the text and answer the following questions.

1. What is folk music?
2. What role does folk music play in a nation's culture?
3. What is the objective of this study?
4. How was the study conducted?
5. Can you summarize the results of this study?
6. What are the conclusion and suggestion of this study?

II Discuss the following questions with your partner.

1. Do you think the research topic in this article is important? Why or why not?
2. What is your viewpoint of the research methods used in this article?
3. Could you suggest other research methods in this research?
4. How do you comment on the results?
5. What do you think of the overall organization of this article?

III Paraphrase the following sentences.

1. The family or parents and grandparents, being a child's first teachers, are a key

factor in introducing a child to folk art during preschool. Kindergartens also play an important role in preserving folk traditions, encouraging, developing, and arousing love of folk music among preschool children by way of systematic music education.

2. Children's playful creativity, socializing, or merrymaking is often distracted by television, radio, and computer. In order to preserve our folk tradition through our children and create a positive attitude towards cultural heritage, we need a systematic approach to the planning, implementation, and evaluation of music education.

3. Our survey results suggest that musical activities related to folk music are not sufficiently incorporated into education process or home environment. Children should learn more folk songs in the kindergarten, and sing them more frequently. Preschool teachers should be familiar with the criteria for the selection of appropriate folk songs, taking into consideration the level of children's musical skills.

4. Based on our survey results we can further conclude that a majority of children never play folk instruments or listen to folk music at home. We can partly attribute that to the inactivity of the parents who do not encourage children to produce or listen to folk music by setting an example and to teachers who rarely incorporate listening to folk music and playing folk instruments in the education process.

5. In the past, the family and the life within a community were two paramount factors in preserving music as cultural heritage. Nowadays, however, our lifestyles have been changing continuously while our taste in music has been increasingly influenced by the media, kindergarten, school, and cultural institutions.

Ⅳ Draw a mind map according to the empirical underpinnings of the text.

Ⅴ Write an outline for the text following the structure below.

Title: The Use of Folk Music in Kindergartens and Family Settings

Thesis Statement: Children's folk music education should be implemented in kindergartens and family settings.

1. **Introduction**

   One of the main goals of music education in the preschool period is to _____
   _____.

2. **Aims and Method**

   This study is to raise the awareness of _____.

   A survey was conducted on preschool teachers and parents of preschool children

attending kindergarten. The research sample included _____.
_____ were used to collect information from the teachers and parents. The data was processed _____ and summarized _____.

3. **Results**

   (1) Most teachers _____
   _____.

   (2) On average, preschool children learned _____.

   (3) More attention should be paid to _____.

   (4) Most parents _____.
   In addition, they rarely _____.

   (5) A majority of children never _____ at home.

   (6) The majority of parents (91.9%) do attribute great importance to _____.

4. **Conclusion**

   The survey results show that _____
   _____. Preserving the nation's cultural heritage deserves great attention.

Ⅵ Write a summary for the text in 150–200 words.

Part 3 Further Reading

Education and the Arts: Educating Every Child in the Spirit of Inquiry and Joy[1]

Abstract

This paper explores the political and social forces that have led to the well-documented

---

1 This paper is from Hardiman, M. M. 2016. Education and the arts: Educating every child in the spirit of inquiry and joy. *Creative Education*, 7: 1913–1928.

narrowing of the curriculum, squeezing out arts programming in schools. While not intended to be an exhaustive literature review, this work highlights important findings that correlate arts learning with biological changes as well as cognitive and academic advantages. Further, it explores how the arts may be the key to promoting 21-century skills of creative thinking and problem solving. From this review, we hope that educators and policymakers will reconsider how arts education and arts-integrated learning can influence educational practices and policies.

Keywords: arts education, arts integration, education, neuro-education, educational policy, pedagogy

Reflections and Practice

Read the full article and answer the following questions.

1. What is the aim of this review article?
2. What previous studies are reviewed?
3. How are they structured?
4. What important findings are revealed?
5. What suggestions for further research are proposed?

Unit 5
Language Learning

Learning Objectives

- Differentiate between conceptual research and empirical research;

- Get familiar with the structure of conceptual articles;

- Analyze conceptual articles in terms of research design;

- Evaluate conceptual articles.

Part 1 Reading Skills and Strategies

Reading Conceptual Articles

1. Features of Conceptual Research

Empirical research and conceptual research are two approaches that are commonly employed while conducting research. Conceptual research is also referred to as analytical research, while empirical research is to test a given hypothesis through observation and experimentation. Both approaches are very popular, but there are no hard and fast rules to their application and they are not mutually exclusive, so they can be employed in different aspects of a particular research.

Conceptual research is defined as a methodology wherein research is conducted by observing and analyzing existing information on a given topic. Conceptual research does not involve conducting any practical experiments. It is concerned with abstract concepts or ideas. Philosophers have long used conceptual research to develop new theories or to interpret existing theories in a different light. For example, Copernicus used conceptual research to develop the concepts about stellar constellations based on his observations of the universe. Down the line, Galileo simplified Copernicus's research by making his own conceptual observations which gave rise to more experimental research and confirmed the predictions made at that time. The most famous example of conceptual research is that of Sir Issac Newton. He observed his surroundings to conceptualize and develop theories about gravitation and motion. Einstein is widely known and appreciated for his work on conceptual research. Although his theories were based on conceptual observations, Einstein also proposed experiments to come up with theories to test the conceptual research.

2. Structure of Conceptual Articles

The significance of a conceptual article lies in its ability to develop logical and complete arguments rather than to test them empirically. Researchers use analytical tools called conceptual frameworks to make conceptual distinctions and organize ideas required for research purposes. Miller & Salkind (2002) proposed four main types of research design in conceptual papers: theory synthesis, theory adaptation, typology, and model. Theory synthesis refers to the conceptual integration across multiple theoretical perspectives to summaries and integrate current understanding. Theory adaptation, on the other hand, refers to revising the scope of perspective of an existing theory by informing it with other theories. Typology aims to explain differences between variants of a concept, and the model aims to build a theoretical framework that predicts relationships between constructs. These types are categorized for easier reference or clarity on how the argument is structured and developed. Drawing on personal reflections on daily editorial activities, Whetten (1989) suggested seven factors by which conceptual papers should be evaluated: (1) What's new? (2) So what? (3) Why so? (4) Well done? (5) Done well? (6) Why now? (7) Who cares? Table 5.1 below illustrates guiding questions for each factor that contributes to a publishable conceptual paper.

Table 5.1 Seven factors in evaluation of conceptual papers

Factors	Guiding questions
What's new?	Does the paper make a significant, value-added contribution to current thinking?
So what?	Will the theory likely change the practice of organizational science in this area?
Why so?	Are the underlying logic and supporting evidence compelling? Are the author's assumptions explicit? Are the author's views believable?
Well done?	Does the paper reflect sound thinking, conveying completeness and thoroughness? Are multiple theoretical elements (What, How, Why, When, Where, Who) covered, giving the paper a conceptually well-rounded, rather than superficial quality?
Done well?	Is the paper well written? Does it flow logically? Are the central ideas easily accessed? Is it enjoyable to read? Is the paper long enough to cover the subject but short enough to be interesting? Does the paper's appearance reflect high professional standards? Are the format and content of the paper consistent with the specifications in the Notice to Contributors?
Why now?	Is this topic of contemporary interest to scholars in this area? Is it likely to advance current discussions, stimulate new discussions, or revive old discussions?
Who cares?	What percentage of academic readers will be interested in this topic?

Part 2 Intensive Reading

Pre-reading questions:

✓ What are the key concepts of this article?

✓ What are some key questions relevant to the concepts?

✓ What might be the purpose of this article?

A Conceptual Framework to Explore the English Language Learning Experiences of International Students in Malaysia[1]

1. Introduction

Globalization has flattened the world of education, opening up increased opportunities for exchanges and transfers. These activities have led to student mobility (Verbik & Lasanowski, 2007). It refers to the movement of students to other countries in the pursuance of knowledge. Foreign students have been going to countries like the UK, the US, Australia, and Canada. Indeed, United Nations Educational, Scientific and Cultural Organization (UNESCO) as cited in Verbik & Lasanowski (2007) reports that in 2005, there were 2.7 million people studying in countries that were not their home land. Seeing the potential in terms of **revenue** and cultural transfer (Andrade, 2006; Bell, 2008; Trevaskes et al., 2003), Malaysia is on its way to become the hub of education regionally (Kerr, 2011) and also internationally (Model for Success, 2008).

In achieving this, Malaysia is opening its doors to students from other countries. These international students come from more than 150 countries all around the world [Ministry of Higher Education (MoHE) Statistics, 2010]. The 2010 statistics further indicate that there were 86,923 foreigners registered as international students in public and private higher institutions in Malaysia in 2010.

---

1 This paper is from Saad, N. S. M., Sidek, H. M., Baharun, H., Idrus, M. M. & Yunus, M. M. 2016. A conceptual framework to explore the English language learning experiences of international students in Malaysia. *International Journal of Advances in Education*, 2(6): 453–464.

The coming of international students into the education institutions in Malaysia would mean that there is a need for a common language for interaction. In this case, English can be the common language as it is the language of technology and second most spoken language in the world (English Language History, n.d.). Thus, Malaysian universities have set the English language requirement for international students. Most universities accept the exam scores of International English Language Testing System (IELTS) and Test of English as a Foreign Language (TOEFL). However, in many institutions, when these international students do not fulfill the requirement, they will undergo English classes provided by department assigned by the management of the institution. This is the phase that is going to be captured in the study where the experiences of these international students utilizing language learning strategies to learn English are highlighted.

The language learning experiences are not straightforward as international students bring along with them their languages, religions, cultures, conventions, habits and other resources. This diversity provides avenues for all to learn, explore, understand and increase awareness about linguistics and culture differences and thus find a way to interact, accept, survive and even adapt to the plural cultures (Bell, 2008; Schmidt & Jansen, 2005). Thus, it is the intention of this article to present the conceptual framework that underlays the study to unearth the experiences of a group of international students learning the English language in a new academic **milieu** and how the experience of each participant depicts the acculturation at the end of his or her first semester studies in a public university in Malaysia. The conceptual framework presented in this article is the initial stage of a bigger study.

2. Problem Statement

The backdrop of this study is based on the areas of language learning strategies and international students. Both have a strong body of research; with the former dating back three decades ago (Macaro, 2006; Oxford, 2011b) and the latter began even earlier, for example in 1950s in Australia with the inception of The Colombo Plan (Cuthbert et al., 2008; Dawson & Hacket, 2006). In Malaysia, literature on language learning strategies started to **gain momentum** in late 1990s with the landmark doctorate study by Mohamed Amin in 1996. On the other hand, research on international students began to take shape when there was a steady flow of them into Malaysia since 1996 (Morshidi Sirat, 2008). The body of literature in Malaysia is still in its first phase (Noor Saazai et. al, 2012) as it touches only on the overall picture of the international students here. However, from the extant literature in Malaysia on language learning strategies and international students, there seems to be a **dearth** in the conflation of these two areas in relation to Malaysia.

3. Literature Review

This part will **succinctly** highlight the **tenets** from the four theories/model and the themes from the areas of language learning strategies and international students that give rise to the four notions (hybrid environment, agency, out-of-class language learning strategies and acculturation strategies) that form the conceptual framework.

3.1 Theoretical Underpinnings

3.1.1 Experiential Learning Theory (ELT)

This theory highlights the role of experience in the process of learning (Kolb et al., 2000).

Kolb (1984) listed six characteristics of ELT and Kolb & Kolb (2005) discussed them again. These characteristics are the propositions derived from three earlier theorists—John Dewey, Kurt Lewin and Jean Piaget. The main tenet from ELT that is parallel to the discussion of this study is learning involves transactions between the person & the environment (Kolb, 1984; Kolb & Kolb, 2005). This also echoes in Beard & Wilson's (2007) handbook on ELT that says learning is a "sense-making process of active engagement between the inner world of the person and the outer world of the environment" (p. 2). Kolb et al. (2005) further strengthen this concept by discussing learning space theory that emphasizes the setting that the learner is in; for example, immediate setting which is termed as microsystem involving the course and the classroom. Besides the environment, it also takes into account the people around the learner like in mesosystem that includes family members. In other words, the concept of environment in ELT also comprises of the people around the learner.

3.1.2 Sociocultural Theory (SCT)

Lantolf (2000) **elucidates** six **germane** tenets of SCT. SCT was **propounded** by Lev Vygotsky: mediated mind, genetic domains, unit of analysis, Activity Theory, internalization and inner speech, and Zone of **Proximal** Development (ZPD). However, this study only embraces characteristics from Activity Theory and ZPD. The former proposes that a person behaves and reacts based on his biological, social and cultural needs (Lantolf, 2000). The latter, on the other hand, is in line with the concept of mediation which is central to SCT, where the mediator can be a tool or a person (Mamour, 2008). According to Vygotsky (1978), ZPD "is a distance between the actual developmental level…and the level of potential development as determined through problem solving under adult guidance or in collaboration with more capable peers" (p. 33). In other words, ZPD highlights the role of other people—teachers and friends, in enhancing the learning process.

3.1.3 Second Language Acquisition (SLA) Model

A lot of studies on language learning strategies employ the SLA Model by Rod Ellis (1994) to build the framework for investigating learners' choice or use of language learning strategies, for example, Mohamed Amin (1996, 2000), El-Saleh (2002), Zamri (2004), Johari Afrizal (2005), and Izawati & Siti Zawiyah (2008). This model identifies three sets of dimensions that explain the process of second language learning: individual learner differences, learner strategies, and outcome.

The first set deals with the individual learner differences that come in seven different categories: age, aptitude, motivation, learning styles, beliefs, affective states and personality. In learning the second language, these diverse individuals operate in different situational and social environment which affects the strategies that they choose. The choice of strategies is the second set of the dimensions. Some researchers doing studies on language learning strategies have broken down this set into the type of classification/typology that they have chosen; Zamri (2004) for example has chosen to look at in-class, out-of-class and test preparation, whereas Izawati & Siti Zawiyah (2008) look at cognitive, metacognitive, affective, memory, compensation and social strategies. This then goes to the third set which is the outcome. This deals with the level of achievement in attaining the second language. It has a two-way relationship with the earlier set. In other words, the result of acquiring the second language depends on the strategies used.

3.1.4 Social Cognitive Theory

The core view of this theory is that "mind, body and world function integratively" (Atkinson, 2011, p. 143). It is to say that the cognitive, physical being and environment affect each other. Moreover, Bandura (2001, p. 2) states that "human functioning is analyzed as social interdependent, richly contextualized and conditionally orchestrated within the dynamics of various societal subsystems and their complex interplay".

Albert Bandura discussed Social Cognitive Theory in light of the agentic perspective. Being an agent, according to Bandura (2001), is for the person to make things happen with intention. Therefore, a person is responsible for one's own development, adaptation and change which depend on the environment and situation. In other words, a person can choose to act or not to act based on a reason or reasons that arise from within that is inspired by or as a resistance towards the world around him.

There are four core features of **agency** which are associated closely to the mind and body: intentionality, forethought, self-reactiveness, and self-reflectiveness (Bandura, 2001, 2005, 2006). These features propel people to have a big role in their own self-development, adaptation and self-renewal with changing times. Being intentional suggests that a person has a reason for doing something or for not doing it. The power to do so is in the hand of that person. In line with that, the second feature—forethought which implies having goals for oneself, provides a reason for the agentic behaviour. Thus, the action or inaction, or selection of action works **in tandem with** the goals that one has set. However, this should not be like the cliché "the end justifies the means", where one can do anything to achieve the goal. The third feature, self-reactiveness provides the monitoring factor to the agency that one has. The monitoring is to ensure that one works within one's cognitive and environmental conditions. Self-reactiveness is also related to motivation. The last feature is self-reflectiveness. It is to examine and evaluate the action to be taken or not to be taken. So, in exercising agency, a person is a planner, forethinker, motivator, self-regulator and self-examiner with high self-efficacy (Bandura, 2001).

3.2 Language Learning Strategies (LLS)

Language learning strategy is seen to be a facilitating technique to ease language learning. Its orchestrated and effective usage leads to success in language learning (Kashefian-Naeeini et al., 2011; Su, 2005; Vann & Abraham, 1990; Oxford, 1990). One of the most prominent **proponents** of this area, Oxford (2011b) posits that the field of LLS is influenced by three landmark concepts in the education world: Piaget's cognitive processes, self-regulation theory by Vygotsky and self-governance or better known as the autonomy concept in 1990s. All these concepts are **underpinned** by the notion of learners' individuality which has myriad of interrelating factors; thus opening doors to research spanning all over the world and investigating all possible factors and elements from all sides and angles. However, this article will look into only one main area: site of research and participants involved.

Research in LLS has seen variation in many aspects. The most apparent is the site of research and participants involved which implicates the factor of learning environment. It is one of the elements that influence learners' individuality and language learning strategy use. This is explicitly mentioned in studies and research by Oxford (1996, 2011b), El-Saleh (2002), Mohamed Amin (1996, 2000), and Green & Oxford (1995). Besides, the importance of learning environment is **evinced** by the many studies conducted in different parts of the world as each location provides a unique **ambiance** for language learning experience, for example, Oman (Adel Abu Radwan, 2011), Turkey (Irgin, 2011), Jordan (El-Saleh, 2002), Indonesia (Johari Afrizal, 2005), Japan (Tanahashi, 2009), Lebanon (Nada, 2006), China (Gu, 2002), Thailand (Pawapatcharaudom, 2007), Korea (Lee, 2003), Palestine (Shmais, 2003), Iran (Kashefian-Naeeini & Nooreiny, 2010) and Malaysia (Mohamed Amin, 2000; Kamarul Shukri et al., 2009; Manprit & Mohamed Amin, 2011; Zamri, 2004).

In light of the research site and participants involved in learning English as a second or foreign language, the studies can be broken down into three big groups. Firstly, the nationals studying English as a second or foreign language in their own countries as in the cases of Malaysians studying English in Malaysia and Japanese learning English in Japan; and secondly, the students of other nationalities studying English in English-speaking countries like studies done by Bernat et al. (2009), Gao (2006), Griffiths (2003), and Wu (2011), involving foreign students in Australia, Britain, New Zealand and America respectively. The third group also consists of students of other nationalities studying English but not in English-speaking countries. Instead, they study English in "hybrid"-speaking countries (Mohamed Amin, 2000; Green & Oxford, 1995) like Puerto Rico. When the studies are tabulated in this manner, it can be **surmised** that while there is a **conglomeration** of studies for the first two groups, there is **a paucity of** research in the third group.

There are many classifications of strategies advocated by the **gurus** in the field of LLS, for instance, Bialystok (1978), O'Malley & Chamot (1990), Oxford (1990), and Mohamed Amin (2000). Each has a **cognizance** of strategies used by students in their social surroundings; they are termed as social strategies (Oxford, 1990), out-of-class strategies (Mohamed Amin, 2000) and included under socio-affective strategies, inference strategies and extended practice strategies by O'Malley & Chamot (1990), Bialystok (1978) and Tragant & Victori (2012) respectively. Thus, out of the many classifications listed in the literature, this study looks at the out-of-class strategies category as it is in line with this research that **accentuates** the importance of learning environment.

3.3 Hybrid Environment

Although it has been "said" in literature on English in Malaysia that English is a second language (ESL) in Malaysia (Thirusanku & Melor, 2011, p. 2); (other examples are Foo & Richards, 2004; Murugesan, 2003), the reality is not very clear cut so that not everyone is able to converse in English and not every place is English-friendly. English is learned and used instrumentally (Mohamed Amin, 2000; Lee Su Kim et al., 2010) for example to excel in exams and land a good-paying job. Furthermore, drawing from Green & Oxford's (1995, p. 268) description of Puerto Rico, the environment on that island is branded as hybrid because "a great deal of potential English input is available for learners who wish to take advantage of it. Thus, it is ESL. On the other hand, Puerto Rican learners can easily survive without using English for communication, so the island might in this respect appear to have characteristics of an EFL (English as a foreign language) setting". It is of a similar case with Malaysia because Malaysian learners can survive without using English but in the case of this study, can the international students survive too? If they do, how do they survive? Thus, it is intriguing to discover how these **sojourners** use English in their out-of-class activities in relation to language learning.

3.4 International Students (ISs)

The students of other nationalities or foreign students as mentioned earlier are better known as international students (henceforth ISs). ISs are students who have crossed geographical borders in pursuit of education. Their destination is usually the English-speaking countries like the UK, the US, and Australia (Arkoudis & Tran, 2007; Harman, 2005). There is a strong growth of research regarding them in these countries and the issues addressed range widely; for instance, preparation in adaptation to new environment (Carroll, 2005; Myles & Cheng, 2003), transition period (Guilfoyle & Harryba, 2009; Hellsten, 2008; Andrade, 2006), problems faced by ISs (Sawir, 2005; Novera, 2004); motivation and global issues (Jiang et al., 2009; Sayers & Franklin, 2007), and programme intervention (Sakurai et al., 2009). There are two broad themes emerging from these studies: social and academic matters. Both issues affect each other but this study concentrates on the latter.

Research on ISs concerning their academic matters has highlighted controversial issues like "soft-marking", plagiarism and their general inability to cope with Western way of studying (Birrell, 2006; Doherty & Singh, 2005; Trevaskes et al., 2003). Moreover, the lack of their English skills has caused concerns as documented by Ballard & Clanchy (1997) and Bradley & Bradley (1984). These studies might be decades old but the concern for the ISs' low proficiency level of English still prevails in current writings, for example, Andrade (2006), Ferman (2003), and Thompson (2009).

Although not an English-speaking country, Malaysia, like other receiving countries, puts emphasis on English as it is the language to be used in the academic milieu. Furthermore, Yusliza & Chelliah (2010) propose proficiency in the English language as one of the seven variables that can predict the adaptation level of ISs in Malaysia. Mapping the discussion of ISs in the above mentioned studies onto the scenario in Malaysia, ISs need to obtain, for example, at least a 5.5 for IELTS to secure a place in a Malaysian higher institution. However, some are accepted into the university or higher learning institution without taking IELTS or other English language tests or the score that they get does not fulfill the language requirement as **stipulated** by the university but their offer is conditional. In cases like this, they need to undergo an English course at the university.

Currently, a big portion of literature about ISs in Malaysia deals mainly about their demographic information and the reasons for their decision to study here [for example, Zainurin & Muhamad Abduh (2011); Rohana Jani et al. (2010); Mohd Taib et al. (2009); Rohaizat et al. (2011)]. A very insignificant number of studies have actually examined the problems among ISs in Malaysia, for instance, Alavi & Syed Mohamed (2011), Mousavi & Kashefian-Naeeni (2011), Zuria et al. (2010), Khairi & Rechards (2010), Manjula & Slethaug (2011). A few of these studies have highlighted that English language is a problem for ISs. The participants in a study by Zuria et al. (2010), for instance, have highlighted that Malaysians do not speak English, Malaysians speak English with Malay accent, and lack of English usage on signage and documents. Thus, it is worthwhile to look into ISs' English language learning experiences in Malaysia.

3.5 Acculturation

Acculturation is a term defined as "socio-cultural adjustment and acquisition of dominant cultural norms by members of a non-dominant group" (Gul & Kolb, 2009, p. 1). Therefore, it implies that the members of the minority group experience changes in dealing with the new environment. The changes are seen in five general aspects according to Berry et al. (1987): physical changes like a new place to live; cultural changes; different sets of social relationships; biological changes like new nutritional status and changes in one's psychology, behaviour and mental health status. Among the above mentioned elements, this proposed study is directly and largely linked to the change in "behaviour" in the ISs' language learning experiences as seen in their language learning strategy use. Thus, although the discussion on acculturation can be associated with other aspects like culture and psychology, this study only looks at the ISs' acculturation into their academic milieu.

Berry (2005) cautions that acculturation process is not identical for each individual as it depends on many factors, for example, attitudes and behaviours. Mapping it onto the proposed study, it is how the ISs feel towards assimilating into the new academic environment and what they actually do to assimilate. Their attitudes and behaviours will be determined by the analysis of their language learning strategy used and agency exercised.

Since acculturation occurs differently for individuals, Berry (2005) posits four variations termed as Acculturation Strategies: integration, assimilation, separation and marginalization. These strategies are placed on two continuums. Each continuum has a pair of contradictory strategies. This is illustrated by Figure 1.

The horizontal continuum is about the attitude of ISs towards own old habits (in this case, the language learning strategy use in home country)—whether to retain old habits or move away from them. The vertical continuum is about the attitude of IS in embracing new habits (in this case, the language learning strategy use to suit the new environment) or rejecting them. The first strategy, integration, suggests that an IS retains old habits and also embodies new ones. Whereas, if an IS leaves old habits and embraces new ones totally, then, the strategy is assimilation. On the other hand, separation strategy is when an IS does not want to adapt to the new habits and prefers to maintain his or her old ones. And lastly, if an IS does not prefer both, then he or she is using the marginalization strategy in acculturation. The acculturation strategy that is employed by each IS is determined by the comparison of out-of-class language learning strategy use in home country and in Malaysia by the end of the period of this study.

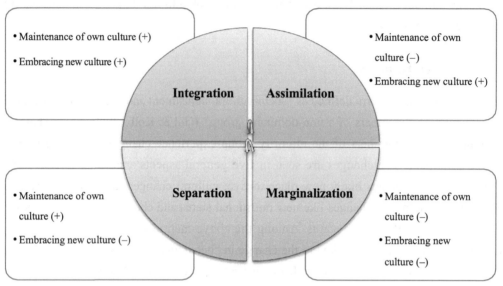

Figure 1   Four acculturation strategies adapted from Berry (2005)

3.6 Agency

According to Davies (1990), having agency is being able to set a goal and plan "a line of action, know how to achieve it and have the power and authority and right to execute it" (p. 343). It is a concept that cuts across the fields of LLS and ISs. This is because in employing language learning strategies and going through acculturation as an international student, one has a goal that is to learn the English language and be able to function in the new environment respectively. Hence, having or exercising one's agency suggests the push from within oneself that is influenced by the need of an end to be fulfilled and the action taken is within the permitted perimeter of the environment. In exercising one's agency, one can resist, negotiate, change and transform oneself (Pavlenko & Blackledge, 2004) in order to meet the goal.

From research done involving agency and ISs, two elements have been gathered to be prevalent in their exercise of agency: imagined community and investment. Studies by Arkoudis & Love (2008) and Gu (2008) are examples of the former; while Gao et al. (2008) and Pierce (1995) discuss the latter. As an illustration, Arkoudis & Love (2008) found that the lack of use of English among students in a mathematics class was due to their "imagined community" because they foresaw that English would not be totally important in their future.

In other words, they visualized that English would be secondary when they pursued their future endeavors in mathematics, thus there was little need for them to speak the language. And on the element of investment, a study by Gao et al. (2008) is a good example. It is about Chinese students from the Chinese Mainland studying in a Hong Kong university setting up a group to practice and use English to upgrade their command of the language. The first writer, who was also one of the participants, revealed the effort put in and the time spent in pursuing their goal in being competent in the language. The effort and time are considered the "investments" put in.

Furthermore, a qualitative study in LLS reported by Oxford et al. in Oxford (2011a) discovers that the student's lack of ability to handle second language learning crisis is due to among others, lack of "investment". As discussed above, "investment" is an element related to agency. Hence, this suggests that the notion of agency can be utilized to explain the choice and usage of LLS.

In encapsulation, using the definition by Bandura (2001, 2005, 2006) that posits personal human agency, the notion of agency can be seen in both fields discussed earlier. In fact, the studies cited show the existence of connection between agency and issues on ISs, and agency in LLS. Thus, agency is one of the aspects that differentiate the individual's English language learning experiences in this study.

4. Conceptual Framework

Espousing from the four theories/model of ELT by Kolb, SCT by Vygotsky, SLA Model by Ellis and Social Cognitive Theory by Bandura, and the themes discussed above, the conceptual framework illustrates the relationship among the notions of hybrid environment, agency, out-of-class language learning strategies and acculturation strategies. This part begins with a discussion on the smaller elements in each notion and then proceeds to establish the connections that exist among the notions. Both the notions and the connections are visualized in Figure 2.

With the aim to explore the English language learning experiences of ISs, and looking through the lenses of the ELT, SCT and Social Cognitive Theory, the integration of mind, body and environment happens in the process of learning. Thus, the big picture here is the environment. "Environment" in this study encompasses Malaysia as the place of study and a Malaysian public university as the institution. Both Malaysia and the institution provide a hybrid environment for international students where ESL meets EFL. Furthermore, being in an institution, the environment involves aspects like the academic conventions, the classroom culture, and the activities in the institution, the lecturers and the peers.

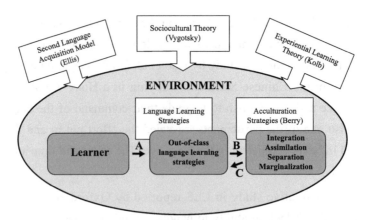

Figure 2　Conceptual framework

With the importance of environment established as the backdrop of the study, the discussion moves on to the process of language learning. In illuminating this, the SLA Model is adapted. There are three sets in the process. The first set is individual differences which in this conceptual framework are made up of personal human agency as advocated by Bandura (2001, 2005) in his Social Cognitive Theory. The exploration of human agency involves knowing the person's motivation, goals in the learning process and one's will to adapt to the new environment—to use all resources in achieving the goals.

The second set is as specified in the original model by Ellis in 1994. This study also uses LLS as the bridge in learning. However, the focus is on one type of strategy—out-of-class language learning strategies. It is significant as to illustrate the influence of the hybrid environment on the strategies chosen.

The third set in the adapted model is the acculturation strategies. Acculturation is an inevitable process for international students as they try to adapt to the new environment. However, each goes through acculturation differently. This set lists four acculturation strategies that might be embraced by the students at the end of this study. They are integration, assimilation, separation and marginalization.

The notions in the conceptual framework are meaningless without the elucidation of how they are connected. Referring to Figure 2, firstly, it is clear that the process of learning for the international students occurs in the hybrid environment as the three sets of dimensions are located in the big oval representing the environment. This also portrays the influence of setting on the language learning process of ISs. Secondly, arrow A indicates the relationship between individual personal agency and the strategies used. Then, arrow B shows the connection between the out-of-class strategies used and the acculturation strategies that the students adopt. This is seen in the maintenance and/or rejection of the old (in home country) and new (in Malaysia) language learning strategies. Lastly, the study is also interested in exploring the two-way relationship between the acculturation strategies and the two notions: language learning strategies and agency (shown by arrow C). This is to be done by narrating the process undergone by students who have used different acculturation strategies and this serves as the answer to fulfill the purpose of exploring how ISs experience English language learning in a hybrid environment.

5. Conclusion

The conceptual framework presented in this article is an initial but crucial part of a bigger research. This article has emphasized the tenets from four theories/model that underpin the study and discussed the major themes of language learning strategies (LLS) and international students (ISs) with their peripheral aspects of hybrid environment, acculturation and agency. The deliberation of both the theories and themes has highlighted the four notions (hybrid environment, agency, out-of-class language learning strategies and acculturation strategies) that become the pillars of the conceptual framework in exploring the English language learning experiences of international students in Malaysia.

(Scan the QR code to access the list of references.)

Words and Expressions

revenue	n.	the income that a government or company receives regularly
milieu	n.	the people, physical, and social conditions and events that provide the environment in which someone acts or lives
gain momentum		to get the force that keeps an event developing after it has started
dearth	n.	an amount or supply that is not large enough
succinctly	adv.	in a way that expresses what needs to be said clearly and without unnecessary words
tenet	n.	one of the principles on which a belief or theory is based
elucidate	v.	to explain something or make something clear
germane	adj.	connected with and important to something
propound	v.	to suggest a theory, belief, or opinion for other people to consider
proximal	adj.	near to the center of the body or to the point of attachment of a bone or muscle
agency	n.	the ability to take action or to choose what action to take
in tandem with		(things) happening at the same time or people working together

proponent	n.	a person who speaks publicly in support of a particular idea or plan of action
underpin	v.	to give support, strength, or a basic structure to something
evince	v.	to make something obvious or show something clearly
ambiance	n.	the character of a place or the quality it seems to have
surmise	v.	to guess something, without having much or any proof
conglomeration	n.	a large group or mass of different things all collected together in an untidy or unusual way
a paucity of		a lack of
guru	n.	a person skilled in something who gives advice
cognizance	n.	knowledge or understanding of something
accentuate	v.	to emphasize a particular feature of something or to make something more noticeable
sojourner	n.	a person who stays in a particular place for a short period
stipulate	v.	to say exactly how something must be or must be done
in encapsulation		in summary
espouse	v.	to become involved with or support an activity or opinion

Reflections and Practice

❶ Read the text and answer the following questions.

1. What are the theories or models that underpin the current study?
2. How can we differentiate the microsystem and the mesosystem in the learning space theory?
3. What is the main argument of the Zone of Proximal Development (ZPD)?
4. What are the core features of agency in Social Cognitive Theory?
5. Which type of research design (theory synthesis, theory adaptation, typology, model) is adopted in the current study?

❷ Discuss the following questions with your partner.

1. What are the advantages of conducting conceptual research?
2. The individual learner differences come in seven different categories, including age,

aptitude, motivation, learning styles, beliefs, affective states and personality. Select one aspect that you are interested in, look for relevant literatures, and discuss with your group member how this aspect influences second language acquisition.

3. As indicated in the Conclusion, "The conceptual framework presented in this article is an initial but crucial part of a bigger research." How do you think the current study would fit in a bigger picture? What would constitute follow-up studies?

II Paraphrase the following sentences.

1. The language learning experiences are not straightforward as international students bring along with them their languages, religions, cultures, conventions, habits and other resources. This diversity provides avenues for all to learn, explore, understand and increase awareness about linguistics and culture differences and thus find a way to interact, accept, survive and even adapt to the plural cultures (Bell, 2008; Schmidt & Jansen, 2005).

2. However, some are accepted into the university or higher learning institution without taking IELTS or other English language tests or the score that they get does not fulfill the language requirement as stipulated by the university but their offer is conditional. In cases like this, they need to undergo an English course at the university.

3. It implies that the members of the minority group experience changes in dealing with the new environment. The changes are seen in five general aspects according to Berry et al. (1987): physical changes like a new place to live; cultural changes; different sets of social relationships; biological changes like new nutritional status and changes in one's psychology, behaviour and mental health status.

4. The horizontal continuum is about the attitude of ISs towards own old habits (in this case, the language learning strategy use in home country)—whether to retain old habits or move away from them. The vertical continuum is about the attitude of IS in embracing new habits (in this case, the language learning strategy use to suit the new environment) or rejecting them.

5. According to Davies (1990), having agency is being able to set a goal and plan "a line of action, know how to achieve it and have the power and authority and right to execute it" (p. 343). It is a concept that cuts across the fields of LLS and ISs. This is because in employing language learning strategies and going through acculturation as an international student, one has a goal that is to learn the English language and be able to function in the new environment respectively.

IV Fill in the table below with regard to the theoretical underpinnings of the text.

Theories	Key scholar(s)	Main tenets
Experiential Learning Theory (ELT)		
Sociocultural Theory (SCT)		
Second Language Acquisition (SLA) Model		
Social Cognitive Theory (SCT)		

V Write an outline for the text following the structure below.

1. **Introduction**
   Globalization has flattened the world of education opening up _____ _____. The coming of international students into the education institutions in Malaysia _____.

2. **Problem Statement**
   The backdrop of this study is based on the areas of _____ and _____.
   However, the extant literature shows _____.

3. **Literature Review**
   Four theories/model and themes are reviewed: _____, _____, _____, and _____.

4. **Conceptual Framework**
   Drawing on the four theories reviewed earlier, the conceptual framework illustrates the relationship among four notions: _____, _____, _____, and _____.

VI Write a summary for the text in 150–200 words.

Part 3　Further Reading

Twenty-Five Years of Research on Oral and Written Corrective Feedback in *System*[1]

Abstract

　　This article provides a comprehensive and critical review of the research on various aspects of oral and written corrective feedback (CF) based on selected articles published in *System* over the past 25 years. The review starts with a comparison between oral and written CF, demonstrating that despite the discrepancies in the characteristics and pedagogical practices of the two types of CF, they have been examined from similar perspectives in the research. The striking similarity in the research themes makes it possible to follow the same template in organizing the research synthesis for each CF type. The synthesis for each CF type comprises three sections. Section 1 provides a taxonomy of the CF type in question and summarizes the findings of descriptive or observational research regarding how teachers provide CF and how students react to CF. Section 2 synthesizes the findings of experimental CF research regarding whether CF is effective in facilitating learning gains and what factors constrain its effectiveness. Section 3 discusses the research on teachers and students' beliefs about the utility of CF and how it should be implemented in the classroom.

Keywords: corrective feedback, written feedback, second language acquisition, form-focused instruction, task-based language learning and teaching, second language writing

 Reflections and Practice

Read the full article and answer the following questions.

1. What is the aim of this review article?
2. What previous studies are reviewed?

---

[1] This paper is from Li, S. & Vuono, A. 2019. Twenty-five years of research on oral and written corrective feedback in *System*. *System, 84*: 93–109.

3. How are they structured? (Chronologically or by theme?)
4. What important findings are revealed?
5. What suggestions for further research are proposed?

Unit 6
Environment

Learning Objectives

- Understand the overall structure and components of review articles;

- Identify the organizational patterns of review articles;

- Evaluate the ideas and research design in review articles.

Part 1 Reading Skills and Strategies

Reading Review Articles

1. Understanding Review Articles

The purpose of a review article is to discuss the published documents in a research area and provide readers with a comprehensive understanding of this area. Different from an empirical study, a review article is an analysis and comparison extracted from many relevant published works. By reading a review article, readers could get to know both the global and local state of a research subject.

Readers need to realize that review articles basically accommodate two different styles: researcher-oriented and information-oriented (Webster & Watson, 2002). The researcher-oriented style focuses on the development of a researcher's thought, and the interaction and/or transmission between different researchers on the thought. In contrast, the main thread running through the information-oriented review is the evolution of a research subject. Sometimes these two styles overlap and interweave in a review article.

A review article may cover a great variety of research territory. Historically, a review article examines the developing stages of a given topic, illustrating its past, present, and future. Horizontally, a review article examines the current state of the given topic and analyzes its research methodologies and findings. It may also have other research focuses, including the different perspectives of a research, different views of researchers, different approaches of a certain application, etc.

The review initially summarizes and synthesizes the key research outcome from the published documents, establishing the relationship between the different parts. Precise and prudent, the selected documents in a review article should possess appropriate depth and breadth in the relevant field. Meanwhile, the review is not just confined to the description of the selected documents; it must critically look at the documents under review, with the author's thoughts and comments on the documents. Careful and rational, the author's sense of value exerts a great influence on the review. This painstaking work will give readers new insights into the follow-up study. To be brief, a good review article reveals both the writer's comprehension of the related studies and the writer's abilities of critical thinking, dialectical thinking, literature integration, and literature evaluation. It will shed light on subsequent research for the readers. Many readers are very interested in a good review article for its convenient and comprehensive access to a relevant subject area, learning about what has been done, what is being done, and what would be done.

Writing a review article needs much prior reading and information retrieval on a given topic. This extensive literature research would establish the writer's framework for his own review article. Readers should recognize the framework of a review article for the easy and effective information retrieval.

2. Identifying Overall Structure and Components of Review Articles

A review article includes the following parts: Title, Author(s)' Name(s) and Affiliation, Abstract, Introduction, Methods, Mainbody, Conclusion, and References (Wee & Banister, 2015; Randolph, 2009). Each part plays a different role in the review article. For effective reading, readers should first catch the overall structure and overview before going to details. Below is a brief introduction to the main parts, as shown in Figure 6.1.

- ✓ **Title:** It should be specific, informative, and concise.
- ✓ **Abstract:** It introduces the research background, summarizes the present review work, and help readers grasp the central theme.
- ✓ **Introduction:** It should be straightforward and concise. Readers should first find the background of the review and then identify the review topic, research purpose, and research significance. Readers may also catch a glimpse of the current state and development trends of the review topic. Perhaps readers learn about the source and scope of the selected documents on the research topic, as well as the definition of a certain concept.
- ✓ **Methods:** This part explains the methods used in the review of the published documents and the organizational patterns of the reviewed documents.
- ✓ **Mainbody:** Usually, the review could be divided into several sections with subheadings of different focuses. Each section summarizes and synthesizes the published work such as the developing stages, current state, findings, developing trends, methods, applications and/or implications. A qualified review must include the writer's unique and profound analysis of the selected research work. In view of the synthesis and evaluation of the published work, the review may put forward the new problems which need to be addressed in the future, the possible significance of the research progress or the considerable insights for further research. A good review could illuminate the underlying logic of the text. There should be logical links and transitions in between the different parts/sections. In one word, a good review article is

informative, instructive, and attractive.

✓ **Conclusion:** It offers a brief summary of the review and draws a conclusion from the above analysis. This last part leaves readers a sense of completeness of the present work by predicting the future research.

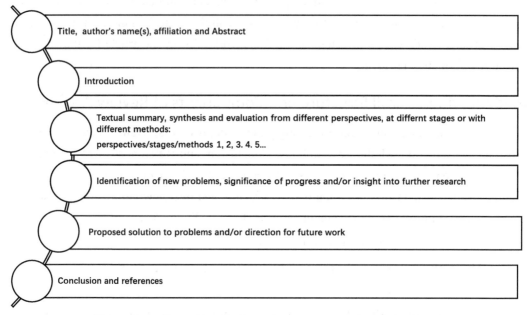

Figure 6.1 Overall structure and components of review articles

3. Recognizing the Organizational Patterns of Review Articles

For the purpose of a better understanding of a review article, readers should recognize the organizational patterns in a review article. Basically, a review article may resort to two patterns: vertical pattern or horizontal pattern. A vertical pattern traces the relevant research in order of chronology or developing stage while a horizontal pattern analyzes and compares different perspectives, different achievements and limitations, different views, or different methods. A review article may deploy both vertical pattern and horizontal pattern. However, one of the patterns should be largely dominant in a certain segment. For example, a vertical pattern may be used in the historical development of a given topic, indicating its past, present and future. It may also be deployed when enumerating a researcher's thoughts at different stages or the interaction process of the thought between different researchers. A horizontal pattern may be employed when analyzing the current state of the research, the different views of researchers, or the different methods in research. It is also useful in the discussion of the significance of research.

Some other patterns are known as chronological pattern, thematic pattern, and methodological pattern, which, more or less, overlap with the above patterns. Readers could also identify these patterns when reading a review article.

Unit 6 Environment

Part 2 Intensive Reading

Pre-reading questions:

✓ What subject matter/area does the research article deal with?

✓ What might be the purpose of this article?

✓ How is the research to be done?

Pesticides: An Overview of the Current Health Problems of Their Use[1]

1. Introduction

The massive use of pesticides is considered one of the main factors affecting the environment (Mahmood et al., 2016). Dichloro-diphenyldichloroethane (DDT) had been widely used since the 1940s for the control of mosquito infestations, and initiated the rapid spread of the use of pesticides throughout the world. Currently, large quantities of them—about 60 chemical classes that group over 2,000 active ingredients are used to protect agricultural crops from a long series of pests (insects, fungal and bacterial attacks, weeds, rodents, etc.) (Vidal & Frenich, 2006; Bolognesi & Merlo, 2011; FAO, 2021).

Worldwide, every year many hundreds of new pesticides are formulated. Because some of them are very uneconomic to produce, they never reach the production line or sales counter. However, even those, which get through the limits imposed by local or state agencies, cannot automatically be considered safe.

Almost all of them, in addition to the declared active ingredient, contain **adjuvant** substances, whose chemical composition is often not well defined and kept **confidential** by the manufacturing companies, making them included under the generic category of **inert** substances (Mesnage et al., 2014). These additives and inert compounds, which make up most of the current commercial formulation (90%–95%), in some cases show even more toxic properties than the active ingredient itself (Meftaul et al., 2020). Pesticides, once released into

---

1 This paper is from Leoci, R. & Ruberti, M. 2021. Pesticides: An overview of the current health problems of their use. *Journal of Geoscience and Environment Protection*, 9: 1–20.

the environment, often decompose into degradation products that may pollute foods, soils, surface waters, and groundwaters (Tiryaki & Temur, 2010).

The EU "Plant Protection Regulation" (PPR) (Regulation 1107/2009/EC) recognizes that pesticides have significant responsibility for environmental degradation.

During 2017–2018, more than one hundred pesticides, some of which are still considered very dangerous and prohibited in several countries, have been approved by US-EPA. A large part (approximately, one third) of these commercial formulations contained a mix of active ingredients (neurotoxic organifisfates and carbamates, paraquat, chloropicrin, fumigants, methyl bromide, etc.), some of which were defined by EPA itself, as "probable" or "known" carcinogen (Donley, 2020).

The European Union Regulation concerns about 1,100 pesticides, presently or previously used in agriculture, and establishes Maximum Residue Levels (MRL) for 315 agricultural products. About 224 different chemical principles have been detected in Italy by the "Istituto Superiore per la Protezione e la Ricerca Ambientale" (ISPRA, 2018) into 60% of surface waters (AMPA, glyphosate, metachlor-esa, imidachloprid, metolachlor, etc.) and 30% of ground deep waters (atrazinedes. desis, flonicamid, metolachlor, terbuthylazine, etc.). Also, researchers from the "Mario Negri" Institute of Pharmacological Research in Milan had previously found, in many water wells in Northern Italy, **conspicuous** concentrations in drinking water of propazine (up to 30 ppt) and simazine (up to 200 ppt). (Silva et al., 2019) evaluated the residue presence of 76 pesticides in 317 agricultural European soil samples. They observed that about 25% of the soil samples examined contained one residue and 58% of the samples contained more than one residue. As evidenced by other research (Stehle & Schulz, 2015), among the substances that most frequently exceed the limits allowed by law, there are glyphosate and neonicotinoids.

This overall situation can be complicated by simultaneous use of different products and complex mixtures with unpredicted cocktails' effects on the environment and life (Maksymiv, 2015; Milo, 2020; Geissen et al., 2021). Regarding the chemical interaction of pesticides, between them and with organic substrate, much obviously depends on the nature of compounds, that is, on their chemical family, on their doses, on climate (Hernandez et al., 2017; Koli et al., 2019) and sensitivity of the organs and tissues subject to intoxication (Ghuman et al., 2013). The impacts of pesticides and environmental stress or so (habitat destruction, invasive alien species, and so on) on animals are equally little known (Ito et al., 2020).

2. Classification and Use in Agriculture

There are many ways to group pesticides. They can be grouped, i.e., according to their chemicals or to the method of application or, more commonly, to the pests species:

Insecticides, Herbicides, Rodenticides, Bactericides, Fungicides and Larvicides. According to (Eurostat, 2008), "pesticide" is a non-specific word concealing:

(1) Products for plant protection (Council Directive 91/414/EEC);

(2) Biocides (Directive 98/8/EC).

In the FAOSTAT Pesticides Use domain (FAO, 2021), there is information about the following main pesticides groups (Table 1).

Table 1 Pesticides groups

(1) Insetticides	Organo—phosphates, Chlorinated hydrocarbons, Pyrethroids, Carbamates—insecticides, Biological products and Others
(2) Mineral Oils	
(3) Herbicides	Triazines, Phenoxy hormones, Carbamates-herbicides, Amides, Urea derivatives, Sulfonyl urea, Uracil, Dinitroanilines, Bipiridils and Others
(4) Fungicides and Bactericides	Inorganic, Benzimidazoles, Dithiocarbamates, Diazines Morpholines, Triazoles Diazoles, and Others
(5) Seed Treatment-Fungicides	Benzimidazoles, Dithiocarbamates, Diazines Morpholines, Botanical products and biological, Triazoles Diazoles, and Others
(6) Seed Treatment-Insecticides	Carbamates-insecticides, Organo-phosphates, Pyrethroids, and Others
(7) Plant Growth Regulalors	
(8) Rodenticides	C Cyanide Generators, Anti-coagulants, Narcotics, Hypercalcaemics, and Others yanide Generators, Anti-coagulants Narcotics, Hypercalcaemics, and Others
(9) Other Pesticides NES	
(10) Disinfectants	

At the beginning of the 1990s, a new revolution occurred in this field: Neocotinoids (such as acetamiprid, imidacloprid, thiamethoxam, and nitrosoguanidine) were introduced (Frederickson et al., 2016). The main difference between these new substances and those used previously (chlorine compounds, such as DDT, and organo-phosphate insecticides) consists in their lower dose of use: a few grams of chemical compound per hectare in comparison to several kilograms per hectare (Reynoso et al., 2019).

According to (FAO, 2021), 4.1 million tonnes of pesticides have been used in agriculture globally in 2018, which was 35% greater than in 2000 (Maggi, Tang, La Cecilia & McBratney, 2019).

The most used pesticides are herbicides and insecticides (FAO, 2021). Among herbicides, the most common ones are glyphosate and isoproturon, the effects of which we discussed in previous notes (Leoci & Ruberti, 2020a; Leoci & Ruberti, 2020b). Among insecticides, chloropicrin (trichloronitromethane) is widely used as fumigant, despite numerous limitations (Ayres, 1919; Leoci & Ruberti, 2020b).

According to (FAO, 2021), the average annual use of pesticides per area of cropland has grown continuously from 1990 to 2018 for all the countries of the different continents, marking the highest quotas for the Asian ones (from about 2.2 kg/ha in 1990 to about 3.6 kg/ha during 2018, with a maximum of 3.8 kg/ha during the years 2011–2012). The lowest use rates are those of African countries, about 0.4 kg/ha/year from 1990 to 2018. Consumption has been fairly constant in European countries as a whole, with values of about 1.4–1.8 kg/ha/year from 1990 to 2018.

3. Economic Aspects

3.1 Global Market

According to (FAO, 2021), at the global level, total pesticides trade reached approximately 5.9 million tonnes in 2018, with a value of $37.6 billion. The global trade of hazardous pesticides, monitored under the Rotterdam Convention, decreased substantially during the period 2007–2018. Since 2016, Asia became an equally important exporter, reflecting the high economic growth of this region. Pesticides exports increased by 2.5 fold in the Asia region in the period 2011–2018 compared to 2001–2010. Asia, nonetheless, remained below Europe in terms of total export value, reflecting the high-quality pesticides produced under the EU Common Agricultural Policy.

In 2018 around $15 billion was spent on pesticides in the USA, representing a five-fold increase since 1960 when adjusting for inflation (Gro, 2021). According to (MacArthur & Murray, 1993), USA constituted approximately one-third of world pesticides production, 75% of which was sold domestically and 25% exported.

According to (FAO, 2021), the top five countries for total pesticides imports in 2018 were Brazil, France, Germany, Canada, and the USA, with trade values ranging $1.4–$3.0 billion. In these countries, imported quantities roughly doubled during the period 1990–2018. The top five exporting countries in 2018 were China, Germany, the USA, France and India, with values ranging $3.0–5.5 billion. With regards to the thirty-five hazardous pesticides covered under the Rotterdam Convention, the top five importing countries in 2018 were Myanmar, Malaysia, the Philippines, Thailand and Costa Rica, with values ranging $20–80 million. Imports decreased during 2007–2018 in all these countries, with the exception of

Myanmar, which is not a **signatory** to the Convention. The top five countries exporting hazardous pesticides in 2018 were the USA, Thailand, South Africa, Nigeria and Malaysia, with values ranging $10–30 million (FAO, 2021).

As for the EU (27 EU Member States), according to (Eurostat, 2020), during 2011–2018, the consumption of pesticides persisted to be substantially stable at around 360,000 t/y, remaining concentrated (over two thirds) in only four countries (Germany, France, Italy and Spain). The best-selling chemical formulations were fungicides (45%), herbicides (32%) and insecticides (11%).

3.2 Environmental Costs

Even if the economic costs of biodiversity loss are very uncertain, variable and dependent by historical context, in the United States of America, some studies have estimated that the economic impact on ecosystems, in terms of loss of insects pollinators, aquatic life and birds could amount to hundreds of billions of dollars per year (Chapin et al., 2020).

According to other estimations, biodiversity and ecosystems have an economic assessment of 10–100 times greater than the costs of the conservation of natural habitats (Gomez-Baggethun & Martin-Lopez, 2010). The added value to economic production brought by **pollinating** insects, for example, is considerable, contributing, to about 5%–8% of world agricultural production, equal to 235–577 billion dollars in 2015 (OECD, 2019).

In addition to these consequences, there are supplementary economic effects correlated to the recreational use of ecosystems and wildlife: hiking, hunting, fishing, birdwatching, etc. All these activities strongly depend on the presence of insects in ecosystems; insects represent a very important food base of natural ecosystems. Unfortunately, the massive and often indiscriminate use of insecticides has **drastically** risen numerous populations of insects all over the world.

However, the problem is even more serious: In fact, the IUCN Red List, while it has estimated that only about 8,000 species of insects are at risk of extinction, has hypothesized, in the medium-long term and in countries with input-intensive agricultural systems, the total disappearance of many mammals and bird species. It has been estimated, for example, thanks to the research of amateur **entomologists**, that insect populations in Germany have fallen by 75% in just 25 years (Hallmann et al., 2017; Hance, 2019).

4. Adverse Effects on Environment

As is well known, pesticides are not only an excellent weapon for the defense of crops and to guarantee high levels of harvest, but in many cases they are also the only available tool when it is necessary to intervene in emergency situations to eradicate parasitic attacks.

However, as is also well known, pesticides seriously undermine the health and well-being of natural habitats and biodiversity, also because they easily migrate to other environmental compartments due to runoff and leaching phenomena (Ewald et al., 2015; Hallmann et al., 2017).

In the meantime, wind and evaporation can transfer pesticides into the atmosphere, causing **contamination** of other ecosystems and sites very far from the place where they were used (Dubus et al., 2000; Ritter, et al., 2002). An example is given by chlorothalonil (2,4,5,6-tetrachloroisophthalonitrile), also found in traces in the Evian's waters, considered pure as they come from the heart of the French Alps (De Neri, 2020).

The excessive use of pesticides and their consequent relative cocktails has also had heavy **repercussions** on the qualitative characteristics of soils for agricultural use (Geiger et al., 2010) impairing the ability of the soil to host a wide variety of crops (Dinis-Oliveira et al., 2006) and to perform other ecosystem services with long-term implications even in soils of organic farms, as some scholars (Geissen et al., 2021) have shown.

Other researches (Hussain et al., 2017) showed that pesticides interact with the microflora, microfauna and macrofauna of the soil by modifying the chemistry of the soil and the exchange of soil substances with the roots of the plants and hindering, for example, the processes of biological fixation of atmospheric nitrogen by rhizo-bacteria.

5. Adverse Effects on Animal Health

Regarding the specific effects on humans and/or animals, we report the following most recent research (last five years), referring to the bibliography cited for an in-depth study of certain aspects. Just to get an idea of the huge number of scientific articles published in the last five years, using keywords as "pesticides", "effects" and "humans" / "animals", on Pubmed we found, respectively, over 9,000 and 13,000 papers, while through the Sciencedirect search engine we found 38,000 and 25,000 papers. It is not easy to **disentangle** in this scenario, so we have sought and selected only those articles that are most significant for us and most cited by recent scientific bibliography.

According to some authors (Beketov et al., 2013; Vogel, 2017), the use of pesticides within the European territory, in the period 1989–2013, led to very substantial reductions in biodiversity: up to 40% for **invertebrates**, up to almost 80% for insects and up to nearly 90% for pollinating insects such as bees.

Some authors, such as (Lushchak et al., 2018), have considered the adverse health effects on animal organisms of pesticides after ingestion, inhalation or dermal contact. This intoxication can lead to cancer, neurotoxicity, reproductive effects, endocrine disorders, liver and kidney damage, and teratogenicity.

5.1 On Birds

After the alarm raised by (Carson, 1962), the worsening of the situation has also been observed by other scholars. A few decades later, in Great Britain, confirming the findings of other studies, a rapid and significant decline in the populations of birds that feed on the seeds of weeds destroyed by herbicides was observed (MacKinnon & Freedman, 1993). Even in tropical and sub-tropical areas, the indiscriminate use of herbicides has greatly reduced the agricultural areas used by wintering migratory birds (Newton, 2004).

Already (Blus & Harry, 1997) showed that even when low-toxic herbicides were used in forestry, significant reductions in bird populations occurred probably due to the corresponding reduction in many plant species used as their food sources.

More recently, some researchers (Eng et al., 2019) of the University of Saskatchewan and York University (Canada) have examined the singing behavior of a migratory bird: the "white-crowned sparrow" (Zonotrichia leucophrys). Imidacloprid **ingested** in the wild by this bird, in realistic amounts of 1.2 or 3.9 mg/kg bw, influenced not only the amount of body fat deposits but also the migratory and reproductive capacity of males of this species and their own survival rate. In fact, neocotinoids, through an articulated neurotoxic mechanism of stimulation of the nicotinic acetyl-choline receptor (nAChR), cause an overstimulation of the nervous system, not only of insects, but also of vertebrates such as birds (Tomizawa & Casida, 2003).

5.2 On Bees and Bats

Another research (Eng et al., 2017) has confirmed the suspicions about the adverse effects of neonicotinoids on the behavior and survival of birds and pollinators such as bees, so that the EU banned three of these compounds in 2018. The damage of neonicotinoids on bees, bumblebees and other species of beneficial insects has now been confirmed by many other studies (Long & Krupke, 2016; Arce et al., 2017; Phelps et al., 2020).

As it was to be supposed, not even bats escape the action of pesticides, having an **omnivorous** diet and thus exposing themselves to a wide range of contaminants as has been ascertained by (Oliveira et al., 2020), even if the populations of these mammals are still the least studied regarding the effects of pesticide residues on their health. The negative effects of pesticides, in fact, also occur on taxons, like bats, which are usually overlooked in toxicity studies, although they are important living species that play a large role in ecosystems as they disperse plant seeds and keep controlling the spread of pests. According to (Berny, 2007) and others (Van Oers et al., 2005), the abuse of pesticides is responsible, depending on the geographic area, for the poisoning of 18%–68% of wild animals.

6. Adverse Effects on Human Health

The environmental risks and health effects on humans of several pesticides are not well known. In 2006 an alarming paper appeared in the *Lancet* (Grandjean & Landrigan, 2006) presenting a list of 202 substances known to be toxic to the human brain, 90 of which were pesticides.

Considering the presence of hundreds of active ingredients available and the continuous placing on the market of new molecules, the detailed knowledge of their toxic action on humans is undoubtedly complex and difficult to be exhaustive. At the same time, many scientific studies have highlighted that these molecules can act in a wide range on all the vital functions of human cells by inducing a long series of alterations: genetic and epigenetic modifications, imbalances in receptor function with an action of "endocrine interference", mitochondrial dysfunction, disturbance of neuronal conduction due to alteration of ion channels, alteration of enzymatic activity, especially due to interference with acetylcholinesterase, oxidative stress, stress of the endoplasmic reticulum and impaired aggregation of proteins and others (Bianco, 2018).

Since food is the main route of intake of pesticides for consumers, their residues in food can represent dangers to human health (Bjorling-Poulsen et al., 2008) and the presence of them in feed products can involve risks for the health of farmed animals and risks for the consumers themselves because they can enter into the food chain (NRC, 1993). Unfortunately, currently, the regulatory systems for stating average exposure to pesticides do not take into consideration personal situations and types of consumption that differ from the average, as well as particular lifestyles, age, presence of **concomitant** diseases, etc. Obviously, children are usually the most exposed, due to their fast growth, their lower weight, the greater consumption of fruit in relation to their weight, etc. (Mridula et al., 2013).

As we will learn more lately, exposure to pesticides, which mimic the chemical structure of hormones classified as endocrine disruptors, causes a series of deformations and a rising of the associated costs for human health (Trasande et al., 2015).

7. Adverse Effects on Reproduction

In general and in principle, with regard to the mechanisms of action of pesticides, the ideal situation would be to have highly selective molecules, i.e. highly efficient, and therefore very toxic, for target organisms (pests) and, at the same time, harmless or at least slightly toxic for non-target organisms, obviously including humans. To achieve this goal, the chemical formulation of the active ingredients of many pesticides currently on the market is designed to damage enzymes present only into target organisms and not present in non-target organisms. However, in the natural environment, also due to complex mechanisms and interactions that occur and which are difficult to predict, the molecules of pesticides and their **metabolites** affect the vital and reproductive functions even of non-target organisms, also very useful for maintaining the delicate eco-systemic balances (Das, 2013).

In fact, as underlined by (Frazier, 2007), many categories of pesticides (pyrethroids, herbicides, organophosphates, fungicides, carbamates, fumigants and especially organochlorines) are potentially able to have adverse effects on development and reproductive endpoints. Reproduction is the essential function that allows continuity of living organisms. Its **perturbation** or dysfunction leads to negative consequences for human, animal and plant productivity and survival.

Many factors can be responsible for this perturbation (Gardella & Hill, 2000). Among these, certain pesticides, present in the food chain at sufficient doses, represent a high risk of harm to human and animal health. In fact, they can increase the occurrence of cases of infertility, spontaneous abortions, **teratogenicity** and delays in fetal development. In the late 1900s, (Gray & Ostby, 1998) confirmed that a multitude of toxic substances, including pesticides, can profoundly alter the development of the nervous and reproductive systems in several species of laboratory guinea pigs.

Pyrethroids, according to what emerges from various studies, are those that cause the most serious **pathological** effects to mother (ovaries, uterus and hormonal system) (Ahmad et al., 2012) and fetus (abortion and teratogenesis) (Auso et al., 2004; Mnif et al., 2011).

A survey, conducted in the USA on women who had undergone treatments to solve infertility problems, found that consumption of fruit and vegetables, probably affected by pesticides, compared to the average, correspondingly increased the risks of termination of pregnancy or missed pregnancies (Yu-Han et al., 2018). Environmental exposure assessments and epidemiological studies show that one of the major culprits of these infertility and miscarriage problems is oxidative stress in excess of the **scavenging** capacity of antioxidants present within a human or animal organism (Szalardy, 2006; Banerjee & Bhattacharya, 2020).

7.1 Endocrine Disorders and Infertility

One of the most feared side effects of pesticides is their ability to act as "Endocrine Disrupting Chemicals" (EDCs) (Rattan et al., 2017; Sifakis et al., 2017). In fact, numerous **endocrine** disruptors, i.e. chemicals (like pesticides) that interfere with the regulation and stability of the endocrine systems of animals (Kavlock et al., 1996), act negatively, as has been shown by many scientific studies conducted in the United States, on the reproductive systems of reptiles, fish and amphibians.

With regard to these endocrine disruptors, much subsequent research is identifying which specific substances can alter the fertility conditions of animals and humans. According to (Upadhyay, 2019), precisely high levels of pesticides, having adverse effects on the endocrine system, are one of the main causes, **albeit** indirect, of infertility problems for women because they greatly increase the levels of oxidative damage.

Some years earlier, (Gray, 1996; Steer, 1993), continuing the research about pseudo-hermaphroditism following exposure to active substances on hormonal systems, have presented scientific evidence regarding the role and mechanisms of action of pesticides on the reproductive system through the binding of the Ah receptor, antiandrogenicity and toxicity of germ cells.

In the same decade, other authors (Wolf et al., 1999) provided experimental data of about ten antiandrogenic substances: ketoconazole, procymidone, congener polychlorinated biphenyl n. 169, linuron, clozolinate, p, p'-DDE, diethylhexyl phthalate, iprodione, dibutyl phthalate (DBP). For example, linuron treatment caused testicular atrophy and **malformed** epididymis, involving RA binding.

According to (Bretveld et al., 2007), pesticides can lead to a series of hormonal disorders and negatively affect the functioning of the central nervous system and thyroid function, the binding and recognition systems of receptors, the correct way of interaction of cells of Leidig and Sertoli.

However, the results of some above experimental studies have been the subject of controversy and denial (Bates et al., 2005).

7.2 Disorders of Sexual Functions

Particularly, (Lindbohm & Sallmen, 2017) have highlighted that the generic exposure of workers, due to their specific professional activities, to chemically or biologically active substances, like pesticides, can cause genetic **mutations** and problems with fertility and sexual function: decrease in sexual potency and **libido**, lowering of sexual hormone levels, alteration of menstrual flow, ovarian dysfunction, delayed menarche, premature menopause, impaired sperm vitality and drastic reduction in male and female fertility. These effects are already known (Sharara et al., 1998).

(Li et al., 2020) identified the residual concentrations of the metabolites of 11 pesticides (including pyrethroids, organophosphate insecticides and herbicides) by examining the urine of a sample of 619 women of childbearing age in the states of California and Utah, detecting high concentrations of chlorpyrifos and chlorpyrifos-methyl (compounds progenitors of TCPY) and diazinon (the parent compound of IMPY), known to be associated with endometriosis phenomena.

(Hu et al., 2020), examining the metabolites present in the spermatic fluid of 346 men of reproductive age in Shanghai (China), correlated the presence of pyrethroids to the reduced fertility parameters of their semen.

7.3 Fetal Malformations

Reproductive anomalies and hermaphroditic deformities have been found in many species of animals living in US rivers: mammals, fish, frogs, reptiles, molluscs, etc. (Mnif et al., 2011).

The pesticide residues, then, taken through food, can cause neurotoxicity and interfere with the normal development of cognitive functions of fetus (Bjorling-Poulsen et al., 2008).

(Bretveld et al., 2006) found that several pesticides interfere with the proper functioning of sex hormones, significantly disturbing the timing of pregnancy, menstruation and even causing miscarriages and developmental defects in the fetus.

Other previous studies (Yoshida et al., 1987) have investigated possible fetal malformations related to the inhaled administration of chloropicrin for six hours a day during 6–15 days before gestation and found no noteworthy adverse effects for doses below the NOAEL. In another multigenerational study (Anastassiadou et al., 2020) administered by inhalation in rats, no adverse effects on reproductive function and fetal development were observed, nor any teratogenic effects during development, although pulmonary inflammation was observed in parental females of rats a NOAEC of 1.0 ppm.

More recently, some Chinese scholars (Tang et al., 2020) identified adverse effects of certain pesticides during pregnancy on the placenta and the development of the fetus, investigating the mechanisms of action of the following estrogenic endocrine disruptors: organochlorine pesticides, bisphenol A, phthalates and diethylstilbestrol.

(Sharma et al., 2020) have focused attention on insecticides as they are associated with metabolic disorders, psychological and neurological diseases and hormonal imbalances also for humans. Oxidative stresses and endocrine alterations of insecticides alter the correct functioning of ovarian activities, of the relative cycle, of the ovulation process and follicular maturation, increasing the risk of spontaneous abruptions and malformations of the fetuses.

7.4 Disorders of Sexual Development and Behavior

(Hu et al., 2020; Conley et al., 2018), using a mixture of different types of pesticides, drugs and phthalates (procymidone, p, p'-DDE, prochloraz, vinclozolin, finasteride, benzyl butyl, dixyl, flutamide and others), at different dilution doses, on male rats after birth, found a conspicuous variety of adverse effects, both during the **neonatal** phase and during the **pubertal** one, concerning consistent reductions in reproductive tissues and malformations of the genital organs even at very low doses of administration.

(Madhubabu & Yenugu, 2017) evaluated the reproductive toxicity of adult male rats of allethrin at an administration of 25–150 mg/kg bw for 60 days, noting a significant reduction in steroidogenesis (StAR, 3'-HSD, 17'-HSD), testosterone and sperm count. From numerous studies, it appears that propiconazole (PROP) interferes with the endocrine system, altering the CYP51 enzyme. For example, (Vieira et al., 2017) identified a possible toxicity of PROP by administering this fungicide to two generations of male rats by investigating the most common morphological parameters of possible mutations, such as anogenital distance and plasma testosterone levels, sperm count and morphology, body weight, etc.

(Hass et al., 2017) experimentally found that, by administering a mixture of six pesticides (quinoclamine, ziram, tiram, primacarb, MCPB and cyromazine) to Wistar rats, there was a significant decrease in birth weight even at doses below the NOAEL.

(Andrade et al., 2006) investigated the reproductive effects of di-(2-ethylhexyl) phthalate (DEHP) exposure in utero and during the lactation phase for the offspring of male rats. The authors recorded a daily decrease in semen of 19%–25% compared to the control guinea pig population, although no obvious abnormalities in sexual behavior were observed at any dose of administration.

8. Conclusions

Pesticide molecules have now permanently entered our environment. They act at infinitesimal doses and are now present in real cocktails of active ingredients and interfere with important and very delicate functions such as hormonal, reproductive, and metabolic functions.

Pesticides, in addition to having strong repercussions on biodiversity and short-term toxic effects on those organisms that are affected by direct exposure, could also have long-term effects, such as the transformation of food chain and disappearance of particular habitats. There is no doubt that the relationship between human health and pesticides has been the subject of numerous studies, especially with regard to the onset of tumors.

It is very urgent and necessary to intensify studies and research on the possible adverse effects—especially those of long-term, low-dose and on non-target living species, animals and plants of pesticides on both humans and animals and environment. On the other hand, international regulatory policy should also constantly adapt to the evolution of scientific knowledge in order to protect human health and safeguard the environment.

(Scan the QR code to access the list of references.)

Unit 6 Environment

 ## Words and Expressions

adjuvant	*adj.*	serving to aid or contribute
confidential	*adj.*	meant to be kept secret
inert	*adj.*	without active chemical or other properties
conspicuous	*adj.*	easy to see or notice
signatory	*n.*	a person, a country or an organization that has signed an official agreement
pollinate	*v.*	to put pollen into a flower or plant so that it produces seeds
drastically	*adv.*	sharply or dramatically
entomologist	*n.*	a scientist who studies insects
contamination	*n.*	the process or fact of making a substance or place dirty or no longer pure by adding a substance that is dangerous or carries disease
repercussion	*n.*	an indirect and usually bad result of an action that may happen some time afterwards
disentangle	*v.*	to tease out something
invertebrate	*n.*	any animal with no backbone
ingest	*v.*	to take food, drugs, etc. into the body, usually by swallowing
omnivorous	*adj.*	eating all types of food, especially both plants and meat
concomitant	*adj.*	happening at the same time as something else, especially because one thing is related to the other
metabolite	*n.*	a product of metabolism
perturbation	*n.*	a small change in or disturbance of something
teratogenicity	*n.*	production of developmental malformations
pathological	*adj.*	caused by, or connected with, disease or illness
scavenging	*adj.*	removing or cleaning away something
endocrine	*adj.*	connected with glands that put hormones and other products directly into blood
albeit	*conj.*	although
malformed	*adj.*	badly formed or shaped
mutation	*n.*	a process in which the genetic material of a person, etc. changes in structure when it is passed onto children
libido	*n.*	sexual desire

| neonatal | *adj.* | connected with a child that has just been born |
| pubertal | *adj.* | of or relating to puberty |

Reflections and Practice

I Read the text and answer the following questions.

1. What would happen when pesticides are released into the environment?
2. What is the main difference between acetamiprid and DDT?
3. How do pesticides degrade environment?
4. Why does bird population decline significantly?
5. How are bats affected by pesticides?
6. In what ways are pesticides detrimental to human health?
7. What are the adverse effects of pesticides on reproduction?

II Discuss the following questions with your partner.

1. Do you think the literature in this article is sufficient and reliable? Why?
2. What do you think are the useful/useless ideas in this article?
3. What is the significance of this review article?
4. What do you think of the overall organization of this article?
5. What do you think of the language in this review article?

III Paraphrase the following sentences.

1. Other researches (Hussain et al., 2017) showed that pesticides interact with the microflora, microfauna and macrofauna of the soil by modifying the chemistry of the soil and the exchange of soil substances with the roots of the plants and hindering, for example, the processes of biological fixation of atmospheric nitrogen by rhizobacteria.
2. Another research (Eng et al., 2017) has confirmed the suspicions about the adverse effects of neonicotinoids on the behavior and survival of birds and pollinators such as bees, so that the EU banned three of these compounds in 2018.
3. A survey, conducted in the USA on women who had undergone treatments to solve infertility problems, found that consumption of fruit and vegetables, probably

affected by pesticides, compared to the average, correspondingly increased the risks of termination of pregnancy or missed pregnancies (Yu-Han et al., 2018).

4. With regard to these endocrine disruptors, much subsequent research is identifying which specific substances can alter the fertility conditions of animals and humans. According to (Upadhyay, 2019), precisely high levels of pesticides, having adverse effects on the endocrine system, are one of the main causes, albeit indirect, of infertility problems for women because they greatly increase the levels of oxidative damage.

5. (Li et al., 2020) identified the residual concentrations of the metabolites of 11 pesticides (including pyrethroids, organophosphate insecticides and herbicides) by examining the urine of a sample of 619 women of childbearing age in the states of California and Utah, detecting high concentrations of chlorpyrifos and chlorpyrifos-methyl (compounds progenitors of TCPY) and diazinon (the parent compound of IMPY), known to be associated with endometriosis phenomena.

IV Draw a mind map according to the review underpinnings of the text.

V Write an outline for the text following the structure below.

Title: Pesticides: An Overview of the Current Health Problems of Their Use

Thesis Statement: Pesticides have direct responsibility for environmental degradation.

1. **Introduction**

   _____

   _____.

2. **Classification and Use in Agriculture**

   _____

   _____.

3. **Economic Aspects**

   _____

   _____.

4. **Adverse Effects on Environment**

   _____

   _____.

5. Adverse Effects on Animal Health
   _____
   _____.

6. Adverse Effects on Human Health
   _____
   _____.

7. Adverse Effects on Reproduction
   _____
   _____.

8. Conclusion
   _____
   _____.

Ⅶ Write a summary for the text in 150–200 words.

Review on Mould Contamination and Hygrothermal Effect in Indoor Environment[1]

Abstract

Mould is an important factor which affects building environment and indoor air quality. Firstly, a variety of damages of mould contamination to human and building are reviewed. Then, the crucial factors of mould growth are analyzed; temperature and humidity are key factors. After that, the indoor mould growth models were analyzed. Heat and moisture transfer in building envelope is a key factor which affects mould growth environment; wall is sensitive

---

1 This paper is from Luo, Y. Y., Ge, Q. H., Chen, P. H. & Wang, H. Q. 2018. Review on mould contamination and hygrothermal effect in indoor environment. *Journal of Environmental Protection, 9*: 100–110.

Unit 6 Environment

to reach the critical condition which leads to mould growth and reproduction, and results in contamination.

Keywords: mould contamination, building environment, mould growth model, heat and moisture transfer

 Reflections and Practice

Read the full article and answer the following questions.

1. What is the aim of this review article?
2. What previous studies are reviewed?
3. How are they structured?
4. What important findings are revealed?
5. Are there any suggestions for further research?

Unit 7
English for Academic Purposes

Learning Objectives

- Understand the purpose and structure of response articles;

- Explore the language features of response articles;

- Consider the issues surrounding the standards of English in academic writing;

- Practice writing a response article.

Part 1 Reading Skills and Strategies

Reading Response Articles

1. Understanding the Purpose of Response Articles

A response article is an important type of academic writing that is written in response to a previously published text. Usually, a response article presents a reader's reaction to a piece of writing based on his or her critical reading, understanding, and analysis of the target text. Although response articles often involve the presentation of different opinions and disagreements, the content is beyond the scope of criticism. Rather, it is the reader's evaluation of the concepts, ideas, arguments, evidence, and suggestions provided by the author of the target text.

Some academic journals invite scholars to write a short response to an article previously published in the same journal. Sometimes, the response article is published in tandem with the target article, thus forming an interesting and insightful academic discussion. For example, the *Journal of Second Language Writing* features a special section called "Disciplinary Dialogues" that publishes a focus paper and its responses on an important and controversial topic in the field of second language writing. The editors of this special section first invite a scholar to write the focus paper and then seek responses from other scholars who "represent different theoretical and disciplinary perspectives" (Xu & Matsuda, 2017: 79) to further explore the topic. The response articles play an important role in stimulating a critical understanding of the target topic by presenting different viewpoints and evidence. They also help readers gain a better understanding of the complexity of the issues under discussion.

2. Understanding the Structure of Response Articles

Response articles can be structured in different ways. However, as a response article often involves summarizing the main points and arguments of the target text and presenting the author's reaction to the text, it usually consists of five basic components:

✓ **Introduction:** The introduction provides the context and purpose of the response article. It allows readers to understand to which text the article was written in response,

and why the author wanted to write a response to that text.
- ✓ **Summary:** The summary presents an overview of the target text by highlighting its main ideas and key supporting evidence.
- ✓ **Thesis:** The thesis expresses the author's opinions on the target text and presents his or her viewpoints on the topic under discussion.
- ✓ **Response:** The response presents the author's detailed analysis and evaluation of the ideas and supporting points offered by the author of the target text. When responding to the text, the author may refer to the original text by using direct quotations or paraphrases. In addition, the author may also refer to external sources to support his or her argument.
- ✓ **Conclusion:** The conclusion restates the thesis of the response article and highlights the significance or implications of the response article.

3. Identifying the Language Features of Response Articles

The language features of response articles are largely associated with their purpose of expressing the author's opinions and attitudes. When expressing opinions, "I think" is often used by novice writers, though it is not commonly seen in academic journal articles. More experienced writers, however, use various ways to express ideas, make comments, and take positions.

A key language feature of response articles is the use of reporting verbs, which serve as a signal of referring to other people's ideas. Another key language feature of response articles is the use of evaluative language, which is used to facilitate the expression of the author's comments on the target text. In addition, hedging words and phrases are also used when establishing the author's positions and expressing the author's viewpoints. Identifying these features would greatly facilitate readers' understanding of the ideas in response articles, where the opinions of the author of the response article and the author of the target text are often intertwined.

1) Reporting verbs

Reporting verbs are used to signal the presentation of someone else's ideas or words. They are often used in response articles when referring back to the original author's statements. Here are some examples you may spot in the intensive reading article in this unit: "McKinley and Rose *note* that…", "as McKinley and Rose *argue*…". It is worth noting that the selection of reporting verbs often indicates the author's stances such as agreement or disagreement and the strength of their positions. For example, "recognize" is weaker than "support" when indicating agreement, while "criticize" is much stronger than "doubt" when showing disagreement. Understanding what the reporting verbs imply helps readers recognize the author's reaction to the source text.

2) Evaluative language

Evaluative language implies a positive or negative judgement and expresses the author's attitudes and stances (Pounds, 2015). It features the use of adjectives, adverbs, or verbs in a way that conveys the author's particular attitude towards the issues under discussion. Here are some examples of sentences that use evaluative language:

✓ The researcher *clearly* indicates that…

✓ The *effective* use of the self-regulation strategies led to…

✓ *Surprisingly*, the findings show that…

✓ The researchers' *careful* consideration of the potential challenges allowed…

✓ The authors *strongly advocated* for more tolerance…

To obtain a critical understanding of response articles, it is essential to recognize the author's reactions to the target text and his or her attitudes towards the topic. Therefore, it is worth paying special attention to the author's use of evaluative language based on a clear understanding that these adjectives, adverbs, or verbs are carefully selected by the author to imply his or her stances. Meanwhile, it is important to identify the role of evaluative language and make a reasonable judgement on what is being discussed without being influenced by the author's attitudes and stances.

3) Hedging words and phrases

The notion of hedging, as introduced by Lakoff (1973: 471), was to describe "words whose job is to make things fuzzier or less fuzzy". By using hedging language, authors are able "to take a rhetorical stance, to downplay their statements and anticipate audience responses by adjusting the degree of certainty they give to their claims" (Hyland, 1994: 241). In other words, using hedging language allows authors to soften their claims and avoid sounding too direct or overconfident.

Hedging is a common feature in response articles, as authors of response articles would need to express their comments on the target text. By using hedges, they are able to show politeness and express tentativeness and possibility, even when they are expressing disagreement or presenting opposing views.

Hedging can be achieved by using certain introductory verbs, lexical verbs, modal verbs/adjectives/nouns, adverbs of frequency, *that* clauses, and other phrases. See Table 7.1 for examples.

Unit 7 English for Academic Purposes

Table 7.1 Hedging language (Adapted from Gillett, 2022)

Introductory verbs	seem, tend to, look like, appear to be, think, believe, doubt, indicate, suggest	The results *seem* to support that…
Lexical verbs	believe, assume, suggest	The study *suggests* that…
Modal verbs	will, must, would, may, might, could	This discrepancy *could* be the result of…
Modal adverbs	clearly, probably, possibly, perhaps, conceivably	The grades will *possibly* decrease…
Modal adjectives	clear, probable, possible, likely, unlikely	The participants were *unlikely* to…
Modal nouns	assumption, possibility, probability	There was great *possibility* of…
Adverbs of frequency	often, sometimes, usually, seldom, generally, occasionally	This issue is *often* examined from the perspective of…
That clauses	It could be the case that… It might be suggested that… It is generally agreed that…	It is *generally* accepted that…
Other phrases	approximately, somewhat, in our opinion, in my view, based on the limited data…	*Based on our limited data*, there is a positive correlation between…

Part 2 Intensive Reading

Pre-reading questions:

✓ What are the key concepts of this article?
✓ What are some key questions relevant to the concepts?
✓ What might be the purpose of this article?

Standards of English in Academic Writing: A Response to McKinley and Rose[1]

1. Introduction

In a recent article, McKinley and Rose (2018) bring to light an issue of interest to both native and non-native English speakers **pertaining to** the accuracy of the language used in academic writing. In essence, they argue that the highly standardized language conventions required by academic journals serve to disadvantage L2 writers who come from a variety of backgrounds. Via a review of the submissions guidelines in 210 journals across 27 disciplines, they found the instructions to authors to be overly **rigid**. This inflexibility led them to urge journals to "become more open to diverse usage of English" (p. 9). Further, they problematized words such as "error" and "good" in reference to standards of academic English, which they claim "**elevate** native norms as the only acceptable standard" (p. 9). McKinley and Rose concluded by calling for a relaxation of the requirements laid out in journal submission guidelines, and in so doing, suggested adopting a more flexible and inclusive approach to the non-standard Englishes used by L2 scholars (p. 10). In raising this issue, McKinley and Rose **reinvigorate** an important discussion of considerable concern to a huge population of scholars who, in order to publish in leading journals, are forced to write in a foreign language. Their conclusions are also supported by a body of literature suggesting that L2 writers are at a distinct disadvantage when attempting to enter the world of academic publishing, which is dominated by the English language and requires them to **conform to** specific standards of English (Belcher, 2007; Canagarajah, 1996; Salager-Meyer, 2008; Seidlhofer, 2011).

In this **rejoinder**, however, I argue that a relaxation of the present language standards established in academic journals, as advocated by McKinley and Rose, fails to fully consider the importance of **retaining** a standard language for conveying scientific findings. Further, I critique their suggestion that advocates the avoidance of certain terms, such as "good" and "error-free" in reference to English usage because if acted upon, it could risk eroding the standards of language that the academic community has established and largely agreed upon. I begin this response by recalling a personal anecdote regarding certain spellings and the usage of the word "besides", and then draw an analogy to the English spelling system to underscore the importance of establishing and retaining standards.

---

1   This paper is from Stapleton, P. 2019. Standards of English in academic writing: A response to McKinley and Rose. *Journal of Second Language Writing*, 44: 110–113.

2. Differing Standards

When I first arrived in Hong Kong, China, a few years ago to take up an academic post, I had to make a few small adjustments in my spelling when writing reports and **corresponding with** colleagues. One word that stands out is "program", which in Hong Kong is spelled (or spelt) "programme", using British spelling. This was a minor **nuisance**, although no one ever corrected me when I **inadvertently** used American spellings. As an aside, McKinley and Rose note that these two forms of English are elevated by journals as the required standard forms in their submission guidelines (p. 9).

Further, I noticed a few unusual usages of words. One of these was "besides", which has a slightly different, and I dare say, incorrect usage in Hong Kong among Chinese speakers when used as a linking adverbial (as opposed to a preposition). "Besides" is also one of a few examples offered by McKinley and Rose in reference to a need for a more flexible approach towards English usage by academic journals.

Take the following typical example from the Hong Kong **Observatory**'s weather report:

Winds are weak over the coast of Guangdong. Besides, pressure over southeastern China is rising. A fresh easterly airstream is expected to reach the coast of Guangdong later today. (Feb. 4, 2019)

Here, "besides" is used in place of a word such as "furthermore".

Unlike the British spelling of "program", which I adopted quickly and easily, I have had more difficulty in adapting to the local usage of "besides" because the much wider meaning attributed to it by Chinese writers is rather marked in academic writing. Other researchers have also noted this marked usage and conducted studies particularly focusing on this one word (Hannay, Martínez Caro, & Mackenzie, 2014; Yeung, 2009). As Yeung (2009), for example, notes, the common usage of "besides" tends to be confined to a context related to reasoning. Moreover, it is "often used in a spoken or narrative context to reinforce an argument, giving it a sense of finality" (p. 330). However, among Chinese writers, it tends to be used as a common conjunctive adverb. Thus, when readers who are unfamiliar with this wider usage of "besides" by Chinese writers encounter it in academic articles, they may believe it has been used incorrectly. The following is an example extracted from one of my student's essays (one of five instances) in which "besides" was used descriptively, not argumentatively. Furthermore, it was not the final point in her description.

The mind maps used here were author-designed with some suggestions from the English teacher and some students. Besides, a pilot mind map class was offered as a taste of a mind map before the experiment.

Proper and precise usage of words in academic articles has to be learned by both native and non-native speakers. To illustrate, when discussing the choice of words to use in academic articles in a course I have taught over the past few years entitled "Conceptualizing Research", I stress the importance of precision in academic writing. One example concerns the word "respectively", which I provide examples for, both correct and erroneous, because I frequently see it misused by both native and non-native speakers of English, most frequently when parallelism is not required. The following example extracted from a student's paper illustrates the mistake.

The two classes of students scored on average 128.11 and 128.66 out of 150 respectively in the English examination.

Another example is the word "prove", often seen in drafts from students when describing studies in the literature. Here, students need to internalize the importance of hedging by using a less definitive term when discussing matters related to findings in research studies. The following example extracted from a student's essay would benefit from a more conservative reporting of past research.

Many researchers have proved that mind maps (MM) have positive effects on educational practices.

Hyland (2016, p. 61) neatly summarizes the point at issue here when he claims "the register of academic writing is a specific domain of expertise". Hyland, drawing on interviews with 25 English as an additional language scholars, along with a few native English speaking ones, casts doubt on the beliefs of those who contend L2 scholars are victims of linguistic injustice, and further observes that "writing for publication is a specialized competence which both native and non-native English speakers must acquire" (p. 61). Thus, although native speakers of English are clearly advantaged in learning to write in a style acceptable by international journals, written academic English remains a distinct form of writing that all those wishing to be published need to use correctly.

McKinley and Rose make little effort in their Introduction to disguise their position on the issue before explaining their study. For example, they describe the "struggle" that L2 writers, readers, teachers and reviewers have with the standards of academic English. They frequently italicize the word "error" and "correct" in reference to the usage of English in academic contexts as if there is an ongoing controversy in academia about what is and isn't correct usage of English. And although they appropriately state that journal submission guidelines should not specifically recommend checks by native speakers of English, their call for a relaxation of language norms by way of eliminating demands for error-free writing, appears to **contravene** efforts in the academic community to establish standards in the way it communicates.

The word "standards" stands out in their paper, and appears in the title. "Standards" is an appropriate word because when this discussion is stripped down to its fundamentals, it is the standards of correctness that fuel the disagreement I have with McKinley and Rose. To illustrate the weakness in their position, this debate may benefit from another standardization of the English language that has been acted out over the past few centuries. I speak of the English spelling system.

3. The Importance of Standardization: English Spelling

When Chaucer's *Canterbury Tales* appeared in the 14th century, the vast majority of people could not read. And those who could would struggle with any version of text that came from outside their immediate geographical area. Horobin (2013, p. 82), for instance, claims there were 500 different spellings for the word "such" (*sech*, *sich*, *soch*, *swich*, etc.). Nevertheless, the narrow circle of Chaucer's **literati** would have been familiar with the following version of Middle English spelling in the opening sentences of his classic novel.

Whan that Aprill with his shoures soote. The droghte of March hath perced to the roote.

However, less than a century later, Gutenberg's printing press sparked an explosion of literacy over the following centuries leading to a need for spelling standardization.

Despite the efforts of our forebears to standardize spelling over the **ensuing** six centuries, today it is still far from perfect. One of the many reasons for its lack of transparency is that the English sound system has over 40 phonemes in most of its dialects that have to be conveyed in the written form by only 26 letters of the alphabet.

Other reasons are related to the economic and political power of decision makers centuries ago. For example, the silent "gh" found in many English words, such as "light", "taught", and "weight", was actually pronounced as a voiceless velar fricative before it disappeared in certain dialects; however, the sound was still pronounced in the political and economic hub of the era, London, when spelling was being standardized, which is reflected in the spelling to this day (Horobin, 2013, p. 84, 102). In fact, many decisions about English spelling emerged from the center of power at the time (1430s), London as well as East Midlands, and it was their dialects that were used in an effort to standardize government documents across regions.

Thus, efforts to **devise** a spelling system comprehensible to all readers of English has always been the goal, and like other efforts to standardize—the metric system's advantages over the imperial one being another good parallel—it creates a universal means to communicate that everyone agrees upon and follows. However, when we look at the historical development of our efforts to communicate, choices have to be made among variables and often it is the system possessed by those with the most power that **prevails**. Returning to the main argument about the standards used in academic writing, a conceptual parallel can be drawn with the efforts made to standardize the English spelling system. Presently, several centuries after the spelling system was largely established, we do not question these standards even though they excluded large sectors of the population at the outset. Likewise, today, the English language happens to be a source of power that the academic community has attached itself to, and a particular form of that language, called "academic English", has become the standard that scholars must adhere to when submitting their work to journals.

4. Critiquing McKinley and Rose

Certainly, as McKinley and Rose argue, in the present environment of global inclusiveness, we should make every effort to avoid marginalizing those without power. And they reason very effectively when they rightly **disparage** the use of the term "native" as a desired benchmark in the guidelines to authors in many journals. After all, "many literate and well-educated NES (native English speakers) lack the necessary know-how and experience to produce publishable papers while countless EAL (English as an additional language) scholars…find themselves more "academically bilingual" (Hyland, 2016, p. 61–62). However, to go as far as to question the use of the terms "correct", "error" and even "good" in reference to guidelines for authors in journals for English usage seems a step too far.

At this point, readers could be thinking, based on my name, that I argue from a position of privilege based on my apparent native language, English, and background, coming from a first-world country. Thus, under this thinking, it is easy for me to espouse the merits of standardization when I have all the advantages on my side. However, all standards have histories, and it is not a question of whether some of those using the standards are advantaged or not, but whether those standards help us achieve the goals upon which the standards were established. The advancement of knowledge via the publication of research findings should be open to all, but not to the extent that we erode our standards in the name of inclusiveness.

Other scholars appear to **concur**. For example, Flowerdew and Wang (2016), compared early drafts and published versions of articles by Chinese doctoral students and noted 5,160 revisions made in the final copy. Upon completion, they wondered "whether it is appropriate to embrace wholeheartedly the movement toward less emphasis on error correction for L2 writers' academic texts" (p. 50). Further, they questioned "how many non-standard features can be tolerated before a manuscript becomes unintelligible? And how much effort should readers be expected to put in to make a text become intelligible?" (p. 50).

Interestingly, despite their review of guidelines in 210 journals, McKinley and Rose offer none of their own specific examples of the type of language that particularly marks L2 usage in academic writing contexts. Their paper includes references to only three words, "besides", "researches" and "specially", identified by Martinez (2018) whose study isolated a few more marked terms such as "works", "nowadays" and "prove". Another study, Heng Hartse and Kubota (2014), cited by McKinley and Rose, discusses several questionable usages in a dialogue format between the native and non-native English speaking authors; however, all their examples appear to have little to do with marked L2 writing. Rather, the examples provided mostly deal with minor issues of style and wording, such as "getting tenure" versus "getting tenured". In sum, what is striking in the literature is the paucity of examples from the L2 world of English that should be deemed acceptable by the academy. If "researches" is acceptable, surely "evidences" (another common error often seen in L2 writing) is also. The slope could become very slippery.

Thus, similar to the standardization of the English spelling system, which our ancestors took pains to develop despite the challenges, scholars wishing to publish their work over the ages have also developed a uniform means of communication for advancing knowledge, which in the case of "academic writing" happens to use an **arcane** form of the English language. For example, the *APA Publication Manual*, used as a standard by this journal, runs to several hundred pages. One example concerns the use of the word "while", which should be used in a temporal sense, and not as a replacement for "although" (APA, 2009, p. 84). And although it is true that this standardization arose around a center of Anglo-American linguistic power and is based on a language that is certainly more challenging to learn for non-native speakers than native speakers of English, to water down the standards in the name of inclusiveness appears shortsighted and even trivial when, in the interests of science, primacy should be accorded to the content.

A **tangential**, but still important point to consider is the majority of scholars who seldom, if ever, consider the arguments discussed in this debate. Presently, the world of academic publications consists of well over a million articles annually catalogued in the Science Citation Index (UNESCO, n.d.), the majority of which were in English. I am imagining these scholars mostly in the natural sciences, who know nothing of this debate, reading articles written by periphery scholars sprinkled with the **faux pas** mentioned above, such as "researches", or worse, incorrectly using terms such as "besides" and "prove", and noting them as marked forms, and perhaps being distracted by what they perceive as either poor proofreading or naive interpretations respectively.

In a similar vein, I can also imagine the reaction of native speakers of languages other than English who see non-standard usages from the parallel periphery in their own native tongue. I have little doubt that they would immediately be marked as errors. In Chinese, for example, characters that are readable, but written using a non-conventional direction and sequence of strokes would even be considered erroneous. My own efforts to learn Cantonese may serve as a case in point. When speaking it, if I inadvertently substitute a rising tone for a falling one, I'm likely to be given a puzzled look or worse, a chuckle, from my native Chinese interlocutor. **Make no mistake**, however; it's considered an error in the ears of the listener.

In conclusion, McKinley and Rose's **appeal for** more tolerance for L2 writers' non-standard usages during the review process is **laudable**, and even some rewording of journal submission guidelines seems both reasonable and appropriate. However, their call for a redefinition and re-conceptualization of the term "error" and the like, seems a step backward from the standardized way of communicating science and advancing knowledge that the academic community has worked so hard to achieve.

(Scan the QR code to access the list of references.)

Words and Expressions

pertain to		to be connected with a particular subject, event, or situation
rigid	*adj.*	not able to be changed or persuaded
elevate	*v.*	to make someone or something more important or to improve something
reinvigorate	*v.*	to make something stronger, or more exciting or successful again
conform to		to behave according to the usual standards of behavior that are expected by a group or society
rejoinder	*n.*	a quick answer, often given in a way that is competitive or amusing
retain	*v.*	to keep or continue to have something
correspond with		to communicate by writing a letter or sending an email
nuisance	*n.*	something or someone that annoys you or causes trouble for you
inadvertently	*adv.*	in a way that is not intentional
observatory	*n.*	a building from which scientists can watch the planets, the stars, the weather, etc.
contravene	*v.*	to do something that a law or rule does not allow, or to break a law or rule
literati	*n.*	[plural] people with a good education who know a lot about literature
ensuing	*adj.*	happening after or following something else
devise	*v.*	to invent something, especially with intelligence or imagination
prevail	*v.*	to be common among a group of people or area at a particular time

Unit 7 English for Academic Purposes

disparage	*v.*	to criticize someone or something in a way that shows a lack of respect
concur	*v.*	to agree or have the same opinion
arcane	*adj.*	mysterious and known only by a few people
tangential	*adj.*	(of a subject or activity) different from or not directly connected with the one you are talking about or doing
faux pas		a remark or action in a social situation that is a mistake and causes embarrassment or offense
make no mistake		to be used to show that you are certain about something
appeal for		to make a serious or formal request, especially to the public, for money, information, or help
laudable	*adj.*	(of actions and behavior) deserving praise, even if there is little or no success

 Reflections and Practice

❶ Read the text and answer the following questions.

1. This article was written in response to the article by McKinley and Rose (2018). According to the author (Stapleton), what were the main points made by McKinley and Rose?
2. Did Stapleton agree with McKinley and Rose's statements?
3. What evidence did Stapleton provide to support or refute McKinley and Rose's statements?
4. How did Stapleton structure this response article?
5. What were Stapleton's main arguments about the standards used in academic writing?

❷ Discuss the following questions with your partner.

1. In terms of whether there should be a relaxation of the language standards established in academic journals, the author and McKinley and Rose held different views. Whose view is more convincing to you? Why?
2. What do you think are the challenges for EFL writers' academic publication in English? To what extent are these challenges related to the standards of English usage?
3. Is it possible to achieve a balance between maintaining standard language in

academic writing and being more tolerant of L2 writers' non-standard usages during the review process? If your answer is yes, how can you achieve this balance? If your answer is no, why?

4. What are some standards of academic writing in your discipline? Could you give some examples of "errors" that are tolerable and intolerable?

5. If you were the authors of the original text (McKinley and Rose), how would you respond to Stapleton's arguments?

Ⅲ Paraphrase the following sentences.

1. In this rejoinder, however, I argue that a relaxation of the present language standards established in academic journals, as advocated by McKinley and Rose, fails to fully consider the importance of retaining a standard language for conveying scientific findings.

2. Hyland, drawing on interviews with 25 English as an additional language scholars, along with a few native English speaking ones, casts doubt on the beliefs of those who contend L2 scholars are victims of linguistic injustice, and further observes that "writing for publication is a specialized competence which both native and non-native English speakers must acquire" (p. 61).

3. And although they appropriately state that journal submission guidelines should not specifically recommend checks by native speakers of English, their call for a relaxation of language norms by way of eliminating demands for error-free writing, appears to contravene efforts in the academic community to establish standards in the way it communicates.

4. Thus, efforts to devise a spelling system comprehensible to all readers of English has always been the goal, and like other efforts to standardize—the metric system's advantages over the imperial one being another good parallel—it creates a universal means to communicate that everyone agrees upon and follows.

5. However, all standards have histories, and it is not a question of whether some of those using the standards are advantaged or not, but whether those standards help us achieve the goals upon which the standards were established. The advancement of knowledge via the publication of research findings should be open to all, but not to the extent that we erode our standards in the name of inclusiveness.

Unit 7 English for Academic Purposes

IV Read the text and identify some examples where reporting verbs, evaluative language, and hedging words and phrases are used.

Language features	Examples in the text
Reporting verbs	
Evaluative language	
Hedging words and phrases	

V Write an outline for the text following the structure below.

1. Introduction
   Context: _____
   _____.
   Purpose: _____
   _____.

2. Summary
   Authors' arguments in the original text:
   Argument 1: _____
   _____.
   Argument 2: _____
   _____.

3. Thesis
   Author's arguments in the response text:
   Argument 1: _____.
   Argument 2: _____.

4. Response
   _____
   _____.

5. Conclusion

   _____
   _____.

Ⅵ Write a summary for the text in 150–200 words.

Ⅶ Write a short article in response to Stapleton's article (2019). Use sources and cite them appropriately when writing your critical response.

Part 3　Further Reading

Conceptualizations of Language Errors, Standards, Norms and Nativeness in English for Research Publication Purposes: An Analysis of Journal Submission Guidelines[1]

Abstract

　　Adherence to standards in English for research publication purposes (ERPP) can be a substantial barrier for second language (L2) writers and is an area of renewed debate in L2 writing research. This study presents a qualitative text analysis of author guidelines in 210 leading academic journals across 27 disciplines. It explores conceptualizations of language errors, standards, norms and nativeness in journal submission guidelines, and identifies key concepts related to so-called error-free writing. Findings indicate that most of the journal guidelines are inflexible in their acceptance of variant uses of English. Some guidelines state a requirement of meeting an unclear standard of good English, sometimes described as

---

1　This paper is from McKinley, J. & Rose, H. 2018. Conceptualizations of language errors, standards, norms and nativeness in English for research publication purposes: An analysis of journal submission guidelines. *Journal of Second Language Writing, 42*: 1–11.

American or British English. Many guidelines specifically position L2 writers as deficient of native standards, which raises ethical considerations of access to publication in top journals. This study leads to a discussion of a need to reconceptualize error-free writing in ERPP, and to decouple it from concepts such as nativeness. It focuses on a need to relax some author guidelines to encourage all authors to write using an English that can easily be understood by a broad, heterogeneous, global, and multilingual audience.

Keywords: standard English, error-free, English as a lingua franca, English for research publication purposes, journal submission guidelines

Reflections and Practice

Read the full article and answer the following questions.

1. What is the purpose of this article?
2. What does relevant literature suggest regarding the standards in English for research and publication?
3. What are the research questions?
4. How was the study conducted?
5. What are the major findings?
6. What are the limitations and implications of the study?

Unit 8
Psychology

📝 Learning Objectives

- Describe the process functions of reporting verbs;

- Describe the evaluative functions of reporting verbs;

- Increase the awareness of disciplinary preferences for reporting verb forms.

Part 1 Reading Skills and Strategies

Distinguishing Reporting Verbs

As introduced in Unit 7, the use of reporting verbs is a key linguistic feature of response articles. Actually, reference to prior literature is generally accepted as a defining feature of the academic research article (Hyland, 2002; White, 2004). The attribution of propositional content to another source provides an appropriate context for the research, demonstrating how the current work builds on, or departs from prior research. Hyland (2002: 127) indicates that "the selection of a particular reporting verb is a delicate choice as it is a crucial means of both situating one's work appropriately and communicating with one's peers effectively". Therefore, it is critical for readers to know the functions of reporting verbs and be aware of the writer's implied attitude towards the cited sources.

Hyland (2002) classified the reporting verbs into three distinguishable processes: research acts, cognition acts, and discourse acts. Within the process categories, writers can make more delicate decisions, using the evaluative functions of the reporting verbs to take either a supportive, tentative, critical, or neutral attitude towards the reported claims. Table 8.1 summarizes Hyland's (2002) framework of functions of reporting verbs with examples.

Table 8.1 Functions of reporting verbs with examples

Process functions		Evaluative functions	Examples
1. Research Acts: verbs representing experimental activities or actions carried out in the real world	Statement of findings	Writers **acknowledge their acceptance** of the authors' results or conclusion.	demonstrate, establish, show, solve, confirm
		Writers **adopt a counterfactive stance**, portraying the author's judgements as false or incorrect.	fail, misunderstand, ignore, overlook
		Writers **show no clear attitudinal signal**.	find, identify, observe, obtain
	Statement of procedures		analyze, calculate, assay, explore, plot, recover

(Continued)

Process functions	Evaluative functions	Examples
2. **Cognition Acts**: verbs concerned with the researcher's mental processes	Writers represent the author as having a **positive** attitude to the material.	agree, concur, hold, know, think, understand
	Writers represent the author as having a **tentative** view to the material.	believe, doubt, speculate, suppose, suspect
	Writers represent the author as having a **critical** attitude to the material.	disagree, dispute, not think
	Writers represent the author as having a **neural** attitude to the material.	picture, conceive, anticipate, reflect
3. **Discourse Acts**: verbs focusing on the verbal expression of cognitive or research activities	Writers take responsibility for their interpretation of the cited sources. **Tentative**	postulate, hypothesize, indicate, intimate, suggest
	Critical	evade, exaggerate, not account, not make point
	Positive	affirm, note, claim,
	Neutral	state, describe, discuss, report, answer, define, summarize
	Writers ascribe the viewpoint to the author.	deny, critique, challenge, attack, question, warn, refute, rule out

Hyland's (2002) study also reveals disciplinary preferences for reporting verb forms. In terms of process functions, the preference for research act forms in science and engineering papers helps to convey an experimental explanatory schema and contributes to the overall impression in the hard discipline papers of research activity as an inductive, impersonal, and empirically-based endeavor. On the other hand, the preference for discourse verbs in the humanities and social sciences is in accordance with the discursive nature of the subjects, which are more inclined to contextual and human irregularities than those studied in the hard sciences. With regard to evaluative functions, however, less obvious differences are observed, as writers in all disciplines display a clear preference for neutral stances.

Part 2 Intensive Reading

Pre-reading questions:

✓ What are the key concepts of this article?

✓ What are some key questions related to the concepts?

✓ What might be the purpose of this article?

Procrastination, Deadlines, and Performance: Self-Control by Precommitment[1]

Self-control problems arise when preferences are inconsistent across time or context (e.g., Ainslie, 1975; Loewenstein, 1996). For example, before going to a restaurant dieters may choose not to have Crème Brûlée, but when the time comes to have dessert they may give in to the temptation and order it after all, only to regret having eaten it after the meal is over. The issue is not whether having Crème Brûlée is right or wrong, but that ordering it is inconsistent with the decision makers' preferences both before and after the event. One way to think about these issues is that individuals have a set of preferences, X, at some point in time (or under a certain set of environmental conditions) and a different set of preferences, Y, at some other point in time. In the case of the Crème Brûlée, dieters may prefer not to consume it (Y) before going to the restaurant, prefer to eat it (X) when ordering dessert and consuming it at the restaurant, and prefer not to have eaten it after the meal is over (Y). This type of systematic preference **reversal** is often described by **hyperbolic** time discounting (e.g., Ainslie, 1975; Kirby, 1997; Laibson, 1997), under which immediately available rewards have a **disproportionate** effect on preferences relative to more delayed rewards, causing a time-inconsistent taste for immediate **gratification**. Crème Brûlée poses but a minor self-control problem. Examples of more important self-control problems include not exercising enough, scratching a rash, nail biting, smoking, engaging in unsafe sex, abusing drugs, overspending, **procrastination**, and so forth.

One of the causes for the apparent changes in preferences over time is changes in the

---

1 This paper is from Ariely, D. & Wertenbroch, K. 2002. Procrastination, deadlines, and performance: Self-control by precommitment. *Psychological Science, 13*(3): 219–224.

saliency of the costs and benefits of the activity in question (Akerlof, 1991). For example, well in advance of actually taking on the responsibility of writing a book, the benefits of completing such a task loom large, and the costs seem small. Consequently, authors take on such tasks. But as the deadline draws closer, the saliency of the costs and benefits changes. Authors become increasingly aware of the costs (the time needed for completing the task), while the benefits become increasingly less clear.

Although such time-inconsistent preferences may form serious obstacles to following a planned course of action, they can be overcome. In addition to exercising willpower to resist temptation (Hoch & Loewenstein, 1991; Muraven & Baumeister, 2000), people can bind, or precommit, their own behavior (Prelec, 1989; Schelling, 1992; Strotz, 1956; Thaler & Shefrin, 1981; Wertenbroch, 1998). For example, people who want to diet, but recognize that Crème Brûlée will tempt them to deviate from their plan, can **preempt** temptation by going to a restaurant with a less tempting menu. A wealth of anecdotes describes examples of binding behaviors, including frequenting health retreats where some food types are not available, saving in non-interest-bearing Christmas clubs, or buying small packages of cigarettes in order to reduce consumption (Wertenbroch, 1998). An extreme example was provided by Schelling (1992), who described drug addicts sending self-incriminating letters to be held in trust (and mailed to the person they fear the most will find out about their addiction) in the event of a **relapse** into drug use. What characterizes binding behavior is the voluntary **imposition** of constraints (that are costly to overcome) on one's future choices in a strategic attempt to resist future temptations.

Although time-inconsistent preferences and self-control have been the subject of much theoretical analysis in psychology and economics (Ainslie, 1975; Bargh & Gollwitzer, 1994; Hoch & Loewenstein, 1991; Muraven & Baumeister, 2000; O'Donoghue & Rabin, 1999, 2000; Prelec, 1989; Strotz, 1956; Thaler & Shefrin, 1981; Tversky & Shafir, 1992), controlled empirical evidence of self-control strategies is **scarce**. The few studies that have looked at self-control show that people do attempt to impose costly restrictions on themselves. In the domain of consumer choice, Wertenbroch (1998) showed with experimental and field data that people are willing to **forgo** quantity discounts on goods that they may be tempted to overconsume, effectively paying a "self-control premium" to implement a precommitment strategy of rationing their own consumption of such "vices". Similarly, Read, Loewenstein, and Kalyanaraman (1999) asked participants to pick three rental movies either simultaneously (for later consumption) or sequentially (for more immediate consumption). Their results showed that participants used the simultaneous choices to precommit to watching more "**highbrow**" (as opposed to more tempting "low-brow") movies. In the domain of medical testing, Trope and Fishbach (2000) allowed participants to set the magnitude of self-imposed penalties for failing to undergo small, unpleasant medical procedures. Their results showed that participants used these penalties strategically as precommitment devices, setting higher penalties for more aversive procedures.

What remains unclear from the studies that have documented such self-control behavior is the extent to which attempts to impose restrictions on oneself are successful. The work we report here examined self-control empirically, with a focus on procrastination. In particular, we were interested in the effectiveness of setting potentially costly deadlines as a way to overcome procrastination. To address this issue, we looked at tasks on which performance could be evaluated objectively. Using performance measures, we could test not only whether people use self-imposed deadlines as precommitment mechanisms, but also whether or not these mechanisms improve performance. We asked three questions regarding procrastination, self-control, and performance:

✓ Do people self-impose costly deadlines on tasks in which procrastination may **impede** performance?

✓ Are people correct in imposing deadlines on themselves? In other words, are self-imposed deadlines effective in improving task performance?

✓ Do people set their deadlines **optimally**, for maximum performance enhancement?

Pilot Studies

The two pilot studies took place within the context of a semester-long course (14 weeks) at the Massachusetts Institute of Technology (MIT). Participants were students in the class, and as part of their course requirement had to write either three short papers (Pilot Study 1) or one short paper (Pilot Study 2). The instructor explained that each student was free to choose the dates by which he or she committed to hand in the short papers, but that the deadlines had to be announced in advance and were binding.

Each of the deadlines was scored by taking its distance (number of days) from the last day of class. Thus, a score of zero implies a planned submission on the last day of class (as would be predicted in the absence of self-control problems). Any other response indicates a more severe deadline than necessary. In the first pilot study, the mean deadline across all three papers was 21.2 days before the end of the course, and significantly earlier than the last possible deadline, $f(83) = 8.05, p < 0.001$. The mean deadline was 32.8 days before the end of the course for the first paper, $f(27) = 5.72, p < 0.001$; 20.4 days before the end for the second paper, $r(27) = 5.04, p < 0.001$; and 10.4 days before the end for the third paper, $f(27) = 4.45, p < 0.001$. These results show that the students set themselves deadlines well before the last day of class.

To rule out the possibility that students self-impose deadlines because of a preference for distributing events evenly over time (Loewenstein & Prelec, 1993), in Pilot Study 2 we gave the students a single task. The mean self-imposed deadline in this case was 41.59 days before the end of the course, $r(21) = 15.44$, $p < 0.001$, suggesting that setting early deadlines is strategic, and not an outcome of a desire to space tasks evenly.

Study 1: The Free-Choice/No-Choice Study

Method

Participants

Study 1 took place during a semester-long executive-education course at MIT. Participants were 99 professionals, most of whom participated in the class via interactive video. The two sections of the course (which, based on records provided by the executive-education program, did not differ in overall academic performance) were each assigned to a different condition (so there was no random assignment of individuals to treatments but rather a random assignment of sections to treatments).

Procedure

During the first lecture, the instructor went over the syllabus, which included instructions for the study. One part of the course requirements was to write three short papers. Students in the no-choice section (48 students) were given fixed, evenly spaced deadlines for the papers (a paper at the end of each third of the course). Students in the free-choice section (51 students) were given detailed instructions about setting their own deadlines (as in the pilot studies). These instructions indicated that each student was free to choose the dates by which he or she wanted to hand in the short papers. Four external constraints were set regarding the dates: First, students had to hand in their papers no later than the last lecture; second, students had to announce the deadlines for submission prior to the second lecture; third, the dates were final and could not be changed; and fourth, the dates were binding, so that each day of delay beyond the deadline would cause a 1% penalty in the paper's overall grade. Finally, it was explained clearly that there were no grade advantages for early submissions because the instructor would not provide grades or feedback on the assignments before the end of the course. Explaining to the students that there would be no feedback before the end of the course was important because it eliminated incentives for students to hand in papers early in order to get feedback that they could use to improve subsequent papers.

In fact, the external incentives for the students in the free-choice section encouraged submission of all three papers on the last possible day. By setting their deadlines as late as possible, the students would have the most time to work on the papers, the highest flexibility in arranging their workload, and the opportunity to learn the most about the topic before submitting the papers. Students also had an incentive to set submission dates late because the penalty would be applied only to late submissions and not to early ones. Finally, students who wanted to submit assignments early could privately plan to do so without precommitting to the instructor. Of course, such private deadlines might be less psychologically meaningful than the deadlines they set with the instructor, and hence more **pliant** and less effective.

Results and Discussion

First, we examined the declared deadlines for each of the three papers. Again, each deadline was scored by taking its distance (number of days) from the last day of class, so that a score of zero indicates a planned submission on the last day of class (perfectly normative). Other responses indicate the severity of the deadlines the students imposed on themselves. The mean deadlines were significantly earlier than the last possible deadline—41.78 days before the end of the course for the first paper, $t(44) = 8.41, p < 0.001$; 26.07 days before the end for the second paper, $t(44) = 8.10, p < 0.001$; and 9.84 days before the end for the third paper, $t(44) = 4.97, p < 0.001$. Figure 1 shows that only 43 deadlines (32%) were set for the final week of class. The majority of the deadlines were set prior to the last lecture, and in fact, only 12 students (27%) chose to submit all three papers on the last day of class.

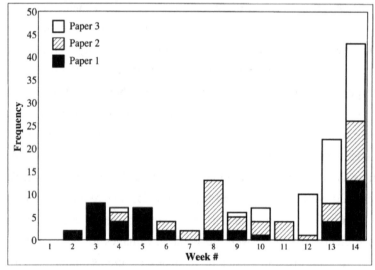

Figure 1 Frequency distribution of the declared deadlines in Study 1 as a function of the week of class (Week 1 is the first week, and Week 14 the last week), plotted separately for the three papers.

These results indicate that people are willing to self-impose deadlines to overcome procrastination, even when these deadlines are costly (our first question). The students could have chosen less binding private deadlines, but instead chose deadlines that involved more commitment and greater potential cost (a grade penalty for being late). It seems that they were willing to take the risk of losing grade points to apply the self-control mechanism of precommitment.

Next, we compared the grades in the two sections to see if flexibility in setting deadlines caused higher or lower grades compared with externally imposed, evenly spaced deadlines. There were three possible predictions: (a) If students do not have self-control problems, greater flexibility should lead to higher grades; (b) if students do have self-control problems, and if they both use deadlines to overcome these problems and set these deadlines optimally, greater flexibility should allow them to achieve higher grades; (c) if students do have self-control problems, and they use deadlines to overcome these problems, but do not set these deadlines optimally, greater flexibility might lead to lower grades. In sum, flexibility, compared with evenly spaced deadlines, should lead to lower grades only if people have self-control problems yet do not set their own deadlines optimally. The result supported the third prediction. The grades in the no-choice section ($M = 88.76$) were higher than the grades in the free-choice section ($M = 85.67$), $t(97) = 3.03, p = 0.003$.

In addition to having a direct effect on performance, deadlines can have a secondary effect on other aspects of performance that also require the investment of time as a resource. A natural candidate for this measure is the students' performance on a final project that was due on the last day of class. Grades for the final project showed the same effect: Scores were lower in the free-choice section ($M = 77$) than in the no-choice section ($M = 86$), $t(95) = 4.15$, $p < 0.001$, suggesting that students with late self-imposed deadlines for the three focal tasks might not have had sufficient time to dedicate to the final project.

Although the students were instructed about the penalties associated with missing the deadlines, it is possible that students in the free-choice section, compared with those in the no-choice section, treated these deadlines as less binding because they were self-imposed. To demonstrate that the better performance in the no-choice section was caused by the timing of the deadlines and not by the perceived force of the externally imposed deadlines, we compared the performance of the students in the no-choice section with the performance of those students in the free-choice section who chose evenly spaced (or almost evenly spaced) dates for submission. This comparison isolates the effect of deadline type (self vs. external) on performance. If these two groups with similarly spaced deadlines differed in their performance, the overall difference between the sections could be attributed to the nature of the deadlines (self vs. external). However, if students who spaced their deadlines evenly showed similar performance regardless of the nature of the deadline, the overall difference between the sections was likely due to the timing of the deadlines. The results showed that the performance difference between the two sections decreased dramatically and became nonsignificant when only those students who had evenly spaced deadlines were included in the analysis (effect size reduced by 59%). This comparison suggests that the overall effect of self-imposing deadlines was due primarily to the timing of the deadlines, not just a weaker perceived potency of self-imposed deadlines.

Study 2: The Proofreading Study

The combined results of the pilot studies and Study 1 suggest that decision makers who face situations in which they can self-impose deadlines recognize two conflicting forces. On the one hand, they realize the value of binding themselves to overcome procrastination; on the other hand, they understand the normative reasons to set the deadlines as late as possible. We propose that decision makers combine these two perspectives and come up with deadlines whose timing is suboptimal (as shown in Study 1) but better than delaying all deadlines to the last possible day. Thus, we hypothesize that performance under self-imposed deadlines is lower than performance under externally imposed, evenly spaced deadlines but higher than performance under maximally delayed deadlines (when all tasks are due simultaneously at the end of the period). To examine this hypothesis, we now focus on our second and third questions: whether self-imposed deadlines improve performance and, if so, whether people know how to set deadlines for maximum performance enhancement. Study 2 was designed to examine these questions in a controlled experimental setup, providing a more sensitive test of the effect of deadlines on performance than Study 1 did, coupled with a more objective performance measure.

Method

Participants

In MIT's newspaper and on bulletin boards, we placed an ad looking for "native English speakers to help us proofread papers by other students to evaluate writing skills". We also noted that payment would be contingent on the quality of the proofreading, with 100 paid per correctly detected error and a $1 penalty for each day of delay. A total of 60 students participated in the study, randomly assigned to the three experimental conditions.

Procedure

We chose a task that people cared about but one whose outcome was not central to their lives (in contrast to the course grades in the previous studies). We also wanted a task for which performance scores would be more objective and for which we could pay participants accordingly. We therefore designed a proofreading task in which we deliberately planted spelling and grammatical mistakes. We used a postmodern text generator to create text that was grammatically correct but not meaningful, as shown by the following sample:

"Sexual identity is intrinsically impossible," says Foucault; however, according to de Selby [1], it is not so much sexual identity that is intrinsically impossible, but rather the dialectic, and some would say the stasis, of sexual identity. Thus, D'Erlette [2] holds that we have to choose between premodern dialectic theory and subcultural feminism imputing the role of the observer as poet.

We created three such texts with a length of about 10 pages each, and inserted in each of them a total of 100 grammatical and spelling errors.

Study 2 included three different conditions. In each condition, we clearly explained to the participants that their payoffs would depend on how many errors they detected and on the time of submission of each proofread text. Participants were told that submitting their tasks early was permitted (without increasing their compensation), but that delay in submission would result in a penalty of $1 for each day of delay. In the evenly-spaced-deadlines condition, participants had to submit one of the three texts every 7 days; in the end-deadline condition, they had to submit all three texts at the end of 3 weeks (21 days); and in the self-imposed-deadlines condition, they had to choose their own deadline for each of the three texts within the 3-week window (as in the previous studies).

Results and Discussion

First, we determined whether the self-imposed-deadlines condition replicated the results of the previous studies. The results showed that participants in this condition chose to **space out** their proofreading tasks, $F(2, 38) = 63.28$, $p < 0.001$, thus showing a preference for self-imposing costly deadlines.

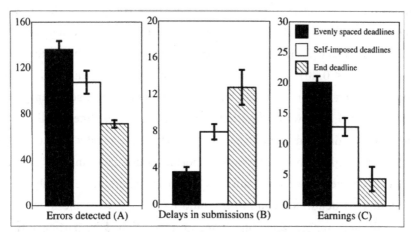

Figure 2   Mean errors detected (A), delays in submissions (B), and earning (C) in Study 2, compared across the three conditions (error bars are based on standard errors). Delays are measured in days, earning in dollars.

We analyzed three aspects of performance across the different conditions: number of errors detected, delays in submissions, and earnings (see Figure 2). All differences were statistically significant (all $ps < 0.01$) in the expected direction. As predicted, the number of errors correctly detected was highest in the evenly-spaced-deadlines condition, followed by the self-imposed-deadlines condition, with the lowest performance in the end-deadline condition. Results were similar for participants' delays in submitting their proofreading work (in this case, shorter delays resulted in higher payoffs). Participants' earnings reflected a combination of error detection and delay and thus show the same pattern of results.

Next, we examined the same measures focusing on the participants in the self-imposed-deadlines condition who had spaced their tasks evenly, or approximately evenly ($n = 10$). Mirroring the results of Study 1, the differences between the evenly-spaced-deadlines condition and the ("sophisticated") self-imposed-deadlines condition decreased dramatically and became nonsignificant for all dependent measures: delay in submissions (effect size reduced by 55%), errors detected (effect size reduced by 79%), and earnings (effect size reduced by 55%). This reduction in effect sizes provides additional evidence that a central cause of the lower performance in the self-imposed-deadlines condition compared with the evenly-spaced-deadlines condition was suboptimal spacing of the tasks.

Finally, we asked participants to evaluate their overall experience on five attributes: How much they liked the task, how interesting it was, how good the quality of the writing was, how good the grammatical quality was, and how effectively the text communicated the ideas contained in it. Responses to all questions were on a 100-point scale, on which higher numbers represented higher quality ratings. An analysis of the average subjective evaluation across the five questions revealed a pattern that was the opposite of the performance results, $F(2,057) = 17.06$, $p < 0.001$. Participants in the evenly-spaced-deadlines condition liked the task the least ($M = 22.1$), followed by the participants in the self-imposed-deadlines condition ($M = 28.12$), followed by participants in the end-deadline condition, who liked the task the most, or disliked it the least ($M = 37.9$). These results are not surprising, as the texts were meaningless and the tasks were boring, if not annoying. We suggest that the pattern would have been reversed if the task had been inherently enjoyable; participants in the evenly-spaced-deadlines condition would have enjoyed it the most, followed by participants in the self-imposed-deadlines condition, and finally by participants in the end-deadline condition.

In addition, we asked participants to estimate how much time they had spent on each of the three texts. The time estimates revealed a mirror image of the subjective evaluations, $F(2,$

57) = 45.76, $p < 0.001$, indicating that increased time spent on the task caused the evaluation to be more negative. Participants in the evenly-spaced-deadlines condition indicated they spent the most time on the task ($M = 84$ min), participants in the self-imposed-deadlines condition spent an intermediate amount of time on the task ($M = 69.9$ min), and participants in the end-deadline condition spent the least time on the task ($M = 50.8$ min). Taken together, the results show that when deadline constraints increased, performance improved, time spent on the task increased, and enjoyment of the task decreased (because of enhanced recognition of the true low quality of the texts). The effectiveness of the constraints themselves depended on the type of constraint—self-imposed deadlines improved performance, but not to the same degree as evenly spaced deadlines.

General Discussion

The studies presented here show that people sometimes impose deadlines on themselves, even when missing these deadlines leads to penalties. In a world without self-control problems, such behavior would seem nonnormative. A rational decision maker with time-consistent preferences would not impose constraints on his or her choices. But if people **impulsively** procrastinate, and if they also are aware of their procrastination problems (e.g., Benabou & Tirole, in press; O'Donoghue & Rabin, 1999), self-imposing costly deadlines can be strategic and reasonable. Study 1 demonstrated that self-imposed deadlines do not enhance performance as much as externally imposed, evenly spaced deadlines. The results from Study 2 show that performance under self-imposed deadlines is lower than performance under evenly spaced deadlines, but higher than performance under maximally delayed deadlines.

We can now return to the three questions posed earlier: (a) Do people self-impose costly deadlines to overcome procrastination? (b) Are self-imposed deadlines effective in improving task performance? (c) Do people set self-imposed deadlines optimally? The answer to the first two questions is "yes", and the answer to the last question is "no". Our findings demonstrate that people understand the value of binding themselves to overcome procrastination, even in the face of strong normative reasons for setting deadlines as late as possible. Our participants showed some sophistication in their understanding of their own procrastination problems, but many did not set their deadlines to bind themselves optimally. Whether our evidence of such "imperfect" sophistication (or "partial naivete") reflects biased self-perception, cognitive limitations in calibrating deadlines, or a deliberate mixed strategy of balancing flexibility and self-control is a question for future research. What is clear from our empirical evidence is that procrastination is a real behavioral problem, that people strategically try to **curb** it by using costly self-imposed deadlines, and that self-imposed deadlines are not always as effective as some external deadlines in **boosting** task performance.

(Scan the QR code to access the list of references.)

Words and Expressions

reversal	n.	the act of changing or making something change to its opposite
hyperbolic	adj.	relating to a way of speaking or writing that makes someone or something sound bigger, better, more, etc., than they are
disproportionate	adj.	too large or too small in comparison to something else, or not deserving its importance or influence
gratification	n.	pleasure or satisfaction, or something which provides this
procrastination	n.	the act of delaying something that must be done, often because it is unpleasant or boring
preempt	v.	to prevent something from happening by taking action first
relapse	n.	the recurrence of a disease after apparent improvement
imposition	n.	a situation in which someone expects another person to do something that he or she does not want to do or that is not convenient
scarce	adj.	not easy to find or get something for its small quantities
forgo	v.	not to have or do something enjoyable
high-brow	adj.	(of books, plays, etc.) involving serious and complicated or artistic ideas, or (of people) interested in serious and complicated subjects
impede	v.	to make it more difficult for something to happen or more difficult for someone to do something
optimally	adv.	in the way that is most likely to bring success or advantage
pliant	adj.	easily influenced or controlled by other people
space out		to arrange things or people so that there is some distance or time between them
impulsively	adv.	suddenly, without any planning and without considering the effects your actions may have
curb	v.	to control or limit something that is not wanted
boost	v.	to improve or increase something

Unit 8 Psychology

 Reflections and Practice

❶ **Read the text and answer the following questions.**

1. What is systematic preference reversal? Can you explain using the example of Crème Brûlée in the first paragraph?
2. What is the research gap identified in the current study?
3. What is the purpose of conducting Pilot Study 2?
4. What are the different conditions and dependent variables in Study 1?
5. What are the different conditions and dependent variables in Study 2?
6. What are the implications of the current study?

❷ **Discuss the following questions with your partner.**

1. What questions did you have as you read?
2. Who would be affected by the results of this study?
3. What are possible limitations of this study?

❸ **Paraphrase the following sentences.**

1. The work we report here examined self-control empirically, with a focus on procrastination. In particular, we were interested in the effectiveness of setting potentially costly deadlines as a way to overcome procrastination.
2. Taken together, the results show that when deadline constraints increased, performance improved, time spent on the task increased, and enjoyment of the task decreased (because of enhanced recognition of the true low quality of the texts).
3. Our findings demonstrate that people understand the value of binding themselves to overcome procrastination, even in the face of strong normative reasons for setting deadlines as late as possible.
4. What is clear from our empirical evidence is that procrastination is a real behavioral problem, that people strategically try to curb it by using costly self-imposed deadlines, and that self-imposed deadlines are not always as effective as some external deadlines in boosting task performance.

IV Rewrite the following sentence, which is in the information-prominent citation style, into sentences in the author-prominent citation style with reporting verbs of different attitudes.

One of the causes for the apparent changes in preferences over time is changes in the saliency of the costs and benefits of the activity in question (Akerlof, 1991).

1. The writer represents the author (Akerlof) as having a neutral attitude towards the material:
   _____
   _____

2. The writer represents the author (Akerlof) as having a speculative attitude towards the material:
   _____
   _____

3. The writer represents the author (Akerlof) as having a positive attitude towards the material:
   _____
   _____

4. The writer represents the author (Akerlof) as having a critical attitude towards the material:
   _____
   _____

V Write an outline for the text following the structure below.

> 1. **Introduction**
>   **Research context:** Self-control problems arise when _____.
>   **Literature review:**
>   (Akerlof, 1991) _____.
>   (Hoch & Loewenstein, 1991; Muraven & Baumeister, 2000) _____
>   _____.
>
>   (Prelec, 1998; Schelling, 1992; Strotz, 1956; Thaler & Shefrin, 1981; Wertenbroch, 1998) _____.
>   **Research niche:**
>   Although much theoretical analysis in psychology and economics has been undertaken, _____ is scarce.
>   What remains unclear is _____.

Research questions: We ask three questions regarding _____, _____, and _____.

2. **Pilot Studies**

    Pilot Study 1: _____.

    Pilot Study 2: _____.

3. **Study 1: The _____ Study**

    Methods

    Participants

    Procedure

    Results and Discussion

4. **Study 2: The _____ Study**

    Methods

    Participants

    Procedure

    Results and Discussion

5. **General Discussion**

    Restatement of the most important findings:

    The results from Study 1 show that _____
    _____.

    The results from Study 2 show that _____
    _____.

    Explanations for the findings:

    _____
    _____.

Ⅶ Write a summary for the text in 150–200 words.

Part 3　Further Reading

Academic Interventions for Academic Procrastination: A Review of the Literature[1]

Abstract

　　Procrastination is a widespread phenomenon in academic settings. It has been studied from many different theoretical angles, and a variety of causes and consequences have been suggested. Recent studies support the notion that academic procrastination can be seen from a situational perspective and as a failure in learning self-regulation. It suggests that interventions should address situational as well as deficits in self-regulation to help students overcome their procrastinating tendencies. The present review examined the recent literature on causes and consequences of academic procrastination and the limited number of studies of academic interventions for academic procrastination. Findings of this review strengthen the need to further study the topic of academic interventions for academic procrastination and to develop effective interventions. At the end of this review, several suggestions for the development of academic interventions are outlined.

Keywords: academic interventions, academic procrastination, young college students

 Reflections and Practice

Read the full article and answer the following questions.

1. What is the aim of this review article?
2. What previous studies are reviewed?
3. How are they structured? (Chronologically or by theme?)
4. What are the key findings?
5. What suggestions for further research are proposed?

1　This paper is from Zacks, S. & Hen, M. 2018. Academic interventions for academic procrastination: A review of the literature. *Journal of Prevention & Intervention in the Community, 46*(2): 117–130.

Unit 9
Carbon Economy

📝 Learning Objectives

- Understand the concept of an annotated bibliography;

- Describe the functions of an annotated bibliography;

- Identify the primary elements in an annotated bibliography;

- Apply effective strategies to write an annotated bibliography.

Part 1 Reading Skills and Strategies

Writing an Annotated Bibliography

1. Introduction to the Annotated Bibliography

A bibliography is usually a list of books and articles cited in a written paper and appended at the end of the paper. A standard bibliography describes the basic information of the cited sources: author(s), title, journal, volume, issue, page numbers, date of publication, etc. The primary functions of bibliographies are to support arguments and claims, to credit the sources, and to assist the reader in finding the sources used in the writing of a paper. An annotated bibliography adds descriptive and evaluative comments (i.e., an annotation) to assess the nature and value of the cited sources. The added comments provide the researcher and reader with a concise summary and a critical evaluation of the source for further research, which is typically done by identifying the research question, methods of investigation, main conclusions, and possible implications of each cited source.

Example 1

McIvor, S. D. (1995). Aboriginal women's rights as "existing rights". *Canadian Woman Studies/Les Cahiers de la Femme 2*(3), 34–38.

This article seeks to define the extent of the civil and political rights returned to aboriginal women in the Constitution Act (1982), in its amendment in 1983, and in amendments to the Indian Act (1985). This legislation reverses prior laws that denied Indian status to aboriginal women who married non-aboriginal men. On the basis of the Supreme Court of Canada's interpretation of the Constitution Act in *R. v. Sparrow* (1991), McIvor argues that the Act recognizes fundamental human rights and existing aboriginal rights, granting to aboriginal women full participation in the aboriginal right to self-government.

Example 2

Waite, Linda J., et al. (1986). Nonfamily living and the erosion of traditional family orientations among young adults. *American Sociological Review, 51*(4), 541–554.

The authors, researchers at the Rand Corporation and Brown University, used data from the National Longitudinal Surveys of Young Women and Young Men to test their hypothesis that young adults who leave their parental home before marriage change their attitudes and expectations towards the traditional sex roles in a marriage. The findings show that the hypothesis is strongly supported in young females, but not in young males. Increasing the time away from parents augmented a sense of individualism and self-sufficiency. However, earlier studies demonstrate no significant changes in sex role attitudes towards marriage.

2. Composition Strategies for the Annotated Bibliography

In an annotated bibliography, each entry consists of a work's citation information followed by a short annotation with three to six sentences summarizing and evaluating the work, which is similar to a literature review except for the shorter length. An annotation should include most of the following:

- ✓ The main research question, purpose, and scope of the cited work;
- ✓ The methods used to address the research question;
- ✓ The major findings and conclusions of the work;
- ✓ The possible impacts of the work, such as the value and significance of the work as a contribution to the subject;
- ✓ Possible shortcomings, bias, or lack of evidence in the work;
- ✓ The authority or background of the author;
- ✓ Comparison or contrast of this work with another one you have cited;
- ✓ Your own impression and reflection of the work, such as how it fits into your research, how it helps you shape your argument, how it changed your opinion about your topic.

An annotated bibliography entry consists of two components: the citation and the annotation. The purpose of an annotated bibliography is to summarize, assess, and reflect the literature published on a particular topic and to inform the reader about the scope and quality of the cited sources. An annotated bibliography should not be confused with an abstract; the former always describes and critically evaluates a work (summary and evaluation), while the latter only gives a summary of the main points of a work. Writing an annotated bibliography can help you think critically about the content of the cited sources, their place within a field of study, and their relation to your own research and ideas. By reading and commenting on a variety of sources on a topic, you start to see what the issues are, what people are arguing about, and you will then be able to develop or improve your own point of view.

Part 2 Intensive Reading

Pre-reading questions:

✓ What is the possible definition of net-negative carbon economy?

✓ What could be the primary purpose of this research?

✓ Have you ever thought of carbon taxes and emission trading systems that treat carbon emission budget as a type of financial loan?

✓ Do you support the idea that people should pay for their carbon emissions and that people can use money to buy extra carbon emission budget?

Operationalizing the Net-Negative Carbon Economy[1]

1. Introduction

Delivering on the many national and corporate net-zero emission **pledges** will probably require the **gross** removal of atmospheric carbon dioxide (CO_2) on top of conventional emission reductions[6,7]. To achieve the Paris Agreement, global gross CO_2 removals will need to exceed gross residual emissions[4,8] after the middle of the century[1,9]. The resultant net-negative emissions **compensate** for the carbon debt[3] **accrued** by CO_2 emissions that overshoot the remaining carbon budget[10,11]. Carbon debt is projected to amount to roughly. the **equivalent** of 9 years of global emissions before the COVID-19 **pandemic** according to the 1.5 °C "middle of the road" scenario P3/S2 of the Intergovernmental Panel on Climate Change (IPCC)[1]. Such large-scale deployment of CDR is controversial mainly for the implied economic and technological risks[12–16] and environmental effects[17,18]; and because reliance

---

1 This paper is from Bednar, J., Obersteiner, M., Baklanov, A., Thomson, M., Wagner, F., Geden, O., Allen, M. & Hall, J. W. 2021. Operationalizing the net-negative carbon economy. *Nature*, *596*(7872): 377–383.

on CDR in **mitigation** scenarios often goes hand-in-hand with a **substantial** shift of the mitigation burden to future generations[19].

Here we would like to highlight a fundamental economic problem **associated with** the existing assessments of climate mitigation scenarios, aiming to inform international climate negotiations. Existing economic policy instruments for emission control are inadequate to **incentivize** a global transformation towards a net-negative carbon economy without imposing excessive **fiscal** burden from 2050 onwards. Currently **envisaged** carbon tax schemes would turn into public **subsidies** under net-negative emissions with potentially prohibitive fiscal implications[5]. Emission trading schemes (ETS), on the other hand, are presently designed to handle only positive emission caps. Negative emissions are merely treated as **offsets**, suggesting that CO_2 emissions from one point in time cannot be compensated by an equivalent quantity of negative emissions at another point in time, as required by most mitigation scenarios. Notably, we observe that pricing the **depletion** of the remaining carbon budget is fundamentally different to pricing overshot emissions after the depletion of the budget, which has profound implications for the consistent **earmarking** of accrued revenues from a price on CO_2.

We argue that establishing the responsibility of emitters for carbon debt is a **prerequisite** to ensuring **viable** net-negative carbon futures. Carbon debt could therefore be treated similar to financial debt, including interest payments on physical liabilities (that is, as a CRO) to internalize the inherent risks. On the basis of this idealized global carbon policy proposal motivated by the IPCC's mitigation scenarios, our numerical results address the shortcomings of the existing climate mitigation literature[20]. Despite the conceptual character of this study, we establish profound implications for national carbon policies, which are strongly influenced by the IPCC's global mitigation pathways in many high-emission countries[21].

2. Methods

Emission reductions induced by a CRO are quantified using a Hotelling-type optimization problem (see ref. 32 for an analytical solution of the model). A global social planner is tasked to implement emission reductions at minimum costs to meet a cumulative emission target. Exogenously given baseline emissions, that is, future emission paths based on "business-as-usual" climate policy assumptions, are reduced by a fraction to obtain net emissions.

The model is solved using the CONOPT solver in GAMS v.26.1. CONOPT is based on the generalized reduced gradient algorithm, one of the most robust and commonly applied methods for solving models with highly nonlinear objective functions or constraints.

3. Results

3.1 Carbon Pricing for Net-Negative Emissions

Integrated assessment models (IAMs) provide global carbon price paths that serve as a proxy for a wider range of cost-effective climate policy options to achieve specified greenhouse gas mitigation goals[9]. Such carbon prices typically increase exponentially with the interest rate as a consequence of the Hotelling rule, which defines the inter-temporally optimal extraction schedule and price of a non-renewable resource[22,23], such as the carbon budget. If understood as a global common, revenues generated from pricing its depletion should consistently add to public budgets, for instance to compensate for the associated welfare effects, which may be unfairly distributed across society. However, in scenarios in which the carbon budget is overshot and subsequently **replenished**, the budget can no longer be regarded as a non-renewable resource. In this case, the Hotelling rule lends itself to an "intertemporal interpretation" for carbon policy: Revenues from carbon pricing after the depletion of the budget can be invested at the market interest rate to finance net carbon removal later in the century. Because marginal **abatement** costs increase at the market interest rate, this calculation is exact under perfect foresight conditions—as assumed in most IAMs—if the retained funds purchase net-negative emissions at marginal costs later on. Because emitters pay for future net CDR through the carbon price, this intertemporal interpretation is **compatible** with the "polluter pays principle". The resultant intertemporal financial transfer thereby addresses concerns of intergenerational equity because public budgets in the near-term no longer **spuriously** benefit from pricing an already depleted resource, while future generations thereafter are forced to replenish the carbon budget through other sources, such as income, sales or payroll taxes. According to the "conventional interpretation" of the Hotelling rule, revenues from carbon pricing are merely treated as contemporaneous additions to public budgets, with no clear earmarking of accrued funds. Notably, as both approaches are simply interpretations of the same underlying carbon price paths, emitters also pay the discounted future costs of net emission removal in case of the conventional interpretation. However, in the absence of consistent earmarking, the financial viability of net CDR in the second half of the 21 century is highly doubtful[5], and intergenerational equity remains unaccounted for.

Unit 9 Carbon Economy

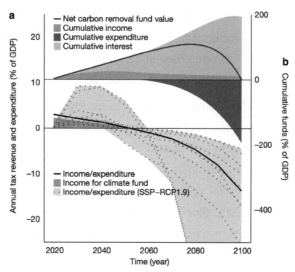

Figure 1   Idealized global tax scheme with net carbon removal fund. a, Bottom, public income and expenditure from a tax on net emissions expressed as a percentage of GDP. Hotelling-compatible (exponential) carbon prices from SSP–RCP 1.9 scenarios are multiplied by net emissions and divided by GDP (grey dashed lines). An idealized income/expenditure curve (black solid line) was derived from these scenarios using a strictly exponential median carbon price, median net emissions and GDP. Instead of reserving 100% of tax revenues after depletion of the carbon budget, we assert that a fraction $\varphi = 0.76$ of revenues is earmarked for net carbon removal, from 2020 onwards. This share of income (■) would need to be accrued into a net carbon removal fund invested at the market rate of interest to account for later expenditure when net emissions turn negative. See Methods for a definition of φ. b, Top, cumulative payments into the net carbon removal fund (■) and interest (■) in theory pay exactly for cumulative tax expenditure (■), so that the net value of the fund (black solid lines) gets exhausted as the warming target is achieved in 2100.

To operationalize a future net-negative carbon economy, carbon tax revenues could be partially retained and transferred over generations to finance net CDR in the style of a nuclear **decommissioning** trust fund or a sovereign wealth fund. The value of such a global net carbon removal fund is potentially enormous, yet in the range of comparable funds, peaking at roughly 100% of global gross domestic product (GDP) in the median of the Shared Socioeconomic Pathway (SSP) scenarios that are compatible with Representative Concentration Pathway 1.9 (RCP 1.9)[24] (Figure 1). For comparison, Norway's large sovereign wealth fund has passed 250% of national GDP[25]. Given this order of magnitude, intermediate investment **portfolios** could be a game changer to lift CDR out of the pilot phase even before pay-out of the fund. However, protecting financial resources from diversion for other purposes as political environments change, or as public finances become stressed, will surely be extremely challenging. For instance, sovereign borrowing to cushion the effects of the

COVID-19 pandemic meant that by the end of 2020 the debt-to-GDP ratio of governments according to the Organisation for Economic Co-operation and Development had increased by about 13.4 percentage points[26]. Severe crises in the future could induce considerable pressure for governments to appropriate savings originally reserved for net CDR.

The success of a net CDR fund also depends on the appropriate choice of several inherently uncertain parameters, including future abatement costs. If costs and other socioeconomic parameters are not estimated in line with the precautionary principle, or if regulators **are reluctant to** adequately reflect future carbon removal in near-term price instruments, insufficient financial resources would be collected as observed for nuclear decommissioning[27]. Because the carbon debt and associated risks would be mutualized by a net CDR fund, missing financial resources would need to be replenished by public budgets.

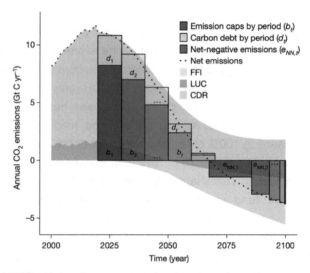

Figure 2 Idealized ETS with intertemporal trade of carbon debt. Illustrative 2 °C pathway with gross carbon emissions from FFI, LUC and non-specified sources of CDR including the schematic architecture of idealized global intertemporal emission trading. ETS emission caps b_t are obtained by distributing the carbon budget in tranches over consecutive periods. The amount by which emission caps b_t are exceeded by net emissions is conceptualized as "carbon debt" (d_t). In this idealized illustration, d_t is compensated later by corresponding net-negative emissions ($e_{NN,t}$) such that $d_t = -e_{NN,t}$. In a conventional ETS, emission caps would be set to $b_t + d_t$, and $e_{NN,t}$ would have to be incentivized by public subsidies. d_t, b_t and $e_{NN,t}$ (in which t indicates 1, 2 and so on) are simplified discrete analogues of the continuous variables $d_{(t)}$, $b_{(t)}$ and $e_{NN(t)}$, respectively, which are described in the Methods. Historical emissions are from a previously published study[39].

3.2 Dynamic Emission Trading

Emission trading with fully liberalized banking and borrowing of allowances can be regarded as a response to these concerns. Decentralized decision-making and price determination in a competitive market is believed to improve efficiency by leveraging the ability of carbon markets to determine cost-effective time paths of mitigation[28]. In an idealized global scheme, the remaining carbon budget would be distributed over time resulting in positive emission caps for consecutive auctioning periods. Emitters would decide in each period what fraction of their CO_2 emissions to compensate for by allowances and how much carbon debt to generate for compensation by future allowances—or future CDR in the absence of a positive emission cap. Effectively, emitters generating carbon debt would remain liable for the timing and delivery of net-negative emissions (Figure 2) and can therefore balance present against future abatement based on individual expectations, such as those concerning technological breakthroughs. Stranded assets can be avoided by harmonizing abatement investments with natural renewal cycles of capital; and fluctuations in the business cycle can be addressed. Fixed price schedules under a carbon tax suggest lower costs for hedging risks related to the long-run costs of negative emissions and low-carbon investments. However, increased intertemporal flexibility in emission trading stabilizes the price—which reflects discounted future marginal abatement costs—compared with currently implemented ETS with no intertemporal trade of allowances[29,30]. At least in principle, this ETS arrangement enables emitters to develop optimal investments over longer time horizons, increasing the dynamic efficiency of emission trading. Although emission caps can be over-shot, the quantity of cumulative emissions remains exactly controlled under an ETS with intertemporal trade of carbon debt, which is, more generally, the main advantage of cap-and-trade schemes compared with carbon taxes. If caps no longer directly control emission reductions, they can be set to equitably distribute ETS revenues over time. However, as the carbon budget diminishes rapidly—the 1.5 °C compatible budget is projected to become depleted roughly within the next 10 years[1]—the importance of carbon debt management increasingly outweighs the requirement of an adequate temporal distribution of the remaining carbon budget.

Privately managed carbon debt within an ETS also has considerable drawbacks: the enforcement of carbon debt, assessment of creditworthiness of emitters, the potential for speculation on future softening of emission targets and subsequent deferral of mitigation (time inconsistency)—which is stronger the lower the **solvency** of emitters (adverse selection)—and the resultant incentive to lobby for cancellation of carbon debt (moral hazard) are crucial obstacles that explain why such intertemporal mechanisms are severely restricted in currently implemented ETS[28]. Moreover, intertemporal trade of carbon debt by means of forward and future markets trading negative emissions over potentially long periods at a fixed price **is**

perceived as infeasible, given the deep uncertainty in the parameters guiding a large-scale CDR rollout[31].

3.3 Carbon Removal Obligations

Intertemporal emission trading would necessarily come at the cost of considerable regulation to address these drawbacks. We argue, however, that practices from the financial industry and monetary policy could be leveraged to reduce risks and adaptively balance potentially competing interests of economic development and climate mitigation by treating carbon debt in a similar manner to a financial debt obligation, and thereby invoking an interest on carbon debt. Economic growth, aggregate demand for carbon debt and individual financial ratings of debtors would define a general base rate, individual mark-ups, term structures and debt maturities. To assure its physical conservation and exert control over its aggregate level, carbon debt would initially be issued at the base rate by managing authorities—for example, central banks—to which commercial banks would be held liable in case of insolvent debtors. Commercial banks, or their equivalents, would issue debt to emitters and, assisted by rating agencies, assess and hedge their insolvency risk by determining individual mark-ups on the base rate. Carbon debt would enter the balance sheets of firms as a physical **liability** in tonnes (t) CO_2—a carbon removal obligation, for which interest payments would be due. This chain of legal liabilities across layers of public and private actors reduces the moral hazard that governments would ultimately pick up the bill for net emission removal, and limit the issuance of CROs to debtors who are reluctant to fulfil their (interest) obligations. Individual interest mark-ups would also balance the push of the market for adverse selection and incentivize a debt transfer from agents losing ground under stringent climate policy to low-risk agents; or lead to more near-term abatement (see below) if risks are deemed non-insurable. The rate controls the volatility of the carbon price and therefore directly affects the price–risk costs of scheduled abatement investments. More generally, interest and debt maturities would need to reflect the speculative nature of CDR, leading to short—but potentially renewable—repayment terms and elevated rates in the near-term. A concrete phase-in scenario of CROs in the ETS of the European Union and beyond is described in Box 1.

Box 1 Hypothetical implementation of a CRO-ETS in the European Union and elsewhere

The total carbon debt of the European Union (EU) amounts to 22.5 Gt CO_2 already by 2050, or roughly 7 years[40] of present CO_2 emissions, according to the 1.5 °C-compatible mitigation scenarios LIFE and TECH from the European Commission[41]. [All numbers provided here include the UK and emissions from land use, land-use change and forestry (LULUCF). Carbon debt for compensation in the 2050–2100 period is determined by subtracting the 2018–2100 budget from the higher 2018–2050 budget. Budgets are average values from the 1.5 °C TECH and LIFE scenarios. Annual emissions in 2018 amount to 3.14 Gt CO_2 (ref. 42).] In line with the EU's net-zero greenhouse gas target for 2050, CO_2 emissions must turn net-negative already by 2043[43]. Despite the lack of any adequate mechanism to do so, sectors currently covered by the EU ETS will therefore need to deliver 50 Mt CO_2-equivalent net greenhouse gas removal by 2050 in the more-ambitious 1.5 °C TECH scenario. CDR volumes are expected to increase after 2050 in line with the economy-wide net-negative greenhouse gas emissions objective already enshrined in the EU Climate Law. Beyond 2050, negative caps in the EU ETS[44] will require considerable public funding, which is likely to obstruct the implementation of ambitious net-CO_2 removal targets. With CROs in place, overburdening of public budgets can be avoided.

We envision the following scenario. With the revision for phase IV of the EU ETS initiated in 2021, the linear reduction factor of emission caps is brought in line with the European Commission's long-term cumulative net-CO_2 target of 26 Gt CO_2 (for the 2018–2100 period; 1.5 °C TECH and LIFE scenarios combined, including net removals), while the scheme is gradually extended to full sectoral coverage. The implied increase of the reduction factor is balanced by a simultaneous phase-in of CROs, and carbon debt management is added to the portfolio of the European Central Bank. The European Central Bank issues debt to commercial banks at a base rate, which in turn issue debt to firms that participate in the EU ETS, charging individual mark-ups depending on the financial ratings of those firms. To be able to repay the European Central Bank despite defaulting debtors, banks would have to develop their own CDR portfolios. The resultant increase in CDR supply and expertise in assessing carbon debt risks induces the development of a wider variety of CRO products, with different maturities. For securing the long-term supply with fossil fuels in hard-to-transition sectors, such as long-haul aviation and shipping[45,46], large energy firms would be incentivized to develop CDR for counterbalancing residual emissions[47]. Alternatively, accrued carbon debt would be transferred to other agents, such as wealthy—potentially non-EU—tech firms, with presumably low credit risk and a proclivity for mitigation technology[48]. For CDR suppliers[49,50], CROs are the basis of a business case and, because negative emissions do not have to be delivered immediately, CROs simultaneously act as loans to finance development.

It may be that the global implementation of a CRO-ETS under the United Nations Framework Convention on Climate Change, as conceptualized in this article, is not realistic for the time being. However, given the potential opportunities for the financial sector and CDR investors, as well as the implications for public finance, non-EU countries or regions with ambitious climate targets and (pilot) ETS schemes, such as China, Japan,

> South Korea, Canada or America[51], would probably be under pressure to liberalize intertemporal trade of carbon debt and thereby establish responsibility for overshot emissions. The EU-wide rollout would therefore be followed by attempts to actively influence regulation globally (for example, through "regulatory export"[52]) and subsequent linkage with other national and regional schemes[53].

For intertemporal emission trading to work efficiently—for instance to reduce issues of time inconsistency and price volatility—emission caps would need to be credibly announced as early as possible. As a consequence, regulators would lose the flexibility of adapting caps as new knowledge concerning the Earth system becomes available. In an idealized global scheme, emission caps need to exactly reflect the remaining carbon budget. Budget uncertainties related to the issuing of carbon debt, similar to those of permafrost thaw after a temperature overshoot[2], could be hedged by collecting risk funds through base rate payments and by incentivizing more-ambitious emission reductions to minimize the risk of climate feedback effects (see below). Such uncertainties should remain manageable by risk reserves, allowing for the budget to be replenished by drawing on risk funds rather than requiring a downwards correction of scheduled emissions caps. In the best case, uncertainties and base rates would decrease over time as updated estimates of the carbon budget converge to a value within the expected range of the previously announced budget. However, new findings might realistically also lead to exceeding of the abilities of risk management, requiring a combined effort of future generations to counter potentially abrupt climate change. Management of physical risks therefore remains limited to what is presently perceivable and realistically quantifiable.

3.4 Climate Mitigation Under Carbon Debt

In IAMs, abatement costs are discounted at the market interest rate, implying a cost advantage for abatement in the distant future compared with near-term decarbonization in terms of net present value. The interest rate is therefore a key driver of carbon debt accrual in IAMs[32,33]. This "discounting effect" is balanced by imposing interest on carbon debt. Longer CRO maturities indicate lower net present costs for CDR. Simultaneously, carbon debt interest is paid over a longer period, compensating for these gains. When the market rate of interest and the carbon debt interest rate (r_d) coincide, the gains from discounting are balanced exactly, as we analytically show in the Methods. In Figure 3, we illustrate the sensitivity of 2 °C-compatible global mitigation pathways to interest on carbon debt, with rates constant over the 2020–2100 period ranging from $r_d = 0$ to $r_d = 0.08$. For each rate, 13 scenarios are computed based on different SSPs and IAMs that are used to calibrate the marginal abatement cost curves of our model.

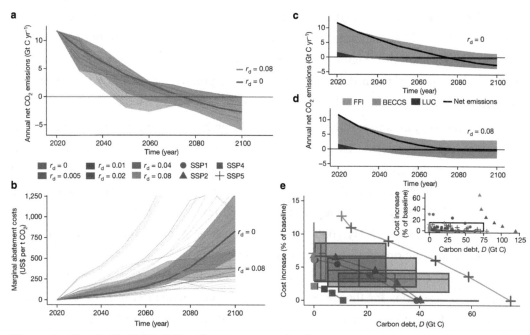

Figure 3 The 2 °C (RCP 2.6) mitigation scenarios for a range of interest rates on carbon debt. a, Net CO_2 emissions of all scenarios with $r_d = 0$ (■) and $r_d = 0.08$ (■), including geometric median paths (bold solid lines) and minimum to maximum ranges (shaded areas). b, Marginal abatement costs of scenarios with $r_d = 0$ (■) and $r_d = 0.08$ (■). Bold solid lines indicate geometric medians, shaded areas indicate 25%–75% interquartile ranges. c, d, Geometric median net emissions as in a, including gross emissions from FFI, BECCS and LUC. c, $r_d = 0$. d, $r_d = 0.08$. e, Total discounted abatement costs (net present value, including interest costs) expressed as a percentage cost increase compared with the baseline ($r_d = 0$) are shown as function of total carbon debt D. The boxes indicate the 25%–75% interquartile ranges around the median values of the costs and D. Symbols linked by grey solid lines indicate the medians grouped by SSP. The entire dataset is shown in the top right corner, in which each scenario is reflected by a symbol, grouped by SSP (symbol type) and r_d (shade color).

For comparison, only the two extreme cases—$r_d = 0$ and $r_d = 0.08$—are illustrated in Figure 3a–d. Notably, when $r_d = 0.08$, the cumulative emission target is achieved without the accrual of carbon debt in the median path (Figure 3d), suggesting that emissions remain at the net-zero level once achieved. This is accomplished by the contemporaneous compensation of residual CO_2 from fossil fuels and industry (FFI) with negative emissions from bioenergy with carbon capture and storage (BECCS) and land-use change (LUC). Complete decarbonization of FFI emissions is, however, not cost-effective owing to the high marginal costs of emission reductions from hard-to-abate sectors. Notably, net-negative emissions of individual scenarios in Figure 3a turn back to zero before 2100, thereby minimizing the "problem of phasedown"[34].

With reduced reliance on net-negative emissions, marginal costs are higher in the near-term due to the more-rapid reduction in FFI emissions and increase in BECCS, but considerably lower in 2100 (Figure 3b). Figure 3e shows a reduction in the total carbon debt D as r_d is gradually increased. Carbon debt risks are therefore greatly reduced at a moderate cost increase of below 12.5% in more than 75% of scenarios in which $r_d > 0.02$.

A similar analysis was performed for the 1.5 °C global warming target; however, direct air capture and storage (DACS) is added to the mitigation technology mix, represented by six different DACS-specific marginal abatement cost curves with low, medium and high costs as well as low- and high-capacity limits. This results in a set of 78 scenarios for each rate r_d. Not surprisingly, the higher the potential for DACS to be deployed, the larger the level of D when $r_d = 0$. By contrast, when interest is invoked, this discounting effect is reversed and scenarios with large-capacity low-cost DACS simultaneously exhibit the lowest levels of D. The pathways in Figure 4 show baseline (Figure 4a, b) and reduced D (Figure 4c, d) scenarios for those scenarios that achieve a reduction in D of at least 30% compared with their associated baselines. For illustration, we interpret the CRO-ETS baseline scenarios, in which $r_d = 0$, as conventional ETS scenarios because both schemes are theoretically equivalent in terms of the resultant emission profiles while they imply a qualitatively different timing of financial flows.

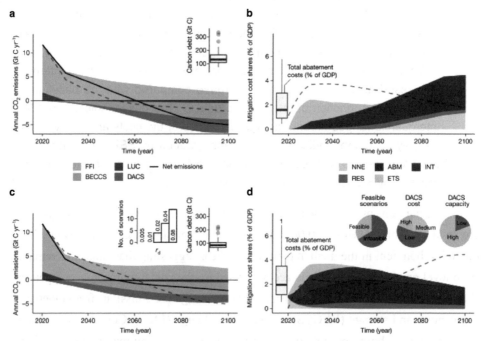

Figure 4   The 1.5 °C (RCP 1.9) pathways under a conventional ETS or a CRO-ETS. a, b, A conventional ETS is used. c, d, A CRO-ETS is used. a, c, Geometric median net emissions (solid line) and gross emissions from FFI, BECCS,

LUC and DACS. Net emissions from a are also displayed in c (dashed line) and vice versa. The total carbon debt D is shown as a box-and-whiskers plot. Boxes indicate the 25%–75% interquartile range around the median values (bold line), whiskers indicate minimum to maximum ranges, points mark the outliers. b, d, Annual mitigation costs as a percentage of GDP, including the share of average abatement costs attributed to emission reductions (ABM), to the compensation of residual emissions by CDR (RES) and to net-negative emissions (NNE), as well as expenditures for allowances (ETS) and interest costs (INT). Total mitigation costs (that is, ABM + RES + NNE + ETS + INT) from d are also displayed in b (dashed line) and vice versa. Box-and-whiskers plots show the total discounted abatement costs (that is, ABM + RES + NNE) as a percentage of GDP, the number above the chart indicates out-of-range outliers. Pie charts in d summarize the properties of the underlying set of scenarios (see Methods). The distribution of r_d in CRO-ETS scenarios is depicted in c.

Despite the earlier increase in DACS in Figure 4c, causing emissions to turn net zero around 2050, an emission overshoot appears to be inevitable if warming is to be limited to 1.5 °C. Remaining net-negative emissions might cause problems of phasedown in 2100, unless CRO maturities are further extended to enable a smooth transition to net-zero emissions; or more net-negative emissions are needed to stabilize the climate in the twenty-second century[35]. Therefore, the median D is equal to roughly 7 years of global net emissions in 2019 in Figure 4c. Yet, the role of CDR changes considerably: Without considering risks, CDR seems to justify late-century compensation of carbon debt. In this case, the median D is equivalent to about 11 years of 2019 global net emissions, with compensation starting roughly 10 years later in Figure 4a. However, when risks are accounted for by imposing interest, CDR supports a rapid decrease in net emissions by balancing the residual emissions. Controversially, the availability of cheap and large-scale CDR options, such as DACS, is key in 1.5 °C scenarios with reduced reliance on the accrual of carbon debt. As illustrated by the pie charts in Figure 4d, the share of high-capacity DACS scenarios among feasible scenarios with respect to the 30% reduction requirement grows to 81% (50% in the underlying set) and the share of low-cost DACS scenarios to 54% (33% in the underlying set). Should CDR not become readily available as asserted in IAMs[36,37,38], this would be reflected in an elevated carbon debt interest rate, incentivizing emission reductions provided by other sources, such as the replacement of fossil fuel with renewable energy sources in hard-to-abate sectors—even if this leads to much higher costs.

3.5 Effect on Financial Flows Over Time

Figure 4, moreover, illustrates the distribution of annual mitigation cost shares, including investments in emission reductions and negative emissions and the financial flows associated with ETS allowances and interest for CROs. The share of abatement costs for emission reductions (ABM), negative emissions compensating for residual emissions (RES) and net-negative emissions (NNE) incurred in the near-versus the long-term increases with larger levels of r_d (compare Figure 4d to Extended Data Figures 3d–5d). Here, CROs with interest induce a more equitable temporal distribution of these cost items, in sum peaking at 2.4% in Figure 4d compared to 4.5% of GDP in Figure 4b. This is partly because the CRO-ETS requires carbon debtors to reserve financial resources early in the century, and such funds earn interest until they are spent for net-negative emissions. By contrast, net-negative emissions expenditures in Figure 4b are incurred at the time of net carbon removal and would need to be funded by public sources in the absence of intertemporal financial transfers. Note that here we show average abatement costs. If marginal costs are paid by incentivizing net CDR on a market, public expenditures are much higher (for comparison, see Figure 1). Pricing overshot emissions under a conventional ETS, moreover, implies much larger revenues ("ETS") than under the CRO-ETS, where emission caps reflect exactly the remaining carbon budget. Median total discounted abatement costs, excluding ETS costs and interest costs ("INT"), increase from 1.6% to 2.0% of GDP when interest is invoked within the CRO-ETS. Median interest costs in these scenarios are substantial, peaking at above 1.3% of GDP, and 0.4% to 1.5% in Extended Data Figures 3–5. These numbers are, however, highly uncertain and will need to be determined considering the viability and scalability of near-term CDR options and other emission reduction technologies.

Enlarging IAM CDR portfolios to reduce technological risks and environmental effects would probably lead to further burdening of future generations in scenarios if CDR remains primarily a motivation for reducing net present costs by accrual of carbon debt. This is especially problematic if such results trickle down through the IPCC and international climate negotiations into national target setting because no viable mechanisms for the repayment of carbon debt have entered the policy debate at the moment. Simultaneously, mitigation pathways with reduced carbon debt heavily rely on CDR, requiring that risks be appropriately managed. Similar pathways result from lowering the market interest rate in IAMs[32] or from adequately setting intermediate climate targets or constraints on net emissions[20]. However, such measures would individually not resolve the more profound issue of finance of net-negative emissions discussed here.

4. Conclusion

In view of the rapid depletion of the global carbon budget, CROs seem to be indispensable for any robust climate mitigation framework. CROs imply a paradigm shift from pricing the permanent to pricing the temporary storage of CO_2 in the atmosphere, with carbon debtors being responsible for delivering net CDR. The implied flexibility for emitters also bears the largest drawback of intertemporal emission trading, if public bailout of carbon debtors becomes necessary. To minimize such risks, the "conservation of carbon debt" needs to take top priority by controlling the total amount of carbon debt and by establishing liability across several layers of actors. Risk management under a CRO-ETS relies on imposing interest on carbon debt. For higher and risk-adjusted carbon debt interest rates, net-negative emission investments no longer benefit from net present cost gains when mitigation is deferred to the distant future. By implication, CDR under a CRO-ETS will need to prove its viability compared with conventional options for the reduction of emissions already in the near-term. This will promote bottom-up CDR market development with the accompanying benefits of price discovery, earlier technological learning, testing of scalability and identification of socio-environmental co-benefits and hazards, and ultimately, eliminating the uncertainties surrounding CDR.

(Scan the QR code to access the list of references.)

Words and Expressions

pledge	*n.*	a solemn promise or undertaking
gross	*adj.*	without deduction of tax or other contributions; total
compensate	*v.*	to give (someone) something, typically money, in recognition of loss or injury
accrue	*v.*	to accumulate or receive (payments or benefits) over time
equivalent	*n.*	a thing, amount, word, etc. that is equal in value, amount, function, meaning, etc. to something else
pandemic	*n.*	a widespread occurrence of an infectious disease over a whole country or the world at a particular time
mitigation	*n.*	the action of reducing the severity, seriousness, or painfulness of something
substantial	*adj.*	of considerable importance, size, or worth
associate with		to involve or connect with
incentivize	*v.*	to motivate or encourage somebody to do something
fiscal	*adj.*	relating to government revenue, especially taxes
envisage	*v.*	to contemplate or conceive of as a possibility or a desirable future event
subsidy	*n.*	a sum of money granted by the state or a public body

offset	n.	a consideration or amount that diminishes or balances the effect of an opposite one
depletion	n.	reduction in the number or quantity of something
earmark	v.	to designate (funds or resources) for a particular purpose
prerequisite	n.	a thing that is required as a prior condition for something else to happen or exist
viable	adj.	capable of working successfully; feasible
replenish	v.	to restore to a former level or condition
abatement	n.	(often in legal use) the ending, reduction, or lessening of something
compatible	adj.	able to exist or occur together without problems or conflict
spuriously	adv.	not being what it purports to be; being false or fake
decommission	v.	to withdraw (something, especially weapons or military equipment) from service
portfolio	n.	a range of investments held by a person or organization
be reluctant to		to be unwilling, hesitant or disinclined to
solvency	n.	the possession of assets in excess of liabilities; ability to pay one's debts
be perceived as		to be regarded or interpreted as
liability	n.	the state of being legally responsible for something

Reflections and Practice

❶ Read the text and answer the following questions.

1. What requires gross removal of atmospheric carbon dioxide (CO_2) on top of conventional emission reductions?
2. What is the fundamental economic problem associated with the existing assessments of climate mitigation scenarios?
3. What do the authors think is a prerequisite to ensuring viable net-negative carbon futures?
4. What is one of the most robust and commonly applied methods for optimizing nonlinear models?
5. Why do the authors think that establishing the responsibility of emitters for carbon debt is a prerequisite to ensuring viable net-negative carbon futures?

6. What does the intertemporal financial transfer address?
7. What is the perceived benefit of decentralized decision-making and pricing for carbon mitigation?
8. In the authors' opinion, what is indispensable for a robust climate mitigation framework?

II Discuss the following questions with your partner.

1. Is it necessary to limit global warming to 1.5°C? Why or why not?
2. Why are net-negative emissions necessary?
3. What are the economic and technological risks by conducting carbon dioxide removal?
4. What are the economic and technological benefits by conducting carbon dioxide removal?
5. Should future generations take more mitigation burden for carbon dioxide than the current generation? Why or why not?
6. Do you think that a country can benefit more if it takes a pioneering role in conducting carbon dioxide removal? Why?

III Paraphrase the following sentences.

1. Delivering on the many national and corporate net-zero emission pledges will probably require the gross removal of atmospheric carbon dioxide (CO_2) on top of conventional emission reductions.
2. Existing economic policy instruments for emission control are inadequate to incentivize a global transformation towards a net-negative carbon economy without imposing excessive fiscal burden from 2050 onwards.
3. Negative emissions are merely treated as offsets, suggesting that CO_2 emissions from one point in time cannot be compensated by an equivalent quantity of negative emissions at another point in time, as required by most mitigation scenarios.
4. Establishing the responsibility of emitters for carbon debt is a prerequisite to ensuring viable net-negative carbon futures. Carbon debt could therefore be treated similar to financial debt, including interest payments on physical liabilities (that is, as a CRO) to internalize the inherent risks.
5. To operationalize a future net-negative carbon economy, carbon tax revenues could be partially retained and transferred over generations to finance net CDR in the style of a nuclear decommissioning trust fund or a sovereign wealth fund. The value of

such a global net carbon removal fund is potentially enormous.

IV Write an annotated bibliography for the text.

V Write an outline for the text following the structure below.

1. **Research Background**
   The remaining carbon budget for _____ will probably be exhausted within this decade. To achieve the Paris Agreement, global gross CO_2 removals will need to exceed gross residual emissions after the middle of the century. Therefore, _____ will be needed in the future.

2. **Research Question**
   How to devise _____ to guarantee potentially very costly net carbon dioxide removal?

3. **Research Objective**
   To propose intertemporal instruments for providing the basis for widely applied _____ to finance a net-negative carbon economy.

4. **Methods**
   To investigate an idealized market approach to incentivize the repayment of previously accrued carbon debt by establishing the responsibility of emitters for the net removal of carbon dioxide through _____.

5. **Major Results and Findings**
   Establishing the responsibility of _____ is a prerequisite to ensuring viable net-negative carbon futures. Carbon debt could therefore be treated similar to _____, including interest payments on physical liabilities to internalize the inherent risks.

6. **Conclusion**
   _____ need to be an indispensable part for any robust climate mitigation framework.

VI Write a summary for the text in 150–200 words.

Unit 9　Carbon Economy

Part 3　Further Reading

The Effects of Assigning Liability for CO_2 Removal[1]

Abstract

The 2015 Paris Agreement on climate change set a goal of limiting global warming to 2 °C, or preferably 1.5 °C, above preindustrial levels. Achieving either of these targets is expected to require not just reductions in carbon emissions, but also technologies that remove carbon dioxide from the atmosphere. Bednar et al. explore policy mechanisms that support the development and implementation of such technologies. They propose an emission trading scheme that provides permits for emissions consistent with a specific global warming goal, but that allows further emissions as long as the emitter commits to removing the extra carbon later on. The authors argue that emitters should be charged for the temporary "storage" of this carbon in the atmosphere. They show that this would lead both to earlier reductions in carbon emissions (decarbonization) and to earlier application of CO_2 removal technologies than would otherwise occur.

Keywords: climate change, global warming, liability, carbon emission, carbon removal

 Reflections and Practice

Read the full article and answer the following questions.

1. What is the purpose of this article?
2. What are the key findings?
3. What kinds of technologies will be needed to remove atmospheric carbon dioxide?
4. What arguments are used to support the opinion that we can limit the pace of decarbonization today?
5. What are the implications of the key findings on policy making?

1　This paper is from Stainforth, D. A. 2021. The effects of assigning liability for CO_2 removal. *Nature*, *596*(7872): 346–347.

Unit 10
Artificial Intelligence (AI)

 Learning Objectives

- Get to know different types of English literature;

- Get familiar with some literature databases;

- Write an effective literature review.

Part 1 Reading Skills and Strategies

Selecting Different Types of Literature and Writing an Effective Literature Review

1. Selecting Different Types of Literature for Reading

The focus of this book is literature reading and reviewing. It is necessary to conclude here with the skill of literature reviewing for the sake of completeness. For graduate students, the outcome of reading is to write a literature review, either as a review article or as a section of a thesis or dissertation.

In the reading texts of the first nine units, we have mainly selected scholarly journal articles of different disciplines. However, the literature includes not only scholarly journal articles, but also archival materials, artifacts, autobiographies (books), correspondence, diaries, government documents, interviews, letters, memoirs (books), newspapers, photographs, works of arts (music, painting, poetry, etc.), which are called primary source materials. The research papers of scholarly magazines are often called secondary source materials, which include biographies, books, book reviews, conference proceedings, dissertations, editorials, literary criticism, magazine articles, textbooks, in which the primary source material is analyzed, evaluated and interpreted. The third type is tertiary source materials—summaries or condensed versions of primary and secondary source materials such as abstracts, bibliographies, chronologies, directories, encyclopedias, guidebooks, manuals, indexes, etc.

In this unit, we will talk about how to start reading various types of literature and which ones should be read first.

1) Original academic journals

Among the literature types, academic journals and papers attract the most attention from researchers. Graduate students are often suggested to identify the top academic journals in their fields and keep tracking them for all the latest research findings, or specifically on a research topic they are academically interested in.

However, few students have the idea that there are other different types of academic journals except for the original articles, say, letters/brief reports, review/perspective articles, editorials, correspondence, or communications, whose titles are narrative or a question, whose abstracts are descriptive, informative, or informative-descriptive, and which usually follow an aim/problem-method-results-conclusion format. All of these types are worth reading when you start work on your thesis or dissertation.

In fact, according to our personal experience, there is a sequential order to consult various documents. Let's introduce the different types of academic papers one by one in the general order of viewing.

(1) Review/perspective articles

Aside from the academic journal papers, review articles or opinion/perspective articles are also worth reading. Although these articles are secondary literature which is based on previously published work, this does not mean these types of articles are not important. These articles should often be read first, because they are probably written by a leader in a certain field, covering the latest developments in this field and can help you quickly know the development trend of the subject matter you are engaged in.

(2) Letters/brief reports

A letter refers to a short academic report, which includes two types: the review letter and the research letter. A review letter is a review of a paper published in a journal. A research letter is a short research paper with fewer words, usually around 800 words. However, the valuable literature is not about the length. The paper on Watson's discovery of the double-helix structure of DNA was only one page. Occasionally, some researchers might submit a paper and hope it will be published as an original article, but might be requested by a journal to revise it as a brief report.

(3) Editorials

Editorials are also one of the types of articles that can be quoted. According to statistics, among the papers published in the *Journal of Virology*, the majority of them are original articles (more than 40,000 papers have been published in total), and there are also many notes, as well as some reviews, letters, etc.

(4) Correspondence and communication

Correspondence is like a letter, such as expressing personal views and opinions on articles originally published in journals, or talking about the main idea in the research. It is just a few paragraphs in length. However, a communication looks like a long article that requires systematic research. And it is also required to be novel and forward-looking, so that innovative research can be published as soon as possible. However, in contrast to the original research papers, the amount of data in communication articles is somewhat less than that of long articles.

In a word, all the above four types of articles are worth reading for getting the latest trends of development in various disciplines. Never ignore any types of them!

2) Archival materials

Both the museum and the library have acquired archival materials throughout their history, especially manuscripts, often in the form of large collections. Such materials, often collected in the past simultaneously with related objects, have effectively complemented the many object-based collections. Today, original material is acquired in the areas of the history of science, technology, medicine and industry without specialist repository. Tracing back to the source is a rigorous academic attitude. As a scholar, archival materials cannot be ignored.

3) Artifacts

Artifacts are not only important for archaeological and historical research, but also very important for the literature reviews in the field of summarizing software artifacts. For example, the newspaper *Summarizing Software Artifacts: A Literature Review* focuses on error reports, source code, mailing lists and developers' discussion of artifacts from January 2010 to April 2016. Many summary technologies, approaches and tools were proposed to meet the ongoing needs of developers to understand these problems and improve software performance and excellence at hand. Later, the above-mentioned artifacts contained organized and unorganized data. At the same time, researchers used different machine learning and data mining technologies to generate summaries. Therefore, the newspaper like *Summarizing Software Artifacts: A Literature Review* first intends to provide a general view on the current situation, describing artifacts, ways of abstracting, and types of common parts of the experimental process shared among these artifacts. For research in deep learning, which is very popular nowadays, these artifacts reviews are also very import for reading.

4) Autobiographies and memoirs

Both the autobiography and the memoir belong to the primary source material. The difference between the autobiography and the memoir lies in their emphasis and narrative techniques. An autobiography is mainly about the authors' own life stories and works, so the first person is generally used. And for a memoir, the third person is used. The ancients often wrote a preface after writing a book, and some of them were autobiographies. For example, Sima Qian's "*Records of the Historians*: Preface of the Grand Historian" is autobiographical. It's quoted by countless literati and writers. Autobiographical works take many forms, ranging from private writing (including letters, diaries, notes and memoirs) that is not necessarily published before death to formal autobiography. The outstanding examples of this genre include St. Augustine's *Confessions* and Nabakov's *Memoirs*, which is also quoted by numerous Western scholars.

Memoirs are true portrayals of a period of history, the indispensable materials for the comprehensive study of dynastic history and academic achievements which are very valuable for reading. In the fourth century BC, Keseno, a student of the ancient Greek philosopher Socrates, wrote a book, which completely and faithfully recorded Socrates' words and experiences. The book is called *Memoirs*. This is probably the first book in history to be titled as a memoir. In China, *The Analects of Confucius* is also a work with the nature of memoir. Sima Qian, a historian of the Western Han Dynasty, can be regarded as a memoir. In modern and contemporary times, the style of the memoir has developed greatly. The readers will always remember the great people who made outstanding contributions to the people. Therefore, those who worked with and contacted these great people wrote memoirs to express their feelings of respect, and also contributed valuable literature to future generations.

2. Some Literature Databases

To help you have a smooth start of retrieving your literature tour, here we provide some literature databases.

Table 10.1 Some retrieval databases recommended

Comprehensive Retrieval Databases
Google Scholar
Elsevier
SCI (Science Citation Index)
SSCI (Social Science Citation Index)
Web of Science
A&HCI (Arts & Humanities Citation Index)
IEEE
Scopus
ScienceDirect
SpringerLink
Ebsco

These databases cover most of the research areas, of which we introduce some of them.

The first one is Scopus. Scopus database is a scientific research retrieval analysis and discipline planning management database launched by Elsevier Publishing House. It is a peer-reviewed journal abstracts and citations database, including:

✓ Nearly 78 million records (updated daily, about 10,000 entries/day);

✓ 24,000+ journals from more than 5,000 international publishers, including more than 20,000 peer-reviewed journals;

✓ 5,527 golden open access journals, more than 9 million pieces of open access literature;

✓ 8,075 journals in editing (obtained 1–4 months before publication);

✓ 23,0000+ books;

✓ More than 9.8 million conference papers;

✓ More than 44 million international patents;

✓ More than 600 Chinese peer-reviewed core journals (including those under the China Outstanding Journals Program).

The Scopus database includes information about more than 7,000 institutions and more than 30 million scholars, providing each scholar with an independent Scopus Author ID. It supports one click generation of author's literature output analysis and citation report, and can flexibly choose to remove self-citation and book citation. Researchers can quickly obtain the characteristics of scientific research output of individuals, peers and institutions, and explore potential partners.

The second one is ScienceDirect. Elsevier's leading information solution empowers over 15 million researchers, teachers, students, healthcare professionals and information professionals around the world to ensure that their work has more impact. ScienceDirect combines authoritative, full-text scientific, technical and health publications with smart, intuitive functionality so users can stay more informed and can work more effectively and efficiently. With over 14 million publications from over 3,800 journals and more than 35,000 books from Elsevier, their imprints and their society partners, ScienceDireect empowers smarter research.

The third one is SpringerLink. SpringerLink is the world's largest online science, technology and medicine (STM) academic resource platform. With flexible subscription mode, reliable network foundation and convenient management system, SpringerLink has become the most popular product of all libraries. SpringerLink is a leader in science publishing and has always enjoyed a reputation for excellence. SpringerLink has published more than 150 Nobel laureates. Through the IP gateway of SpringerLink, readers can quickly access important online research materials.

The last one is Ebsco. Ebsco database is a full-text database and a secondary abstract database. The full-text database, Academic Search Premier (ASP for short), provides academic full-text journals. Business Source Premier (BSP for short) provides a full-text library of business resources, including business, management, economics, finance, accounting, etc.

3. Writing an Effective Literature Review

After you have collected a number of materials on your research subject from the library and the Internet and spent several weeks reading the sources, you want to start writing the literature review. It is crucial now to have a clear and overall picture of what a literature review is, so that you will know exactly what information you need and how to select it.

1) What is a literature review?

A literature review is an overview of the previously published works on a specific topic. The term can refer to a full scholarly paper or a section of a scholarly work such as a book, or an article. Either way, a literature review is supposed to:

- ✓ Provide the researcher/author and the audiences with a general image of the existing knowledge on the topic under question;
- ✓ Ask a proper research question;
- ✓ Choose a proper theoretical framework and/or research methodology;
- ✓ Serve to situate the current study within the body of the relevant literature and to provide context of the relevant literature for the reader;
- ✓ Not report new or original experimental work.

In such case, the review usually precedes the Methodology and Results sections of the work. Producing a literature review is often a part of graduate and postgraduate student work, including in the preparation of a thesis, dissertation, or a journal article. Literature reviews are also common in a research proposal or prospectus (the document that is approved before a student formally begins a dissertation or thesis).

2) Types of literature reviews

A literature review can be a type of a review article. In this sense, a literature review is a scholarly paper that presents the current knowledge including substantive findings as well as theoretical and methodological contributions to a particular topic. Literature reviews are a basis for research in nearly every academic field. There are five main types of literature reviews: evaluative, exploratory, instrumental, systematic and integrative.

- ✓ Evaluative review is an assessment of the values, qualities, and significance of the literature.
- ✓ Exploratory review is done with the intention of examining something in order to find out more about it or to learn the truth about it.
- ✓ Instrumental review is a system of pragmatic philosophy that considers ideas to be instruments, which should guide our actions; their value is measured by their success.
- ✓ Systematic review is a literature review focused on a research question, trying to identify, appraise, select and synthesize all high-quality research evidence and arguments relevant to that question. A meta-analysis is typically a systematic review using statistical methods to effectively combine the data used on all selected studies to produce a more reliable result.
- ✓ Integrative review is to generate new knowledge on a topic through the process of review, critique, and then synthesis of the literature under investigation.

3) Process and product

Shields et al. (2013) distinguish between the process of reviewing the literature and a finished work or product known as a literature review. The process of reviewing the literature is often ongoing and informs many aspects of the empirical research project.

The process of reviewing the literature requires different kinds of activities and ways of thinking. Shields and Rangarajan (2013) and Granello (2001) link the activities of doing a literature review with Benjamin Bloom's revised taxonomy of the cognitive domain—ways of thinking: remembering, understanding, applying, analyzing, evaluating, and creating.

As for products, the empirical study of literature is an interdisciplinary field of research which includes the psychology, sociology, and philosophy of texts, the contextual study of literature, and the history of reading literary texts. The International Society for the Empirical Study of Literature and Media (IGEL) is one learned association which brings together experts in this field. Major journals in the field are *Poetics: Journal of Empirical Research on Culture, The Media and the Arts*, *Poetics Today: International Journal for Theory and Analysis of Literature and Communication*, and *Scientific Study of Literature*.

4) Living review

In academic publishing, a living review is a review article, published electronically, that is updated at intervals to reflect the current state of research. Unlike in a print journal, a reader reading an old version of a review will automatically be aware that a newer version exists. While different versions of the review have to be cited separately, a living review acts as version control for the existing state of research.

Unit 10 Artificial Intelligence (AI)

For instance, the first article published in *Living Reviews in Relativity* was:

Rovelli, C. (26 January 1998). "Loop Quantum Gravity". *Living Reviews in Relativity.* 1:1. arXiv: gr-qc/9710008. Bibcode: 1998LRR.....1....1R. doi: 10.12942/lrr-1998-1. PMC 5567241. PMID 28937180.

In 2008, an updated version was produced:

Rovelli, C. (15 July 2008). "Loop Quantum Gravity". *Living Reviews in Relativity.* 11: 5. Bibcode: 2008LRR....11....5R. doi: 10.12942/lrr-2008-5. PMC 5256093. PMID 28179822.

The authors and titles of living reviews will typically remain the same from version to version, although this is not an absolute rule. Authors could change due to additional researchers joining a collaboration, retirement, or death. The title of the review will also typically remain the same, although development in the field may require adjusting the title to reflect the current state of research, or an adjustment in the scope of the review.

Some academic journals that publish living reviews are the *Living Reviews* astrophysics journal series, and the *Cochrane Database of Systematic Reviews* in medicine.

Part 2 Intensive Reading

Responsible Urban Innovation with Local Government Artificial Intelligence (AI): A Conceptual Framework and Research Agenda[1]

Pre-reading questions:

- ✓ What are the key concepts of this article?
- ✓ What are some key questions relevant to the concepts?
- ✓ What might be the purpose of this article?
- ✓ What is the methodological approach of this perspective article?

---

1 This paper is from Yigitcanlar, T., Corchado, J. M., Mehmood, R., Li, R. Y. M., Mossberger, K. & Desouza, K. 2021. Responsible urban innovation with local government artificial intelligence (AI): A conceptual framework and research agenda. *Journal of Open Innovation: Technology, Market, and Complexity,* 7(1): 71.

1. Introduction

Over the last 50 years, the pace of technological development has increased significantly. We owe this remarkable progress to the efforts of the stakeholders of the global innovation ecosystem that activated two ground-breaking digital revolutions[1-3]. The First Digital Revolution occurred in the 1980s and 1990s—some scholars even date it back to the 1970s, when the development of the personal computer commenced[4]. These technological developments resulted in mass digitization, an increasing number of products and services being encoded in the cyberspace, and the diffusion of the Internet on a pervasive scale[5]. Today, the world is on the verge of the Second Digital Revolution—where an increasing number of computing- and Internet-enabled objects and devices allow for **ubiquitous** computing and open innovation opportunities in our everyday lives[6-8].

Moreover, Makridakis[9] estimates that the next digital revolution will take place within the next couple of decades, and calls it the "artificial intelligence (AI) revolution". He further predicts that it will have a greater impact than both the first and the second digital revolutions combined. However, we are already on track towards the AI revolution. For instance, the Internet-of-Things (IoT) links objects wirelessly to a network that enables data sharing, and within this network AI is simultaneously analyzing IoT data and making decisions autonomously[10-12]. The smart home can be offered as an example of the popular application areas for this technology[13-14]. While highly innovative technologies—e.g., artificially intelligent Internet-of-things (AI-IoT)[15]—are disrupting the industrial processes—i.e., Industry 4.0[16]—, they are disrupting our cities and societies as well—i.e., smart city and smart community[17-19].

Nonetheless, this disruption is not necessarily solely generating positive externalities and delivering the desired outcomes or the desired outcomes for all[20]. For instance, on the one hand, autonomous vehicles—in the form of autonomous shuttle buses—could increase public transport coverage and **patronage**, and hence decrease the carbon emissions associated with transport[21-22]. On the other hand, autonomous vehicles—in the form of private autonomous cars—could increase mobility and urban sprawl, and thus increase transport carbon emissions[23]. Issues similar to these bring up the need for technological innovation in the context of cities, or in other words urban innovation, to become responsible for maximizing the desired outcomes and positive impacts for all and minimizing the unwanted ones[24-26].

Responsible innovation is vital in order to tackle the challenges our cities face, **irrespective** of whether they are related to natural resource degradation, climate change, economic progress or social welfare[27]. According to Von Schomberg[28] (p. 51), "responsible innovation is a transparent, interactive process by which societal actors and innovators become mutually responsive to each other with a view to the ethical acceptability, sustainability and societal desirability of the innovation process and its marketable products in order to allow for the proper embedding of scientific and technological advances in our society." Responsible urban innovation can be defined as "a collective commitment of care for the urban futures through responsive **stewardship** of science, technology and innovation in the present"[29] (p. 27). That is to say, responsible urban innovation challenges us not only to generate science, technology and innovation which can have a positive impact on our cities and societies today, but also makes us think about and act upon our responsibility to build the desired urban futures for all[30].

This perspective paper is written with the purpose of contributing to the existing responsible urban innovation discourse—that is an understudied and a relatively underadvocated area. With a specific focus on technology for responsible urban innovation, the paper concentrates on AI and its use as part of local government systems. The rationale behind this selection is as follows: (a) AI, a technology with an increasing number of applications in the urban context, is referred to as one of the most powerful technologies of our time with both positive and negative externalities for cities[31-32]; (b) AI is an integral part of a smart city structure that provides the required efficiencies and automation ability in the delivery of local infrastructures, services and amenities[33-34], and (c) there is a trend among local government agencies to adopt AI for managing routine, complex and complicated urban issues, where the knowledge and the experience of the staff in the area of responsible innovation, in general, are fairly limited[35-37].

As for the methodological approach, this perspective paper undertakes a review of the literature, research, developments, trends and applications concerning responsible urban innovation with local government AI systems, and develops a conceptual framework. In the light of the findings, the paper advocates the need for balancing the costs, benefits, risks and impacts of developing, adopting, deploying and managing local government AI systems targeting responsible urban innovation.

Following this introduction, Section 2 provides an overview of the notion of responsible urban innovation. Subsequently, Section 3 focuses on local government AI systems including their common application areas. Next, Section 4 presents the concept of responsible local government AI and its necessity for obtaining the desired urban outcomes as well as for showcasing responsible urban innovation practices. Section 5 introduces a conceptual framework of responsible urban innovation with local government AI. Lastly, Section 6 closes the paper with some concluding remarks and prospective lines of research.

2. Responsible Urban Innovation

Cities continue to experience significant challenges—e.g., resource demands, governance complexity, socioeconomic inequality and environmental threats—where innovation is seen as an important means of addressing these problems[38-40]. In other words, innovation is considered necessary for tackling urbanization problems and ensuring smart, sustainable and inclusive growth[41-43]. While local governments conducting urban experiments to trial combatting urban problems in a novel way with technological innovation[44], this also created a **lucrative** business opportunity for the high-tech companies—such as Cisco, IBM, Siemens, Huawei and Sidewalk Labs—which merged technology solutions with urban planning and development under the popular "smart city" brand[45-46].

Some initiatives are **renowned** for their success in the use of advanced technologies, such as AI to guide urban planners in making improvements in the city. The following are just some of the success cases: "(a) Massachusetts Institute of Technology (MIT) Media Lab's agent-based **simulation** to explore possible designs for busy public spaces, including a regenerated Champs-Élysées in Paris; (b) the AI application of Topos, a New York based startup, including image recognition and natural language processing, to help understand how the layout of a city affects those living in it, and to identify how different areas of New York were used by the residents; (c) University of Melbourne's AI utilization for future urban design decisions through the use of generative adversarial networks (GANs) to reproduce Google Street View images in the style of Melbourne's neighborhoods with public health characteristics"[47] (p. 4); (d) the Array of Things (AoT) project of the University of Chicago that comprise "a network of interactive, **modular** devices, or nodes, that are installed around Chicago to collect real-time data on the city's environment, infrastructure, and activity. These measurements are also shared as open data for research and public use"[48] (p. 1)—also see Hawthorne[49] for how citizen devices are being used for tracking Chicago's pollution hot spots, and (e) additional examples can be given with the cities' living lab experiments that utilize quadruple helix as a form of local innovation system[50], deploying innovative technology to encourage citizen participation in urban decisions[51], and social innovation initiatives concerning urban problems, such as sustainable development and climate change[52].

Nonetheless, the short-term profit-at-any-cost mindset of many disruptive technology companies has been generating innovation with more negative externalities—e.g., increased energy demand, pollution, damage to physical and mental health, and waste of taxpayers' money—than positive externalities[53-54]. This is to say, innovation without responsibility creates more problems than it solves—e.g., technology push, **negligence** of fundamental ethical principles, policy pull, and lack of precautionary measures and technology foresight[55–56].

Some of the common examples of the negative consequences of urban innovation involving advanced technologies, such as AI, include, but are not exclusively limited to: (a) the failure of algorithmic decision-making and predictive analytics of Pittsburgh, PA, in solving urban poverty, homelessness and violence problems, particularly by misdiagnosing child maltreatment and prescribing the wrong solutions[57]. This issue of automating inequality is discussed in length in the **seminal** work of Eubanks[58]. (b) Bias algorithmic decision-making has become one of the major unintended negative externalities, and the examples range from excluding women[59] to excluding people of color[60], and from excluding religious minorities[61] to excluding indigenous people[62]. (c) In most cases the failure and bias of algorithmic decisions led to the abolition of AI adoption endeavors in local governments. A good example is **scrapping** of the use of algorithms in benefit and welfare decisions in 20 local councils in the UK[63]. Furthermore, as stated by McKnight[64] (p. 1), "as AI has no a moral compass, OpenAI's managers originally refused to release GPT-3 (Generative Pre-trained Transformer 3)—an autoregressive language model that uses deep learning to produce human-like text—**ostensibly** because they were concerned about the generator being used to create fake material, such as reviews of products or election-related commentary. Similarly, AI writing bots may need to be eliminated by humans, as in the case of Microsoft's racist Twitter prototype AI chatbot—i.e., Tay." (d) The other negative externalities include "creating **opaque** decision-making processes, challenges in accountability and trust in AI-enabled decisions, and risks to privacy due to sensitive, **granular** and in-depth data collection practices"[65] (p. 3).

Moreover, even the most celebrated smart city initiatives—that represent urban innovation in management and policy as well as technology—have failed to deliver their promises or have even been abandoned before project initiation—e.g., Songdo, Masdar, PlanIT Valley and Sidewalk Toronto[66–67]. The main reasons behind this failure include technology **myopia**, a top-down approach, solutionism and the lack of clear objectives and socio-spatial responsibility[68]. Consequently, technology giants—e.g., Google's Sidewalk Labs and Cisco—have recently pulled back from the smart city push that did not practice clear responsible urban innovation principles—including accountability, anticipation, reflexivity, transparency, responsiveness, inclusiveness and sustainability[69–71]. As argued by Green[72] (p. 1), we need to "recognize the complexity of urban life rather than merely see the city as something to optimize, truly smart cities are the ones that successfully incorporate technology into a holistic vision of justice and equity".

Responsible urban innovation is central to addressing the current and emerging challenges of cities characterized by complexity, uncertainty, risk and myopia[73]. It

encompasses a public and environmental value-sensitive approach to technology design and adoption, which makes environmental (e.g., eco-responsibility) and societal (e.g., social-responsibility) factors as relevant as the economic (e.g., frugality) ones in the urban innovation and development processes[74–76]. In other words, responsible urban innovation carefully considers the effects of innovation on the environment and society[77]. Responsible urban innovation, thus, is characterized by its sustainability, which is vital for generating long-lasting solutions[78].

Furthermore, as stated by Ziegler[79] (p. 195), there are two roles for responsible urban innovation to play for socio-spatial justice. These are: "(a) to contribute to the long-term stability of the society, and thus to find creative responses to socio-spatial challenges such as climate change, and (b) to find ideas that specifically improve the benefits for the least advantaged members of the community in the present."

3. Local Government Artificial Intelligence Systems

As stated by Das and Rad[80] (p. 1), AI-based algorithms "are transforming the way we approach real-world tasks done by humans; where recent years have seen a surge in the use of these algorithms in automating various facets of science, business, and social workflow". In particular, government agencies are increasingly interested in using AI capabilities to deliver policy and generate efficiencies in high-uncertainty environments[81–82]. A study by De Sousa et al.[83] **disclosed** a growing trend of interest in AI in the public sector, with the US as the most active country. This is also the case with many local government agencies[84]. According to Wirtz et al.[85], the most common AI applications in government agencies are as follows: (a) AI-based knowledge management software; (b) AI process automation systems; (c) chatbots/virtual agents; (d) predictive analytics and data visualization; (e) identity analytics; (f) cognitive robotics and autonomous systems; (g) recommendation systems; (h) intelligent digital assistants; (i) speech analytics; and (j) cognitive security analytics and threat intelligence.

AI offers urban innovation opportunities to generate novel solutions to the problems of our cities[86–87]. It has the potential to create a great impact on the way citizens experience and receive services and interact with their government, as recent advances in AI have resulted in an increasing number of decisions being handed over to algorithms[88–89]. This also applies to local government operations and services[90–91]. Today, AI is not only becoming an integral part of local government operations and services, but is also impacting and shaping the future of our cities and societies[92]—e.g., the forthcoming autonomous vehicle disruption[93–95].

In the context of cities, AI systems were first introduced as part of smart city **initiatives**[96].

Nonetheless, today AI is no longer exclusively associated with smart city projects. For instance, there is an increasing number of local governments, with no smart city agenda, which have utilized AI-driven chatbots in their customer and service delivery services[97–98]. This is because local government agencies are becoming more aware of the benefits of AI. According to the International City/County Management Association (ICMA)[99], these benefits include: (a) local governments can run more efficiently; (b) local governments can focus on their residents; (c) local governments can remove a great deal of bias; and (d) local governments can make data-smart decisions and gain that extra edge for under-resourced departments.

Besides AI-powered chatbots for engaging with the local community, local governments are using AI for automating routine tasks via self-service, and enhancing public services with data and analytics[100–101]. Additionally, hyper-personalized services, predictive maintenance of assets, workforce, schedule and resource optimization, reducing our carbon footprints, optimizing energy usage, and combatting child abuse and financial fraud are among the applications of AI used in local governments[102].

Today, many cities around the world are trying to position themselves as the leaders of urban innovation through the development and utilization of AI[103]. Some of these cities which are experimenting with and adopting AI systems include, but are not exclusively limited to, New York, Washington, Los Angeles, San Antonio, Pittsburgh, Phoenix, London, Singapore, Barcelona, Oslo, Helsinki, Hong Kong, Beijing, Brisbane, Sydney, Melbourne, Bangalore, Dubai and Jeddah[104]. Moreover, the world's first "AI city"—or artificially intelligent city—is being planned in Chongqing (China) with wired AI-IoT, robotics, networking and big data[105].

While the popularity of AI is skyrocketing in the urban context, Allam[106] (p. 31) warns us that, "whilst AI stands as a potential **savior** and as its role is being accentuated in urban planning, governance and management, there are increasing concerns that its practical implications and planning principles are disconnected with sensibilities linked to the dimensions of sustainability". This very issue has also been raised by other urban scholars[107].

Importantly, as today AI-based decision-making is in a trend to become commonplace, local government AI systems should be used "responsibly and ethically that extends beyond compliance with the narrow letter of the law. It also requires the system to be aligned with broadly-accepted social norms, and considerate of impact on individuals, communities and the environment"[108] (p. 1).

Despite the use of AI in local governments being relatively new, it is already possible to find promising examples of responsible practices, which include, but are not limited to:

(a) AI-driven transportation analytics and decision-making systems to address the urban traffic problems of Austin, TX[109]; (b) autonomous shuttle buses are currently being used as first- and last-mile solutions to increase public transport patronage and/or to provide transport service to disadvantaged populations in cities, including Lyon (France), Geneva (Switzerland), Wien (Austria), Oslo (Norway), Las Vegas (USA), Masdar City (UAE), Thuwal (Saudi Arabia), West Kowloon (Hong Kong, China) and Renmark (Australia)[110-111]; and (c) computer vision and machine learning for robots to identify material characteristics while sorting waste and increasing the capacity of recycling of the San Francisco Bay Area[112].

Building on the aforementioned practices which are limited but promising practices, Schmelzer[113] (p. 1) raised the following key issues which must be fully tackled so that many more local governments can successfully implement responsible AI practices: "(a) identifying the unique challenges around data at the local government level; (b) determining the areas that AI has the biggest impact at the local level; (c) understanding the challenges local governments face around data privacy, transparency and security; (d) developing an AI-ready local government workforce, including upskilling the current workforce around data and AI skills; and (e) having a responsive lens when deploying and managing AI technologies." A study by Chen et al.[114] reveals the success factors for AI adoption as: (a) innovation attributes of AI; (b) organizational capability; and (c) external environment.

4. Responsible Local Government Artificial Intelligence

Amid the global push for AI use at the local government level[115], there are growing concerns over AI uptake in the absence of an in-depth understanding of the implementation challenges, contextual local differences, and local government readiness[116]—as well as the lack of responsible urban innovation practices[117].

The upcoming digital urban infrastructure that will be supporting future societies will intrinsically be based on AI[118]. This is evident from the work on the sixth-generation (6G) networks with extreme-scale ubiquitous AI services through the next-generation softwarization, platformization, heterogeneity and configurability of networks[119-121]. Such infrastructure will provide unimaginable opportunities for urban innovation. Nevertheless, a responsible approach is critical when it comes to eliminating the negative externalities of innovation which could otherwise have catastrophic consequences—e.g., worsening socioeconomic inequity, widening digital divides, devastating environmental externalities and increased bias.

Some promising developments are being made at present. A good outcome of the academic discourse is the "Montreal Declaration for Responsible AI", developed under the auspices of the University of Montreal, following the Forum on the Socially Responsible Development of AI of November 2017[122]. Another notable example is AI regulation and ethics frameworks being rolled out in various countries. The most celebrated of these is the European Parliament's initiative on the guidelines for the European Union (EU) on ethics in AI[123]. While thus far, more than 50 countries have developed their national AI strategies—where the intention is mainly economic development and national security[124]—only a few have attempted to form their AI ethics frameworks that advocate responsible AI[125].

Despite the increasing interest in the scholarly debate, responsible urban innovation and responsible local government AI remain highly understudied, and thus far, there is a limited empirical evidence base and few conceptual expansions[126]. Thus, local governments' adoption and use of AI systems[127], in the context of urban innovation, is an important topic of scholarly research, and key to expanding our understanding of the pathways leading to the achievement of responsible urban innovation through these systems.

Moreover, in the absence of an abundance of responsible urban innovation with local government AI, the generation of new insights and evidence is of utmost importance. Prospective research in this interdisciplinary field will aid in conceptualizing and providing a sound understanding of the most appropriate approaches for local governments engaging with AI to achieve responsible urban innovation. Such conceptualization will also aid in the efforts to develop clear pathways for healthy AI design and **deployment**. Furthermore, the outcomes of these future studies will help urban policymakers, managers and planners better understand the crucial role played by local government AI systems in ensuring responsible outcomes. This consolidated understanding will guide the efforts in developing new coordination and delivery practices for local government AI systems to achieve the desired responsible urban innovation outcomes in their cities.

5. Conceptual Framework

We have developed a conceptual framework of responsible urban innovation with local government AI. The main **rationale** behind the development of this high-level information, i.e., the conceptual framework, is to highlight the relationship between the key drivers, components and the fundamental principles of responsible urban innovation in the context of local government AI. We believe this approach will create an interest and curiosity in the academic community to further investigate the topic and subsequently generate new research directions and practical solutions for the government and industry to adopt or benefit from. Hence, the framework, which is illustrated in Figure 1 and elaborated below, shall not be seen as an operational framework to directly guide the AI system development, deployment and management practices of local government agencies.

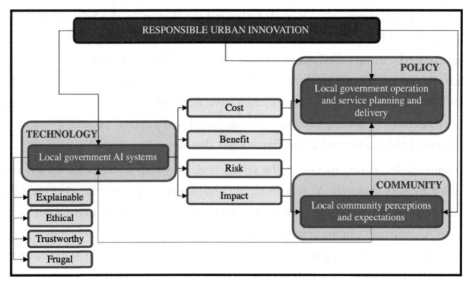

Figure 1　Conceptual framework of responsible urban innovation with local government artificial intelligence (AI)

In this framework, the responsible urban innovation phenomenon is conceptualized through a process that involves technology, policy and community to produce strategies, action plans and initiatives, with balanced costs, benefits, risks and impacts of developing, adopting, deploying and managing local government AI systems.

First, technology, policy and community are envisaged as the key drivers of responsible urban innovation; where local government AI systems represent "technology", local government operation and service planning and delivery decisions represent "policy", and local community perceptions and expectations represent the "community" views and input. This is attributed to the fact that the trio of "technology, policy and community" are being widely seen as the key drivers of smart cities—urban localities that use digital data and technology to create efficiencies for boosting economic development, enhancing the quality of life, and improving the sustainability of the city[128]—or technology-based urban growth practices[129-131] or technology-based public policy[132].

Second, "cost", "benefit", "risk" and "impact" are identified as the central foci of the framework for realizing responsible outcomes concerning local government AI systems. This is attributed to the need for undertaking a cost-benefit analysis before developing, adopting and deploying AI systems in order to ensure the worthiness of the investment[133]. Likewise, being aware of the potential hazards by undertaking a risk analysis is critical when it comes to assuring the success of the AI system[134]. Similarly, forecasting the impact of the AI system on the society and the environment is crucial for identifying both positive and negative externalities[135]. Additionally, rather than only looking at costs and benefits overall, responsible use of AI should also consider the distribution of costs and benefits, and whether some groups or places (e.g., disadvantaged neighborhoods) bear more risk. This is an ethical concern—equity as a public value.

Moreover, this conceptualization advocates that local government AI systems should include the following characteristics: to be (a) explicable; (b) ethical; (c) trustworthy; and (d) frugal. First, the effectiveness of the AI systems is limited by the machine's inability to explain its thoughts and actions to human users. Hence, explainable AI (XAI)—which refers to methods and techniques that generate high-quality interpretable, intuitive, human understandable explanations of AI decisions—is essential for operators and users to understand, trust, and effectively manage local government AI systems[136-137].

Second, the ethical considerations made by the designers and adopters of AI systems, are critical when it comes to avoiding the unethical consequences of AI systems[138-139]. As stated by Floridi et al.[122] (p. 694), "ensuring socially preferable outcomes of AI relies on resolving the tension between incorporating the benefits and mitigating the potential harms of AI, in short, simultaneously avoiding the misuse and underuse of these technologies. In this context, the value of an ethical approach to AI technologies comes into **starker** relief."

Third, today, we are seeing an increasing trend of autonomous decision-making, but we are not there yet. This is especially true for most government services[140-141]. In particular, local governments around the world are looking at technological solutions, including decisions being made autonomously by AI systems with limited or null human involvement, to address a range of social and policy challenges. While this **handover** of decisions to AI provides benefits—e.g., reduction in human error, faster decision-making, 24/7 availability, completion of repetitive tasks—it also creates risks, e.g., algorithmic bias caused by bad/limited data and training, privacy violations, removing human responsibility, and a lack of transparency[142]. The public is already becoming increasingly distrustful of many AI decisions; robodebt and systematic racism traumas caused by AI systems in Australia and the US are among the recent examples[143-146]. In order to prevent these risks from occurring and gaining public confidence, AI must be trustworthy[147-149].

Fourth, at present comprehensive AI systems are significant investments for local governments, with many of these organizations having limited budgets and responsibilities for justifying the investment and management cost to their citizens and taxpayers. For a wide-scale AI adoption in local governments, AI systems should become accessible and affordable, or in other words frugal[150]. In this context, frugality is the minimum use of scarce resources—e.g., capital, time, workforce and energy. Alternatively, the resources can be **leveraged** in new ways or other solutions can be found that do not jeopardize the delivery of high value outputs[151].

The framework, illustrated in Figure 1 and elaborated above, underlines the key drivers, components and the fundamental principles of responsible urban innovation with local government AI. It **sheds light on** the overall principles of the development and deployment of AI systems that assure the delivery of not only the desired urban outcomes, but also the desired urban outcomes for all citizens, stakeholders, users and the environment. The approach outlined in this framework is invaluable for local government agencies when it comes to being aware of the issues around responsible innovation; as local governments continue in the phase of experimentation with AI technologies, they need guidance on how best to design, develop, and deploy these solutions in a responsible manner that advances public value. Nevertheless, it should be noted that the framework presented here is a conceptual one developed with the goal of contributing to the academic discourse on the topic and generating directions for future research agendas. Thus, prospective research is needed to develop more operational frameworks involving specific guidelines for local governments so that they can make informed decisions regarding their investments in AI systems.

6. Concluding Remarks and Research Agenda

With the advent of powerful technologies and the strong short-term profit-at-any-cost mindset of many disruptive technology companies, ensuring responsible urban innovation will continue to be a major challenge in the third decade of the 21st century as well[152]. In particular, there are some important issues, in the context of responsible urban innovation with local government AI, that require urgent attention.

With the aforementioned urgency in mind, in this perspective paper, we underlined the importance of local government agencies making informed decisions while developing, adopting, deploying and managing AI systems. This is becoming a highly critical issue, as stated by Arrieta et al.[137] (p. 82), in recent years, the "sophistication of AI systems has increased to such an extent that almost no human intervention is required for their design and deployment. When decisions derived from such systems ultimately affect humans' lives, there is an emerging need for understanding how such decisions are furnished" and how responsible they are. Moreover, this also increases the danger that unintended consequences can grow and multiply through policy inattention or delayed recognition.

Nevertheless, at present there are no operational frameworks and clear guidelines to assist local governments in achieving responsible innovation through AI practices. In the absence of such guidelines, the conceptual framework illustrated in Figure 1 is a step towards increasing awareness on the matter and triggering potential research agendas for the development of operational frameworks and guidelines. In this instance, we underline some of the fundamental issues, as listed below, where focusing on these could pave the way for a new research agenda concerning responsible urban innovation with local government AI:

- ✓ How can local governments utilize AI systems effectively, what are the requirements for making them responsible, and how can local government AI support responsible urban innovation efforts?
- ✓ Why do some local governments experiment with and adopt AI systems when the risks are not clearly known, while the others prefer to take a wait and see approach before making this decision?
- ✓ How can local governments conduct **trade-offs** between costs, risks, benefits and impacts, and utilize AI systems in their municipal operations and services, and what externalities do these trade-offs generate?
- ✓ How can the AI systems' costs, risks, benefits and impacts be distributed across the local government service users and communities, and how can the equity concerns be addressed?
- ✓ Further dwelling on the above issue, if some groups or geographic areas bear greater risk or costs, should AI be used anyway, should there be a just compensation in some manner, and if yes, how?
- ✓ How can local governments **align** the public perceptions and expectations of AI, and mitigate the impact of consequential negative externalities of AI systems on the environment and society?
- ✓ How can local governments support and ensure high levels of trust, transparency, and openness in the local community culture and extend these concepts of digital trust to AI?
- ✓ How can local governments successfully adopt, deploy and manage AI systems to generate responsible urban innovation in their cities, and how can the guidelines for successful adoption be developed?
- ✓ How will local government AI systems shape the future of our cities and impact the lives of citizens, and how can the negative externalities of the disruption be alleviated?
- ✓ How can operational frameworks and guidelines be developed for local governments in regard to adopting, deploying and managing AI systems to achieve responsible urban innovation outcomes?

There is very limited to no coverage on either theoretical or applied aspects concerning the aforementioned questions in the literature and practice—as the responsible local government AI notion is still cutting-edge but **incipient** in nature. Most studies reported in the literature, thus far, are drawn from the intuitions and predictions of scholars rather than hard evidence obtained through exhaustive empirical research. We strongly believe that investigation of these issues in prospective research projects, by the scholars of this highly interdisciplinary (more correctly transdisciplinary) field, will shed light on the better conceptualization and practice of responsible urban innovation with local government AI.

Thus, the future research agenda should focus on tackling the aforementioned issues via carefully designed empirical studies in international contexts. In this regard, the conceptual framework, presented in Figure 1, is a useful compass to guide in the design of new empirical investigations. For instance, an example of a prospective research agenda, concerning responsible urban innovation with local government AI, could be as follows.

At present, AI is not only becoming an integral part of urban services, but also is impacting and shaping the future of living and cities[153–154]. Nevertheless, the current AI practice has shown that urban innovation without responsibility generates more problems than it solves. In particular, the absence of a deep understanding of the costs, benefits, risks and impacts of deploying local government AI systems creates concerns. Focusing on the local government case studies, prospective projects can generate new knowledge on the local government use of AI systems, and expand our understanding of the pathways for responsible urban innovation. These studies could also produce invaluable outcomes that include the local government AI adoption and implementation of guiding principles for informed decisions.

In conclusion, the AI revolution is already under way and its disruption will likely be comparable to that of the agricultural and industrial revolutions, which changed the course of human civilization radically[155]. Nevertheless, it should not be forgotten that the AI revolution contains an equal measure of opportunities and challenges[156–157]. According to Walsh[158], the ethical challenges posed by AI—e.g., fairness, transparency, trustworthiness, protection of privacy and respect, and many other fundamental rights—are the biggest issues, and they must be addressed with utmost care and urgency. Importantly, the actions to address these challenges should be adopted before the local government AI systems are actually in use[159–161].

(Scan the QR code to access the list of references.)

 Words and Expressions

ubiquitous	*adj.*	seeming to be everywhere or in several places at the same time
patronage	*n.*	the support, especially financial, that is given to a person or an organization by a patron
irrespective	*adj.*	not taking something into account; regardless of
stewardship	*n.*	the position of steward
lucrative	*adj.*	producing a sizeable profit
renown	*v.*	to the state or quality of being widely honored and acclaimed

Unit 10 Artificial Intelligence (AI)

simulation	*n.*	the act of giving a false appearance
modular	*adj.*	constructed with standardized units or dimensions allowing flexibility and variety in use
negligence	*n.*	the trait of neglecting responsibilities and lacking concern
seminal	*adj.*	containing important new ideas and having a great influence on later work
scrap	*v.*	to get rid of or cancel
ostensibly	*adv.*	in a way that appears or claims to be one thing when it is really something else
opaque		preventing light from travelling through, and therefore not transparent or translucent
granular	*adj.*	made of, or seeming like, granules
myopia	*n.*	a condition in which someone cannot clearly see things that are far away
encompass	*v.*	to include different types of things
disclose	*v.*	to make something known publicly, or to show something that was hidden
initiative	*n.*	a new plan or process to achieve something or solve a problem
savior	*n.*	a person who saves someone from danger or harm
rationale	*n.*	the reasons or intentions that cause a particular set of beliefs or actions
stark	*adj.*	empty, simple, or obvious, especially without decoration or anything that is not necessary
handover	*n.*	the giving of control of or responsibility for something to someone else
leverage	*v.*	to use something that you already have in order to achieve something new or better
shed light on...	*n.*	to provide information about something or to make something easier to understand
trade-off	*n.*	a balancing of two opposing situations or qualities, both of which are desired
align	*v.*	to put two or more things into a straight line, or to form a straight line
incipient	*adj.*	just beginning

Reflections and Practice

I Read the text and answer the following questions.

1. Why is technological innovation vital for the society in the context of cities?
2. What is responsible urban innovation? How is the term defined in the article?
3. Why does this paper focus on AI technology for responsible urban innovation?
4. Can you list some of the high-tech companies that merged technology solutions with urban planning and development under the popular "smart city" brand?
5. What are the negative externalities generated by many disruptive technology companies with the short-term profit-at-any-cost mindset?
6. According to Wirtz et al., what are the most common AI applications in government agencies?
7. What are the key drivers of responsible urban innovation for local government AI systems?

II Discuss the following questions with your partner.

1. The AI revolution is already under way, are you well prepared for it? What are the advantages and disadvantages of the AI technology in every aspect of human life?
2. What factors should be considered for the new research agenda concerning AI in your own study field?
3. Any technology will bring bad effects on human life. AI, a technology with an increasing number of applications in the urban context, is the most powerful technologies of our time. What do you think is the bad impact it may have on people?
4. What ethical challenges will artificial intelligence bring to human beings?

III Paraphrase the following sentences.

1. While local governments conducting urban experiments to trial combatting urban problems in a novel way with technological innovation, this also created a lucrative business opportunity for the high-tech companies—such as Cisco, IBM, Siemens, Huawei and Sidewalk Labs—which merged technology solutions with urban planning and development under the popular "smart city" brand.
2. Nonetheless, the short-term profit-at-any-cost mindset of many disruptive technology companies has been generating innovation with more negative externalities—e.g.,

increased energy demand, pollution, damage to physical and mental health, and waste of taxpayers' money—than positive externalities.

3. Furthermore, as stated by McKnight (p. 1), "as AI has no a moral compass, OpenAI's managers originally refused to release GPT-3 (Generative Pre-trained Transformer 3)—an autoregressive language model that uses deep learning to produce human-like text—ostensibly because they were concerned about the generator being used to create fake material, such as reviews of products or election-related commentary."

4. The upcoming digital urban infrastructure that will be supporting future societies will intrinsically be based on AI. This is evident from the work on the sixth-generation (6G) networks with extreme-scale ubiquitous AI services through the next-generation softwarization, platformization, heterogeneity and configurability of networks.

5. Thus, the future research agenda should focus on tackling the aforementioned issues via carefully designed empirical studies in international contexts. In this regard, the conceptual framework, presented in Figure 1, is a useful compass to guide in the design of new empirical investigations.

Ⅳ Write a review to reflect the current state of AI research and practice. You may give a title of your own.

Ⅴ Write an outline for the text following the structure below.

1. **Introduction**

    The "artificial intelligence (AI) revolution" will have a greater impact than both the First Digital Revolution (the invention of the personal computer) and the Second Digital Revolutions (_____) combined. However, we are already on track towards the AI revolution and are facing a lot of challenges such as _____.

2. **Research Objective**

    To propose a conception framework to make urban innovation become responsible for maximizing the desired outcomes and positive impacts for all and minimizing the unwanted ones.

3. **Methodological Approach**

    This perspective paper undertakes a review of the literature, research, developments, _____ concerning responsible urban innovation with local government AI systems, and develops a(n) _____.

4. Conceptual Framework

_____
_____ .

5. Conclusion

_____
_____ .

Ⅵ Write a summary for the text in 150–200 words.

Part 3 Further Reading

A Systematic Literature Review of AI in the Sharing Economy[1]

Abstract: Although artificial intelligence (AI) has been adopted in sharing economy platforms, few studies have investigated this phenomenon in this context. Consequently, there is no thorough overview of how AI has been used in the sharing economy. To address this research gap, a systematic literature review was performed for this paper. This method can be useful for the exploration of new and emerging trends within disciplines and allows boundaries to be mapped on what is known thereby identifying gaps on what is yet to be known. After screening, 28 English journal articles were selected in a qualitative synthesis. Results show AI can help the sharing economy platforms by enhancing trust, matching assets, and understanding participants' preferences and attitudes. Based on these findings, potential directions are established. The current study will contribute to both the sharing economy and AI literature, and the results may help practitioners and academia to achieve a greater

---

1 This paper is from Chen, Y., Prentice, C., Weaven, S. & Hsiao, A. 2022. A systematic literature review of AI in the sharing economy. *Journal of Global Scholars of Marketing Science, 32*(3): 434–451.

understanding of this topic.

Keywords: artificial intelligence, sharing economy, systematic literature review, machine learning, deep learning

 Reflections and Practice

Read the full article and answer the following questions.

1. How could the review article claim to have made a systematic literature review of AI in the sharing economy? What is a systemic methodology?
2. How can you make a qualitative synthesis?
3. What do the results suggest us? What are the potential directions of AI applications?
4. What are the significances of having a better understanding of this topic?
5. In which aspect could the systematic literature review help both the practitioners and the academia?

References

北京市高等教育学会研究生英语教学研究分会. 2020. 非英语专业学位研究生英语教学大纲. 北京：中国人民大学出版社.

胡庚申. 2000. 英语论文写作与发表. 北京：高等教育出版社.

李文梅，徐亚琴，王丽明. 2021. 研究生学术交流英语. 北京：清华大学出版社.

庞继贤. 2008. 英文研究论文写作. 杭州：浙江大学出版社.

文秋芳. 2017. 辩证研究法与二语教学研究. 外语界，（4）：2–11.

American Psychological Association. 2020. *Publication Manual of the American Psychological Association* (7th ed.). Washington, D.C.: American Psychological Association.

Berdanier, C. & Lenart, J. 2020. *So, You Have to Write a Literature Review: A Guided Workbook for Engineers*. Hoboken: John Wiley & Sons, Inc.

Cabanac, A. 2017. Arts and scholastic performance. *Creative Education, 8*: 2393–2399.

Cargill, M. & O'Connor, P. 2013. *Writing Scientific Research Articles: Strategy and Steps*. Chichester: John Wiley & Sons, Inc.

Coxhead, A. 2000. A new academic word list. *TESOL Quarterly, 34*(2): 213–238.

DiYanni, R. 2017. Reading responsively, reading responsibly: An approach to critical reading. In R. DiYanni & A. Borst (Eds.), *Critical Reading Across the Curriculum: Humanities* (Vol. 1). Somerset: John Wiley & Sons, Inc, 3–23.

Dong, Y. 2018. *Critical Thinking in Second Language Writing: Concept, Theory, Teaching and Assessment*. Beijing: Foreign Language Teaching and Research Press.

Elder, L. & Paul, R. 2019. *The Thinker's Guide to Intellectual Standards: The Words That Name Them and the Criteria That Define Them*. Dillon Beach: Foundation for Critical Thinking.

Engle, M. 2022. How to prepare an annotated bibliography. *Cornell University Library*. Retrieved September 22, 2022, from Cornell University Website.

Gillett, A. 2022. Features of academic writing: Hedging. *UEfAP*. Retrieved from UEfAP.

He, Y. Y., Luo, Q. H., Ge, P. H., Chen, G. J. & Wang, H. Q. 2018. Review on mould contamination and hygrothermal effect in indoor environment. *Journal of Environmental Protection, 9*: 100–110.

Hyland, K. 1994. Hedging in academic writing and EAF textbooks. *English for Specific Purposes*, *13*(3): 239–256.

Hyland, K. 2002. Activity and evaluation: Reporting practices in academic writing. In J. Flowerdew (Ed.), *Academic Discourse*. Harlow: Longman, 115–130.

Hyland, K. 2004. *Disciplinary Discourse: Social Interactions in Academic Writing*. Ann Arbor: The University of Michigan Press.

Keshav, S. 2007. How to read a paper. *ACM SIGCOMM Computer Communication Review*, *37*(3): 83–84.

Lakoff, G. 1973. Hedges: A study in meaning criteria and the logic of fuzzy concepts. *Journal of Philosophical Logic, 2*(4): 458–508.

Lea, M. R. & Street, B. V. 1998. Student writing in higher education: An academic literacies approach. *Studies in Higher Education, 23*(2): 157–172.

Lin, L. & Evans, S. 2012. Structural patterns in empirical research articles: A cross-disciplinary study. *English for Specific Purposes, 31*(3): 150–160.

Miller, D. C., & Salkind, N. J. 2002. Elements of research design. In D. Miller & N. Salkind (Eds.), *Handbook of Research Design and Social Measurement*. London: Sage, 18.

Neville, C. 2010. *The Complete Guide to Referencing and Avoiding Plagiarism* (2nd ed.). Maidenhead: Open University Press.

Paul, R. & Elder, L. 2001. *Critical Thinking: Tools for Taking Charge of Your Learning and Your Life*. Upper Saddle River: Prentice Hall.

Pirozzi, R., Starks-Martin, G. & Dziewisz, J. 2014. *Critical Reading, Critical Thinking: Focusing on Contemporary Issues* (4th ed.). Harlow: Pearson.

Pounds, G. 2015. Evaluative language. In K. Tracy, C. Ilie. & T. Sandel (Eds.), *The International Encyclopedia of Language and Social Interaction*. Malden: Wiley-Blackwell, 564–568.

Randolph, J. 2009. A guide to writing the dissertation literature review. *Practical Assessment, Research, and Evaluation, 14*: 13.

Shields, P., Rangarajan, N. & Stewart, L. 2012. Open access digital repository: Sharing student research with the world. *Journal of Public Affairs Education, 18*(1): 157–181.

Swales, J. 1990. *Genre Analysis: English in Academic and Research Settings*. Cambridge: Cambridge University Press.

Van Wee, B. & Banister, D. 2016. How to write a literature review paper? *Transport Reviews, 36*(2): 278–288.

Wallace, M. & Wray, A. 2011. *Critical Reading and Writing for Postgraduates* (2nd ed.). London: Sage.

References

Webster, J. & Watson, R. T. 2002. Analyzing the past to prepare for the future: Writing a literature review. *MIS Quarterly, 26*: 13–23.

Wee, B. V. & Banister, D. 2015. How to write a literature review paper. *Transport Reviews, 36*: 2.

Whetten, D. 1989. What constitutes a theoretical contribution? *Academy of Management Review, 14:* 490–495.

White, H. D. 2004. Citation analysis and discourse analysis revisited. *Applied Linguistics, 25*(1): 89–116.

Wu, B.C. 2022. SAT materials: English studying methodologies—key words in reading. *Baidu Wenku.* Retrieved September 7, 2022, from Baidu Wenku Website.

Xu, F., & Matsuda, P. 2017. Disciplinary Dialogues section: Perspectives on multimodal composition. *Journal of Second Language Writing, 38*: 79.